Happy Days

Titles by H. L. Mencken published by the Johns Hopkins University Press

Happy Days: 1880–1892

Prejudices
Selected by James T. Farrell

Thirty-five Years of Newspaper Work
edited by Fred Hobson, Vincent Fitzpatrick, and Bradford Jacobs

Also available:

Mencken: A Life
by Fred Hobson

Maryland Paperback Bookshelf

Publisher's Note

Works published as part of the Maryland Paperback Bookshelf are, we like to think, books that are classics of a kind. While some social attitudes have changed and knowledge of our surroundings has increased, we believe that the value of these books as literature, as history, and as timeless perspectives on our region remains undiminished.

HAPPY

DAYS

1880-1892

H. L. MENCKEN

The Johns Hopkins University Press
Baltimore and London

Some of these chapters have appeared, either wholly or in part, in the *New Yorker*. The author offers his thanks to the editors of that magazine for permission to reprint them.

Originally published in a hardcover edition by Alfred A. Knopf, New York.
Published by arrangement with Alfred A. Knopf, Inc.
Maryland Paperback Bookshelf edition, 1996
05 04 03 02 01 00 99 98 97 96   5 4 3 2 1

The Johns Hopkins University Press
2715 North Charles Street
Baltimore, Maryland 21218-4319
The Johns Hopkins Press Ltd., London

Library of Congress Cataloging-in-Publication Data will be found at the end of this book.

A catalog record for this book is available from the British Library.

ISBN 0-8018-5338-9 (pbk.)

Frontispiece: H. L. Mencken and family, early in 1890. Photograph courtesy of the Enoch Pratt Free Library.

C O N T E N T S

Preface

THESE casual and somewhat chaotic memoirs of days long past are not offered to the nobility and gentry as coldly objective history. They are, on the contrary, excessively subjective, and the record of an event is no doubt often bedizened and adulterated by my response to it. I have made a reasonably honest effort to stick to the cardinal facts, however disgraceful to either the quick or the dead, but no one is better aware than I am of the fallibility of human recollection. Fortunately, I have been able to resort, at many points, to contemporary inscriptions, for my people have lived in one house in Baltimore since 1883, and when I returned to it in 1936, after five years of absence, and began to explore it systematically, I found its cupboards and odd corners full of family memorabilia. My mother, who died in 1925, was one of those old-fashioned housewives who never threw

anything away, and in the years following her
death my sister apparently made only slow progress in excavating and carting off her interminable
accumulations. Moreover, I found that my father,
ordinarily no cherisher of archives, had nevertheless preserved, for some reason unknown, a file of
household bills running from the year of his marriage to the early nineties — not a complete file, by
any means, but still one showing many well-chosen
and instructive specimens.

I have mined this file diligently, and found a
number of surprises in it. One is the discovery that
my memory was grossly at fault, for nearly half a
century, on a salient point of my education. For
all those years I boasted that I could read music at
the age of six at the latest — indeed, I boasted that
I could read it so far back in my nonage that it was
impossible for me to recall the time when I couldn't.
These boasts turned out, on reference to the bill
file, to be mere sound and hooey, signifying nothing. Therein, as plain as day, was a receipt showing beyond cavil that there was no piano in the
house until my *eighth* year — or, to be precise, until I was seven years, four months and one day old.
This disconcerting experience caused me to check
and re-check the whole saga of my infant recollections, partly by the same bill file, partly by the
countless other documents, glyphs and cave-draw-
ings in the house, and partly by the memories of
surviving contemporaries. I unearthed many other

errors, but none so gross as the one about my genesis as a *Tonkünstler*, and on the whole I made a
pretty good average score. As Huck Finn said of
" Tom Sawyer," there are no doubt some stretchers
in this book, but mainly it is fact.

It has, so far as I can make out, no psychological,
sociological or politico-economic significance. My
early life was placid, secure, uneventful and happy.
I remember, of course, some griefs and alarms, but
they were all trivial, and vanished quickly. There
was never an instant in my childhood when I
doubted my father's capacity to resolve any difficulty that menaced me, or to beat off any danger.
He was always the center of his small world, and
in my eyes a man of illimitable puissance and re-
sourcefulness. If we needed anything he got it
forthwith, and usually he threw in something that
we didn't really need, but only wanted. I never
heard of him being ill-treated by a wicked sweat
shop owner, or underpaid, or pursued by rent-col-
lectors, or exploited by the Interests, or badgered
by the police. My mother, like any normal woman,
formulated a large programme of desirable improvements in him, and not infrequently labored
it at the family hearth, but on the whole their marriage, which had been a love match, was a marked
and durable success, and neither of them ever neglected for an instant their duties to their children.
We were encapsulated in affection, and kept fat,
saucy and contented. Thus I got through my non-

age without acquiring an inferiority complex, and
the present chronicle, both in its materials and in
its point of view, must needs fall out of the current fashion, which seems to favor tales of dirty
tenements, wage cuts, lay-offs, lockouts, voracious
landlords, mine police, foreclosed mortgages, evic-
tions, rickets, prostitution, larceny, grafting cops,
anti-Semitism, Bryanism, Hell-fire, droughts, xen-
ophobia, and other such horrors. I was a larva of
the comfortable and complacent bourgeoisie,
though I was quite unaware of the fact until I was
along in my teens, and had begun to read indignant
books. To belong to that great order of mankind is
vaguely discreditable today, but I still maintain
my dues-paying membership in it, and continue to
believe that it was and is authentically human, and
therefore worthy of the attention of philosophers,
at least to the extent that the Mayans, Hittites,
Kallikuks and so on are worthy of it.

How, on one of its levels, it lived and had its being in a great American city in the penultimate
decade of the last century is my theme, in so far as
there is any theme here at all. I shut down my narrative with the year 1892, which saw my twelfth
birthday. I was then at the brink of the terrible
teens, and existence began inevitably to take on a
new and more sinister aspect. It may be that I'll
resume the story later on, but that is not certain,
for on the whole I am more interested in what is
going on now than in what befell me (or anyone

else) in the past. My days of work have been mainly spent, in fact, in recording the current scene, usually in a far from acquiescent spirit. But I must confess, with sixty only around the corner, that I have found existence on this meanest of planets extremely amusing, and, taking one day with another, perfectly satisfactory. If I had my life to live over again I don't think I'd change it in any particular of the slightest consequence. I'd choose the same parents, the same birthplace, the same education (with maybe a few improvements here, chiefly in the direction of foreign languages), the same trade, the same jobs, the same income, the same politics, the same metaphysic, the same wife, the same friends, and (even though it may sound like a mere effort to shock humanity), the same relatives to the last known degree of consanguinity, including those in-law. The Gaseous Vertebrata who own, operate and afflict the universe have treated me with excessive politeness, and when I mount the gallows at last I may well say with the Psalmist (putting it, of course, into the prudent past tense) : The lines have fallen unto me in pleasant places.

Roaring Gap, N. C., 1939.   H. L. M.

Happy Days

I

INTRODUCTION TO THE

𝔘𝔫𝔦𝔳𝔢𝔯𝔰𝔢

AT the instant I first became aware of the cosmos we all infest I was sitting in my mother's lap and blinking at a great burst of lights, some of them red and others green, but most of them only the bright yellow of flaring gas. The time: the evening of Thursday, September 13, 1883, which was the day after my third birthday. The place: a ledge outside the second-story front windows of my father's cigar factory at 368 Baltimore street, Baltimore, Maryland, U. S. A., fenced off from space and disaster by a sign bearing the majestic legend: AUG. MENCKEN & BRO. The occasion: the third and last annual Summer Nights' Carnival of the Order of Orioles, a society that adjourned *sine die*, with a thumping deficit, the very next morning, and has since been forgotten by the whole human race.

At that larval stage of my life, of course, I knew nothing whatever about the Order of Orioles, just as I knew nothing whatever about the United States, though I had been born to their liberties, and was entitled to the protection of their army and navy. All I was aware of, emerging from the unfathomable abyss of nonentity, was the fact that the world I had just burst into seemed to be very brilliant, and that peeping at it over my father's sign was somewhat hard on my still gelatinous bones. So I made signals of distress to my mother and was duly hauled into her lap, where I first dozed and then snored away until the lights went out, and the family buggy wafted me home, still asleep.

The latter details, you will understand, I learned subsequently from historians, but I remember the lights with great clarity, and entirely on my own. They constitute not only the earliest of all my earthly recollections, but also one of my most vivid, and I take no stock in the theories of psychologists who teach that events experienced so early in life are never really recalled, but only reconstructed from family gossip. To be sure, there is a dead line beyond which even the most grasping memory does not reach, but I am sure that in my own case it must have run with my third birthday. Ask me if I recall the occasion, probably before my second, when I was initiated into the game of I-spy by a neighbor boy, and went to hide behind a wire screen, and was astonished when he detected me — ask me about that, and I'll admit freely that I recall nothing of it whatever, but only the ensuing anecdote, which my poor mother was so fond of telling that in the end I hid in the cellar every time she started it. Nor do I remember anything on my own about my baptism (at which ceremonial my father, so I have heard, made efforts to get the rector tight, and was hoist by his own petard), for I was then but a few months old. But not all the psychologists on earth, working in shifts like coal-miners, will ever convince me that I don't remember those lights, and wholly under my own steam.

They made their flash and then went out, and the fog again closed down. I don't recall moving to the new house in Hollins street that was to be my home for so many years, though we took possession of it only a few weeks later. I don't recall going into pants at about a quarter to four years, though it must have been a colossal experience, full of pride and glory. But gradually, as my consciousness jelled, my days began to be speckled with other events that, for one reason or another, stuck. I recall, though only somewhat vaguely, the deck of an excursion-boat, *circa* 1885, its deafening siren, and the wide, gray waters of Chesapeake Bay. I recall very clearly being taken by my father to a clothing-store bright with arc-lights, then a novelty in the world, and seeing great piles of elegant Sunday suits, and coming home with one that was tight across the stern. I recall a straw hat with flowing ribbons, a cat named Pinkie, and my brother Charlie, then still a brat in long clothes, howling like a catamount one hot Summer night, while my mother dosed him with the whole pharmacopoeia of the house, and frisked him for outlaw pins. I recall, again, my introduction to the wonderland of science, with an earthworm (*Lumbricus terrestris*) as my first subject, and the experiment directed toward finding out how long it would take him, laid out in the sun on the backyard walk, to fry to death. And I recall my mother reading to me, on a dark Winter afternoon, out of a book describing the adventures of the Simple Simon who went to a fair, the while she sipped a cup of tea that smelled very cheerful, and I glued my nose to the frosty window pane, watching a lamplighter light the lamps in Union Square across the street and wondering what a fair might be. It was a charming, colorful, Kate Greenaway world that her reading took me into, and to this day I can shut my eyes and still see its little timbered houses, its boys and girls gamboling on village greens, and its unclouded skies of pale blue.

I was on the fattish side as an infant, with a scow-like beam and noticeable jowls. Dr. C. L. Buddenbohn, who fetched me into sentience at 9 p.m., precisely, of Sunday, September 12, 1880, apparently made a good (though, as I hear, somewhat rough) job of it, despite the fact that his surviving bill, dated October 2, shows that all he charged " to one confinement " was ten dollars. The science of infant feeding, in those days, was as rudimentary as bacteriology or social justice, but there can be no doubt that I got plenty of calories and vitamins, and probably even an overdose. There is a photograph of me at eighteen months which looks like the pictures the milk companies print in the rotogravure sections of the Sunday papers, whooping up the zeal of their cows. If cannibalism had not been abolished in Maryland some years before my birth I'd have butchered beautifully.

My mother used to tell me years afterward that my bulk often attracted public notice, especially when it was set off dramatically against her own lack of it, for she was of slight frame and less than average height, and looked, in her blue-eyed blondness, to be even younger than she actually was. Once, hauling me somewhere by horse-car, she was confronted by an old man who gaped at her and me for a while with senile impertinence, and then burst out: " Good God, girl, is that baby *yours?* " This adiposity passed off as I began to run about, and from the age of six onward I was rather skinny, but toward the end of my twenties my cross-section again became a circle, and at thirty I was taking one of the first of the anti-fat cures, and beating it by sly resorts to malt liquor.

My gradually accumulating and clarifying memories of infancy have to do chiefly with the backyard in Hollins street, which had the unusual length, for a yard in a city block, of a hundred feet. Along with my brother Charlie, who followed me into this vale when I was but twenty months old, I spent most of my pre-school leisure in it, and found it a strange, wild land of endless discoveries and enchantments. Even in the dead of Winter we were pastured in it almost daily, bundled up in the thick, scratchy coats, overcoats, mittens, leggings, caps, shirts, over-shirts and under-drawers that the young then wore. We wallowed in the snow whenever there was any to wallow in, and piled it up into crude houses, forts and snow-men, and inscribed it with wavering scrolls and devices by the method followed by infant males since the Würm Glaciation. In Spring we dug worms and watched for robins, in Summer we chased butterflies and stoned sparrows, and in Autumn we made bonfires of the falling leaves. At all times from March to October we made a Dust Bowl of my mother's garden.

The Hollins street neighborhood, in the eighties, was still almost rural, for there were plenty of vacant lots nearby, and the open country began only a few blocks away. Across the street from our house was the wide green of Union Square, with a fishpond, a cast-iron Greek temple housing a drinking-fountain, and a little brick office and tool-house for the square-keeper, looking almost small enough to have been designed by Chick Sale. A block to the westward, and well within range of our upstairs windows, was the vast, mysterious compound of the House of the Good Shepherd, with nuns in flapping habits flitting along its paths and alleys, and a high stone wall shutting it in from the world. In our backyard itself there were a peach tree, a cherry tree, a plum tree, and a pear tree. The pear tree survives to this day, and is still as lush and vigorous as it was in 1883, beside being thirty feet higher and so large around the waist that its branches bulge into the neighboring yards. My brother and I used to begin on the cherries when they were still only pellets of hard green, and had got through three or four powerful bellyaches before the earliest of them was ripe. The peaches, pears and plums came later in the year, but while we were waiting for them we chewed the gum that oozed from the peach-tree trunk, and practised spitting the imbedded flies and June bugs at Pinkie the cat.

There was also a grape-arbor arching the brick walk, with six vines that flourished amazingly, and produced in the Autumn a huge crop of sweet Concord grapes. My brother and I applied ourselves to them diligently from the moment the first blush of color showed on them, and all the sparrows of West Baltimore helped, but there was always enough in the end to fill a couple of large dishpans, and my mother and the hired girl spent a hot afternoon boiling them down, and storing them away in glass tumblers with tin tops. My brother and I, for some reason or other, had no fancy for the grape jelly thus produced with so much travail, but we had to eat it all Winter, for it was supposed, like camomile tea, to be good for us. I don't recall any like embalming of the peaches, plums and pears; in all probability we got them all down before there were any ripe enough to preserve. The grapes escaped simply because some of them hung high, as in the fable of the fox. In later years we collared these high ones by steeple-jacking, and so paid for escape from the jelly with a few additional belly-aches.

But the show-piece of the yard was not the grape-arbor, nor even the fruit-trees; it was the Summer-house, a rococo structure ten feet by ten in area, with a high, pointed roof covered with tin, a wooden floor, an ornate railing, and jig-saw spirals wherever two of its members came together. This Summer-house had been designed and executed by my mother's father, our Grandfather Abhau, who was a very skillful cabinet-maker, and had also made some of the furniture of the house. Everything of his construction was built to last, and when, far on in the Twentieth Century, I hired a gang of house-wreckers to demolish the Summer-house, they sweated half a day with their crowbars

and pickaxes. In the eighties it was the throne-
room and justice-seat of the household, at least in
Summer. There, on fair Sunday mornings, my father and his brother Henry, who lived next door,
met to drink beer, try out new combinations of tobacco for their cigar factory, and discuss the credit
of customers and the infamies of labor agitators.
And there, on his periodical visitations as head of
the family, my Grandfather Mencken sat to deter-
mine all the delicate questions within his jurisdiction.

My mother was an active gardener, and during
her forty-two years in Hollins street must have
pulled at least a million weeds. For this business,
as I first recall her, she had a uniform consisting
of a long gingham apron and an old-time slat-
bonnet — a head-dress that went out with the Nineteenth Century. Apron and slat-bonnet hung on
nails behind the kitchen door, and on a shelf adjoining were her trowels, shears and other such tools,
including always a huge ball of twine. My brother
Charlie and I, as we got on toward school age, were
drafted to help with the weeding, but neither of us
could ever make out any difference between weeds
and non-weeds, so we were presently transferred to
the front of the house, where every plant that came
up between the cobblestones of Hollins street was
indubitably verminous. The crop there was always
large, and keeping it within bounds was not an
easy job. We usually tackled it with broken

kitchen knives, and often cut our hands. We disliked it so much that it finally became convict labor. That is to say, it was saved up for use as punishment. I recall only that the maximum penalty was one hour, and that this was reserved for such grave offenses as stealing ginger-snaps, climbing in the pear-tree, hanging up the cat by its hind leg, or telling lies in a gross and obvious manner.

Charlie was somewhat sturdier than I, and a good deal fiercer. During most of our childhood he could lick me in anything approximating a fair fight, or, at all events, stall me. Civil war was forbidden in Hollins street, but my Grandfather Mencken, who lived in Fayette street, only three blocks away, had no apparent objection to it, save of course when he was taking his afternoon nap. I remember a glorious day when eight or ten head of his grandchildren called on him at once, and began raising hell at once. The affair started as a more or less decorous pillow-fight, but proceeded quickly to much more formidable weapons, including even bed-slats. It ranged all over the house, and must have done a considerable damage to the bric-a-brac, which was all in the Middle Bismarck mode. My grandmother and Aunt Pauline, fixed by my grandfather's pale blue eye, pretended to be amused by it for a while, but when a large china thunder-mug came bouncing down the third-story stairs and a black hair-cloth sofa in the parlor lost a leg they horned in with loud shrieks and lengths of stove-wood, and my grandfather called time.

Charlie and I were very fond of Aunt Pauline, who was immensely hospitable, and the best doughnut cook in all the Baltimores. When the creative urge seized her, which was pretty often, she would make enough doughnuts to fill a large tin washboiler, and then send word down to Hollins street that there was a surprise waiting in Fayette street. It was uphill all the way, but Charlie and I always took it on the run, holding hands and pretending that we were miraculously dashing car-horses. We returned home an hour or so later much more slowly, and never had any appetite for supper. The immemorial tendency of mankind to concoct rituals showed itself in these feasts. After Charlie had got down his first half dozen doughnuts, and was taking time out to catch his breath and scrape the grease and sugar off his face, Aunt Pauline would always ask " How do they taste? " and he would always answer " They taste like more." Whether this catechism was original with the high contracting parties or had been borrowed from some patent-medicine almanac or other reference-work I don't know, but it never varied and it was never forgotten.

There were no kindergartens, playgrounds or other such Devil's Islands for infants in those innocent days, and my brother and I roved and rampaged at will until we were ready for school. Hollins street was quite safe for children, for there was little traffic on it, and that little was slow-moving, and a cart approaching over the cobblestones could be heard a block away. The backyard was enough for us during our earliest years, with the cellar in reserve for rainy days, but we gradually worked our way into the street and then across it to Union Square, and there we picked up all the games then prevailing. A few years ago, happening to cross the square, I encountered a ma'm in horn-rimmed spectacles teaching a gang of little girls ring-around-a-rosy. The sight filled me suddenly with so black an indignation that I was tempted to grab the ma'm and heave her into the goldfish pond. In the days of my own youth no bossy female on the public payroll was needed to teach games to little girls. They taught one another — as they had been doing since the days of Neanderthal Man.

Nevertheless, there was a constant accretion of novelty, at least in detail. When we boys chased Indians we were only following the Sumerian boys who chased Akkadians, but the use of hatchets was certainly new, and so was the ceremony of scalping; moreover, our fiends in human form, Sitting Bull and Rain-in-the-Face, had been as unknown and unimagined to the Sumerian boys as Henry Ward Beecher or John L. Sullivan. The group songs we sang were mainly of English provenance, but they had all degenerated with the years. Here, precisely, is what we made of " King William " in Hollins street, *circa* 1885:

> King William was King James's son;
> Upon a ri' a race he won;
> Upon his breast he wore a star,
> The which was called the life of war.

What a *ri'* was we never knew and never inquired, nor did we attach any rational concept to *the life of war*. A favorite boys' game, called " Playing Se*bast*apool " (with a heavy accent on the *bast*), must have been no older in its outward form than the Crimean War, for Sebastapool was plainly Sevastopol, but in its essence it no doubt came down from Roman times. It could be played only when building or paving was going on in the neighborhood, and a pile of sand lay conveniently near. We would fashion this sand into circular ramparts in some friendly gutter, and then bristle the ramparts with gaudy tissue-paper flags, always home-made. Their poles were slivers of firewood, and their tissue-paper came from Newton's toy-store at Baltimore and Calhoun streets, which served the boys and girls of West Baltimore for seventy years, and did not shut down at last until the Spring of 1939. The hired girls of the block cooked flour paste to fasten the paper to the poles.

To the garrison of a Sebastapool all the smaller boys contributed tin soldiers, including Indians. These soldiers stood in close and peaceful ranks, for there was never any attempt at attack or defense. They were taken in at night by their owners, but the flags remained until rain washed the

15

Sebastapool away, or the milkman's early morning horse squashed it. There were sometimes two or three in a block. Girls took a hand in making the flags, but they were not allowed to pat the ramparts into shape, or to touch the tin soldiers. Indeed, for a little girl of that era to show any interest in military affairs would have been as indecorous as for her to play leap-frog or chew tobacco. The older boys also kept rather aloof, though they stood ready to defend a Sebastapool against raiders. Tin soldiers were only for the very young. The more elderly were beyond such inert and puerile simulacra, which ranked with rag dolls and paper boats. These elders fought in person, and went armed.

In the sacred rubbish of the family there is a specimen of my handwriting dated 1883 — two signatures on a sheet of paper now turned a dismal brown, the one small and rather neat and the other large and ornamented with flourishes. They seem somehow fraudulent, for I was then but three years old, but there they are, and the date, which is in my mother's hand, is very clear. Maybe she guided my stubby fingers. In the same collection there is another specimen dated January 1, 1887. It shows a beginning ease with the pen, though hardly much elegance. My mother also taught me many other humble crafts — for example, how to drive a nail, how to make paper boats, and how to sharpen a lead pencil. She even taught me how to thread a needle, and for a time I hoped to take over darning my own stockings and patching the seats of my own pants, but I never managed to master the use of the thimble, and so I had to give up. Tying knots was another art that stumped me. To this day I can't tie a bow tie, though I have taken lessons over and over again from eminent masters, including such wizards as Joe Hergesheimer and Paul Patterson. When I go to a party someone has to tie my tie for me. Not infrequently I arrive with the ends hanging, and must appeal to my hostess.

This incapacity for minor dexterities has pursued me all my life, often to my considerable embarrassment. In school I could never learn to hold a pen in the orthodox manner: my handwriting satisfied the professors, but my stance outraged them, and I suffered some rough handling until they finally resigned me to my own devices. In later life I learned bricklaying, and also got some fluency in rough carpentering, but I could never do anything verging upon cabinet-work. Thus I inherited nothing of the skill of my Grandfather Abhau. All my genes in that field came from my father, who was probably the most incompetent man with his hands ever seen on earth. I can't recall him teaching me anything in my infancy, not even marbles. He would sometimes brag of his youthful virtuosity at all the customary boys' games, but he always added that he had grown so old (he was thirty-one when I was six) and suffered so much from dead beats, noisy children and ungrateful cigarmakers, drummers and bookkeepers that he had lost it. Nor could he match the endless stories that my mother told me in the years before I could read, or the many songs. The only song I ever heard him sing was this one:

> Rain forty days,
> Rain forty nights,
> Sauerkraut sticking out the smokestack.

Apparently there were additional words, but if so he never sang them. The only *Märchen* in his répertoire had to do with a man who built a tin bridge. I recall nothing of this tale save the fact that the bridge was of tin, which astonished my brother and me all over again every time we heard of it. We tried to figure out how such a thing was possible, for the mention of tin naturally made us think of tomato-cans. But we never learned.

II

THE

Caves of Learning

My first day in school I have forgotten as I have forgotten my first day on earth, but my second I remember very well, for I etched it on my cortex by getting lost, along with my cousin Pauline, who lived next door in Hollins street.

Pauline and I were of an age, and hence entered the caves of learning together. They were situate in the very heart of old Baltimore, a good mile and a half from Hollins street, and the business of getting to them involved a long journey by the Baltimore-street horse-car, with a two-block walk to follow. On the first day we were taken over the route by Pauline's father, my uncle Henry, who gave us careful sailing directions along the way, pointing out all salient lights and landfalls — the City Hall

dome, the *Sun* Iron Building, Oehm's Acme Hall
(which specialized in boys' pants with double
seats), and so on. On the second day, launched on
our own, we recalled enough of this instruction to
board the horse-car going in the right direction,
and even enough to get off correctly at Holliday
street, but after that our faculties failed us, and
we set out afoot toward the right instead of the left.

The result was that we presently found ourselves
in Pratt street, an inferno of carts and trucks, with
the sluggish Back Basin, which smelled like the
canals of Venice, confronting us on the far side.
The Basin looked immense to us, and unmistakably
sinister. Over its dark, greasy waters a score of
Chesapeake Bay packets were in motion, churning
up the slime with their paddles and blowing their
sirens ferociously. It was a fascinating spectacle,
but terrifying, and in a little while we began to
blubber, and a crowd of Aframerican dock-wallop-
ers gathered around us, and a cop was soon pushing
his way through it, inquiring belligerently what in
hell the trouble was now. We must have managed
to tell him the name of our school, though that part
of it is a blank, for he delivered us only a few minutes late to the principal and proprietor thereof,
Professor Friedrich Knapp, and got a shot of
Boonekamp bitters for his pains.

This was my introduction (barring that obliterated first day) to F. Knapp's Institute, a seminary that catered to the boys and girls of the Bal-

timore bourgeoisie for more than sixty years. It
was already beginning, in 1886, to feel the competition of the public schools, but Professor Knapp
was not alarmed, for he believed firmly, and often
predicted, that the public schools would collapse
soon or late under the weight of their own inher-
ent and incurable infamy. They were fit, he argued
freely, only for dealing with boys too stupid, too
lazy, too sassy or too dirty to be admitted to such
academies as his own, and it was their well-deserved
destiny to be shut down eventually by the police, if
not by actual public violence. As for sending girls
to them, he simply could not imagine it; as well
shame and degrade the poor little angels by cutting
off their pigtails or putting them into pants.

The professor discoursed on the obscene subject
very often, and with special heat whenever another
boy left him to tackle the new and cheaper learning.
He always hinted that he had really kicked the
traitor out, and sometimes he followed with a hom-
ily on parents who neglected the upbringing of
their children, and so bred forgers, footpads and
assassins. The worst punishment he ever threatened against a boy who came to school with his hair
uncombed, or supernormal shadows behind his ears,
was expulsion with a certificate so unfavorable that
only the public schools would take him. Every
time there was a hanging at the city jail (which was
pretty often in those days when psychiatrists still
confined themselves to running madhouses), he re-

ferred to the departed, not by his crime but by his education, which was invariably in the public schools. No authentic graduate of F. Knapp's Institute, he let it be known, had ever finished on the gallows.

Otherwise, the professor was a very mild and even amiable man, and much more diligent at praise than at blame. He was a Suabian who had come to Baltimore in 1850, and he still wore, nearly forty years afterward, the classical uniform of a German schoolmaster — a long-tailed coat of black alpaca, a boiled shirt with somewhat fringey cuffs, and a white lawn necktie. The front of his coat was dusty with chalk, and his hands were so caked with it that he had to blow it off every time he took snuff. He was of small stature but large diameter, and wore closely-clipped mutton-chop whiskers. His hands had the curious softness so often observed in pedagogues, barbers, and Y.M.C.A. secretaries. This impressed itself on me the first time he noticed me wiggling a loose milk-tooth with my tongue, and called me up to have it out. He watched for such manifestations sharply, and pulled, I should say, an average of six teeth a week. It was etiquette in the school for boys to bear this barbarity in silence. The girls could yell, but not the boys. Both, however, were free to howl under the bastinado, which was naturally applied to the girls much more lightly and less often than to the boys.

The professor viewed the pedagogical art with

great pride, and was a man of some eminence in the town. He was on easy terms with the Mayor, General Ferdinand C. Latrobe, who once got us an hour's release from learning by dropping in from the City Hall across the street to harangue us darkly on civic virtue. The old professor, in the days when I knew him, had begun to restrict his personal teaching to a few extra abstruse subjects, *e.g.*, fractions, but he always lined up all the boys for inspection in the morning, and he led both boys and girls in the singing that opened every day's session. For this last purpose all hands crowded into the largest classroom. The professor conducted with his violin, and his daughter Bertha helped out at a parlor organ. The songs, as I recall them, were chiefly German favorites of his youth — " Goldene Abend Sonne," " Winter, Adieu!," " Fuchs, du hast die Gans gestohlen," " Hurrah, Hurrah, Hurra-la-la-la-la!," and so on. Most of the pupils knew very little German, though they were taught it fiercely, but they all managed to sing the songs.

As I have said, the institute had already begun to wither around the edges when I first knew it. In 1879 (so I gather from a faded announcement in an old Baltimore directory) it had had a teaching staff of twelve savants, and offered instruction in French, Latin and Hebrew, not to mention German and English, but by my time the staff had evaporated down to six or seven, and French and Latin had been abandoned. There was still, however, a class in Hebrew for the accommodation of a dozen or more Jewish boys, and I sat in on its proceedings (which went on in the same classroom with less exotic proceedings) long enough to learn the Hebrew alphabet. This must have been in my ninth year. By the time I left Knapp's for the Polytechnic the class had been shut down, and I had forgotten all the letters save *aleph, beth, vav, yodh* and *resh*. These I retain more or less to the present day, and whenever I find myself in the society of an orthodox rabbi I always show them off. On other Jews I do not waste them, for other Jews seldom recognize them.

There was no enmity between the Chosen and the *Goyim* in the old professor's establishment, and no sense of difference in his treatment of them, though he was in the habit, on bursting into a classroom that was disorderly, to denounce it violently as a *Judenschule*. He used this word, not because it was invidious, but simply because it described precisely the thing he complained of, and was sound colloquial German. He was also fond of using a number of Hebrew loan-words, for example, *tokos* (backside), *schlemihl* (oaf), *kosher* (clean) and *mashuggah* (crazy), most of which have since come into American. The Jewish boys of Baltimore, in that innocent era, were still palpably and unashamedly Jews, with Hittite noses, curly hair, and such given names as Aaron, Leon, Samuel and

Isaac. I never encountered one named Irving, Sidney, Malcolm or Wesley, nor even Charles or William. The old professor and his aides labored hard to teach these reluctant Yiddo-Americans the principles of their sacred tongue, but apparently with very little success, for the only textbook I ever saw in use was an elementary *Fibel*, with letters almost as large as those in the top line of an oculist's chart. All its victims were of German-Jewish origin, and came of well-to-do families, for in those days Eastern Jews were still rare in Baltimore, and whenever we boys passed one on the street we went Bzzzzzzzz in satirical homage to his beard. I must add in sorrow that the Jewish boys at Knapp's were unanimously *Chazirfresser*.

There was also in the school a group of students, all male, from Latin America, chiefly Cubans and Demerarans. I recall that their handkerchiefs were always well doused with perfume, and that they willingly paid tops, marbles and slate-pencils for the seats nearest the stove in Winter. There was one Cuban whose father had been captured by brigands and carved in a dreadful manner: his detailed description of the paternal wounds was very graphic, and made him something of a hero. For the rest, the student-body included German-Americans, Irish-Americans, French-Americans, Italian-Americans and even a few American-Americans. There was never any centrifugence on racial lines, and the only pupil I can remember who had a nickname hinting at anything of the sort was a husky German girl, lately arrived in the Republic, who went under the style or appellation of Germany-On-Wheels. She had a fist like a pig's foot and was not above clouting any boy who annoyed her. Moreover, she was a mistress of all the German declensions, and hence unpopular. The old professor treated these diverse tribes and species with uniform but benevolent suspicion — all, that is, save the American-Americans, whom he plainly regarded as intellectually underprivileged, to say the least. I also heard him hint more than once that their fathers were behind with their tuition fees.

The Institute, in its heyday, had specialized in German, but by my time all its teaching was in English. I must have learned some German in it, for to this day I can rattle off the German alphabet in par, and reading the Gothic type of a German newspaper is almost as easy to me as reading the Lateinisch. Also, I retain a few declensions in poll-parrot fashion, and can recite them with fearful fluency, especially under malt-and-hops power. Again, I can still write a very fair German script, though reading the script of actual Germans often stumps me. Yet again, I always get the curious feeling, hearing German spoken, that it is not really a foreign language, for all its sounds seem quite natural to me, including even the *ch* of *ich*. But the professor and his goons certainly never taught me to speak German, or even to read it with any ease. They tried to ram it into their pupils as they rammed in the multiplication table — by endless repetition, usually in chorus. To this day I know the conjugation of *haben* down to *Sie würden gehabt haben*, though I couldn't write even a brief note in Hoch Deutsch without resort to a grammar and a dictionary. What little of the language I actually acquired in my youth I picked up mainly from the German hired girls who traipsed through the Hollins street kitchen during the eighties — corralled at the Norddeutscher-Lloyd pier at Locust Point by my father (who spoke next to no German, but knew the chief inspector of immigrants), and then snatched away, after a year or so, by some amorous ice-man, beer-man or ash-man. One actually married a saloonkeeper, learned bartending, survived him, and died rich. My mother complained bitterly that these husky Kunigundas, Käthes, Ottilies and Charlöttchens were hardly house-broken before they flitted away, but some of them, and especially the Bavarians, were prime cooks, and all of them were ready to feed my brother Charlie and me at any moment, and to lie us out of scrapes.

My father, whose mother had been British-born, had a firm grasp upon only the more indecorous expletives of German, so the language was not used in the house. But my mother knew it well enough to palaver with the hired girls, and with the German marketmen, plumbers, tinners, beermen and grocery boys who were always in and out. When her father dropped in he would speak to her in German, but she would usually talk back, for some reason that I never learned, in English. Such bilingual dialogues sometimes went on for hours, to the fascination of my brother and me. We tried to figure out what the old man had said on the basis of what my mother answered. Maybe this taught us some German, but probably not much. One of the family anecdotes has to do with my efforts as a small child to dredge out of this grandfather an explanation of the puzzling differences between his language and ours. " Grandpa," I asked him, " if the German for *kiss* is *Kuss*, why isn't the German for *fish Fush?* " He knew English well enough, but this mystery he could not explain. My brother and I concocted a dreadful dialect for communicating with the German hired girls in their pre-English stages. Its groundwork was a crudely simplified English, but it included many pseudo-German words based on such false analogies as the one I have just mentioned, for example, *Monig* for *money* (from *Honig-honey*) and *Ratz* for *rat* (from *Katz-cat*). How we arrived at *Roch* for *(cock)roach* (pronounced in the German manner, to rhyme with *Loch*) I can't tell you: it must have been a sheer inspiration. To this day, alas, my

German is dreadful (though not quite as bad as my Sanskrit and Old Church Slavonic), and it always amuses me to encounter the assumption that I am a master of it, and even a scholar.

Professor Knapp, to return to him, spent most of his day moseying in and out of his classrooms at the institute, observing the technic of his agents and doing drum-head justice on boys of an evil nature. He was a virtuoso with the rattan, and chose his tool for a given caning with apparent care. He had an arsenal as large as a golfer's bag of clubs, and carried it with him from class to class. But the routine of the operation was always the same, and every boy knew it as familiarly as he knew the rules of run-a-mile or catty. The condemned would be beckoned politely to the place of execution beside the teacher's desk, and at the word *Eins* from the professor he would hold up his hands. At *Zwei* he would lower them until they stuck out straight from his shoulders, and at *Drei* he would bend over until his finger-tips touched his ankles. The punitive swooshes *a posteriori* would follow — sometimes two, three or even four, but more often only one. As I have said, it was etiquette for the condemned to make an outcry. He was also allowed and even expected to massage his *gluteus maximus* violently as he pranced back to his bench. This always led the professor to remark sagely: " You can't rub it out." Criminal girls were punished

29

more gently, with smacks from a ruler on the open palm. They consoled themselves by hugging the insulted hand under the opposite arm.

The professor showed very little moral indignation when he carried on such exercises, and I never heard of a victim denouncing them as unjust. Whenever they took place the whole class seemed to be convinced that they were sound in law and equity, and necessary to peace and civilization. No doubt this was because the professor always took much more visible delight in rewards than in punishments. When, listening in on a recitation, he noted a boy or girl who did well, he grinned like a Santa Claus, and halted the proceedings long enough to give the worthy one a " merit." A merit was simply a card inscribed with the date and the recipient's name, and signed by the professor. Teachers could also award them, but we naturally liked the professor's best. A pupil who accumulated fifty in the course of a year received a book at the close of school, with his parents present to swell with pride. I received my first on June 28, 1888. It was a copy of Grimms' Fairy Tales, horribly translated by a lady of the name of Mrs. H. B. Paull. I got it, as the inscription notifies, " for industry and good deportment." I have it still, and would not part with it for gold and frankincense.

These merits were not plain cards, but works of art in the *Gartenlaube* manner, and very elegant in our eyes. They were lithographed in full color, and commonly showed a spray of flowers, a cat playing with a ball of wool, or a Winter scene in the Black Forest, with the snow represented by powdered mica. Sometimes the art took the form of a separate hand, embossed as well as colored. The hand was anchored to the card at the cuff, which was always laced, and one got at the inscription by turning back the fingers. Merits with hands were especially esteemed, though they had no greater exchange value than the plain ones. One of them still survives as a bookmark in the copy of Grimms' Fairy Tales aforesaid. On my withdrawal from these scenes it will go to the League of Nations.

There were teachers at the institute who came and went mysteriously and have been forgotten, but I remember very clearly all the members of the permanent staff — the old professor's daughter, Miss Bertha; his niece, Miss Elvina; his son, Mr. Willie; his chief-of-staff, Mr. Fox; and his slave, Mr. Paul. Mr. Paul was a tall, smooth-shaven, saturnine German who always wore a long black coat, and was greatly given to scenting himself with *Kölnischeswasser*. There was no science of ventilation in those days, and schoolrooms were kept hermetically sealed. Mr. Paul's powerful aroma thus served admirably as a disinfectant, but toward the end of a laborious day it sometimes made us more or less giddy. He lived at the school, taking part of his emolument in board and lodging, and I heard years later, from a fellow pupil who was a great hand at the keyhole, that his maximum salary in cash was never above $10 a week.

This fact was no doubt responsible for his generally subversive frame of mind, which led him to an unhappy false step in 1888 or thereabout, almost fatal to his career. It took the form of an address to his class advocating the eight-hour day, then an anarchistic novelty in the world, and almost as alarming to the bourgeoisie as the downright confiscation of tax-free securities would be today. Worse, he recited a slogan in support of it, running as follows:

> Eight hours for work;
> Eight hours for sleep;
> Eight hours for what you will.

The boys could make nothing of his argument, but quickly learned the slogan. I did so myself and one evening recited it proudly to my father, looking confidently for his applause. Instead, he leaped from his chair, turned pale, and began to swear and splutter in a fearful manner. I made off in alarm, and it was years afterward before I learned from him why he was so indignant, and what followed from his dudgeon.

It appeared then that he had been convinced in conscience, and was still convinced in conscience, that the eight-hour day was a project of foreign nihilists to undermine and wreck the American Republic. In his own cigar factory nearly all work was piece-work, so he really didn't care how long his men kept at it, but he conceived it to be his duty to holler against the heresy in the interest of other employers. This he did, it appeared, on the very next day, and to Professor Knapp. The professor, who had also heard from other fathers, was much upset, and had Mr. Paul on the carpet. From that time on we heard nothing more of the subject. Mr. Paul applied himself with undivided diligence to his chosen branches — penmanship, free-hand drawing, mathematics up to the multiplication table, and deportment — and discreetly avoided all politico-economic speculations.

He was a kindly man, with some gifts as a draftsman. He taught me to draw complicated, fantastic, incredible flowers with both pen and pencil, and on lazy afternoons he would often suspend his teaching and entertain the boys and girls by covering the blackboard with images of birds carrying letters in their bills, and their plumage bulging out into elaborate curlicues. This art, now in decay, was greatly esteemed in those days. In penmanship Mr. Paul followed classical models. Every downstroke had to be good and thick, and every upstroke as thin as a spider's web.

At Christmas time all the boys and girls were put to writing canned letters of filial duty to their parents. Fancy four-page blanks were provided for this purpose, with the first page lithographed in full color. The text was written on the blackboard, all inkwells were cleaned and refilled, and new pens of great fineness were provided. The first boy who made a blot tasted the rattan, and after that everyone was very careful. As I recall it, the business of concocting these letters occupied the better part of a day. The professor himself dropped in from time to time to praise the young penmen who were doing well, and to pull the ears of those who were making messes. When an error was detected his son, Mr. Willie, was sent for to scratch it out with a sharp penknife. Too many errors caused the whole blank to be condemned and torn up, and the offender had to buy another at a cost of ten cents. We were always glad when this agony was over.

Mr. Willie, when I first knew him, was in his middle thirties. He was short and stocky, wore the silky mustache of the period, and combed his hair in oyster-shell style. He was much more worldly than Mr. Paul, and often entertained us with tales of his adventures. One of his favorite stories recounted his observations and sensations on seeing a surgeon cut off a man's leg. This happened somewhere in the West, where he had served for a year or two as a disbursing agent of the General Land Office. The boys liked the story, and encouraged him to improve its horrors, but the girls clapped their hands over their ears whenever he began it, and professed to shiver. He was also fond of telling about the hazards of navigating the Missouri

river, which he had traversed during the seventies
to the southern frontier of what is now South Da-
kota. In one of his stories he told how the river-
packets of the time, when they ran aground on a
sandbar, put out stilts operated by steam, and
lifted themselves over it. Not a boy in the school
believed this story, and I myself was nearly forty
years old before I discovered that it was really
true. But one of Mr. Willie's actual stretchers I
swallowed without a shadow of doubt. He was dis-
coursing one day on the immense number of books
in the world, and their infinite variety. " On the
single subject of the eye of the dog," he said,
" enough has been written to fill this classroom."
We all believed that one.

The dean or first mate of F. Knapp's Institute
was Mr. Fox, a tall Pennsylvanian with a goatish
beard, greatly resembling the late Admiral Win-
field Scott Schley. He ran the school store, and
carried it about with him in a large black dispatch-
box. The boys believed that he made a large income selling them pens, slate-pencils, pads of
scratch-paper, and other such supplies. They also
believed that he made a great deal of additional
money by serving as the secretary of a lodge of
Freemasons. The business of this lodge occupied
him on dull afternoons, when recitations degenerated into singsong, and there was no rattaning to
be done. He would spend hours addressing post-
cards to the members, notifying them of initiations,

oyster-roasts, funerals, and the like. While he plugged away he would solemnly chew his beard. We boys marvelled that it never grew any shorter.

Mr. Fox assisted the old professor as lord high executioner, and did most of the minor fanning of the wicked. He employed a frayed rattan of small percussive powers, and was but little feared. One day in 1889 I saw demonstrated before him the truth of Oscar Wilde's saying that nature always imitates art. The comic papers of the time had among their stock characters a boy who put a slate, a shingle or a book in his pants to protect himself from justice. This was actually done in my sight by a very small boy whose name, as I recall it, was Johnnie Horlamus. When Mr. Fox turned him over, the seat of his pants bulged out into an incredible square, and Mr. Fox halted the proceedings to investigate. His search produced a third grade geography-book. When he pulled it out the whole class roared, and he had to bite his beard hard to keep from roaring himself. He let Johnnie off with a single very gentle clout.

Mr. Fox was no virtuoso like the professor. He rattaned conscientiously, but without any noticeable style. The professor not only adorned the science, but made a notable contribution to it. This was the invention of mass caning, the use of which was confined to his morning inspection in the schoolyard. It often happened that he would detect three, four or even five boys with unshined

shoes or unwashed ears. He would order them to
step forward a few paces, and then line them up
very precisely. When they had all got into the
position called for by his command of *Drei* he
would try to fetch their fundaments simultaneously
with one swoop of an extra-long rattan. Sometimes he succeeded, and sometimes he failed. The
favorite spot in the line was naturally the one
nearest him, for the boy who had it got the thick
part of the rattan, swinging through a small arc,
and was hence but little hurt. The boy at the far
end got the thin and poisonous tip, swinging over
an orbit long enough to give it the speed of a
baseball and the bite of an adder's fang.

The professor believed that he was responsible
for the policing and sanitation of his pupils from
the time they left home in the morning until they
returned there safely in the afternoon. It was a
felony by the school code for a boy to hook a ride
on a horse-truck. Culprits were detected by the
simple fact that such trucks, being dirty, commonly left marks on the knees of stockings or seats
of pants or both, but the boys preferred to believe
that they were betrayed by stooges among the
girls. Many an innocent girl had her pigtail
severely yanked on that charge. This yanking was
itself a felony, but the victim seldom complained,
for if she did so her pigtail would be surely yanked
again, and with a yo-heave-ho so hearty that it
just fell short of scalping her.

The most serious of all crimes, of course, was fighting on the streets. When detected, it not only brought a Class A rattaning, but also a formal threat of banishment to the Gehenna of the public schools. But the institute's statutes, like the canon law of Holy Church, always provided for exceptions and dispensations. In this case the pummeling, clubbing and even (if it could be imaginably achieved) strangling and dismemberment of a boy from Scheib's School was dismissed as venial. Scheib's was so close to F. Knapp's that the two were separated only by the narrow channel of Orange alley. Professor Knapp and Pastor Scheib were ostensibly on the most fraternal footing, and always spoke of each other in flattering terms, but there was a great deal of pupil-snatching to and fro, and deep down in their chalky pedagogical hearts they were a Guelph and a Ghibelline.

III

RECOLLECTIONS OF

𝕬𝖈𝖆𝖉𝖊𝖒𝖎𝖈 𝕺𝖗𝖌𝖎𝖊𝖘

SOME time ago I read in the New York papers about the death of an Irishman who had been esteemed and honored in life as the inventor of the hot-dog. The papers themselves appeared to believe that he had deserved this veneration, for they gave his peaceful exitus almost as much space as they commonly give to the terminal deliriums of a movie star or United States Senator. They said that he had made his epochal invention in the year 1900 or thereabout, and that it had been first marketed as consumers' goods at the Polo Grounds.

All this made me smile in a sly way, for I devoured hot-dogs in Baltimore 'way back in 1886, and they were then very far from new-fangled. They differed from the hot-dogs of today in one detail only, and that one was hardly of statistical significance. They contained precisely the same rubbery, indigestible pseudo-sausages that millions of Americans now eat, and they leaked the same flabby, puerile mustard. Their single point of difference lay in the fact that their covers were honest German *Wecke* made of wheat-flour baked to crispness, and not the soggy rolls prevailing today, of ground acorns, plaster-of-Paris, flecks of bath-sponge, and atmospheric air all compact.

The name hot-dog, of course, was then still buried in the womb of time: we called them *Weckers*, being ignorant that the true plural of *Weck* was *Wecke*, or in one of the exceptional situations so common in German grammar, *Wecken*. They were on sale at the Baltimore baseball-grounds in the primeval days before even Muggsy McGraw had come to town, and they were also sold at all picnics. In particular, I recall wolfing them at the annual picnic of F. Knapp's Institute. One year I got down six in a row, and suffered a considerable bellyache thereafter, which five bottles of sarsaparilla did not cure. My brother Charlie did even better. He knocked off eight *Wecke*, and then went strutting about with no bellyache at all. But Charlie, in those days, had a gizzard like a concrete-mixer, and I well recall the morning when he ate eighteen buckwheat cakes for breakfast, and gave up even then only because the hired girl had run out of batter.

The annual picnic of F. Knapp's Institute, always holden in early June, was the great event of the school year, and the older pupils began chattering about it soon after Christmas. Tickets were twenty-five cents each, but every pupil could buy them at five for a dollar, and the extra quarter was his profit. It was clearly understood that the money thus amassed was undividedly his own, and that the way he spent it was nobody's damned business. It was not etiquette for the teachers of the institute, or even his parents, to molest him when he set out to clean up the *Wecke*, pretzels, doughnuts and other delicatessen that were on sale on the grounds, or tried to stretch his skin over ten or a dozen bottles of sarsaparilla. If he collapsed there were benches for him to lie on, and a bottle of paregoric to medicate him.

The picnic was always held at Darley Park, a pleasant grove adjoining a suburban brewery. It was outfitted in the stark, Philistine style of the period, with all the trees whitewashed up to a height of six feet. Scattered about were a couple of dozen plain board tables, each outfitted with hard benches. In the middle of the grove was a small pavilion, with a senile excursion-boat piano in the center of it. Along one boundary ran a long brick building, and somewhere within it was a bar. The *Weck*, crab-cake, pretzel, doughnut and sarsaparilla vendors circled about, howling their wares. In a far corner was a portable carrousel with four horses, operated by what was then always called jackass-power. That is to say, it was kept going by a sweating Aframerican turning a crank. He turned it steadily from 10 a.m. to 4 p.m., and there were always plenty of girls and baby-class boys waiting in line. We more elderly roués spent all our money on food and drink. Sarsaparilla had a sharp bite, and, like opium, produced an appetite for itself. So did *Wecke*.

When the great day arrived all the pupils of the institute piled into a string of Gay-street horse-cars and proceeded to Darley Park at high speed. Professor Knapp always traveled by the first car, and took up at once the police duties of the day. He never carried his battery of rattans along, but he had sharp eyes and a good memory, and any boy who pulled too many of the girls' pigtails, or engaged in fisticuffs with another boy, or indulged himself in sassing a teacher was sure to go on trial the next morning, with two or three swooshes to rearward following. But crime was relatively rare at those picnics, and I remember one (I should add in frankness that it was considered exceptional) which didn't produce a single culprit. We played the immemorial games of the schoolyard, but mainly we played follow-your-leader. Sometimes as many as forty boys would be in line, and the course would include hurdles over all the benches in the park, and even up into the pavilion and over the excursion-boat piano. One year the leader, a large, gaunt boy who was generally regarded as feebleminded, led the gang out of the park and into an adjoining brickyard, and there took it through a series of puddles bottomed with red clay. When the procession returned and the professor saw the boys' shoes, he got into a dreadful lather, and soon after sunrise the next morning he broke a rattan over the half-wit's caboose.

At noon or thereabout parents began to arrive, usually in buggies. They were received formally by the whole faculty of the school, and the mothers proceeded at once to track down and inspect their offspring, looking (in the case of boys) for dirty hands, holes in stockings and skinned shins, and (in the case of girls) for torn skirts and lost hair-ribbons. Sometimes a black-hearted boy would sneak into the adjacent brickyard, which was covered in large part with Jimson weeds, plantains and other such vegetable outlaws, and return with a large ball of nigger-lice.[1] One of these nigger-lice, on being thrown at a girl, would stick to her dress. If it hit her hair, getting it out would be a tedious and even painful business. Indeed, it was generally believed by the boys of Baltimore that a nigger-louse lodged in the wool of an actual Negro girl could not be removed without shaving her head. When nigger-lice began to fly about at a school picnic the whole faculty would mobilize instantly, and in a little while the marks-

[1] The burrs of the common burdock (*Arctium minus*).

men would be detected and disarmed, and next morning they would get hearty fannings from the professor.

While the mothers of the pupils were inspecting them, their fathers, following custom, would invite the male pedagogues to the bar, and there ply them with beer. My father always had a low opinion of the Baltimore beers, and complained bitterly whenever he had to drink them. He concocted an elaborate legend about one of the worst of them, to the effect that it was made of the ammoniacal liquor discharged from the Baltimore gasworks, with mill-feed for malt and picric acid for hops. Once, when I was still a small boy, I was riding proudly with him on the platform of a horse-car, when he encountered a *Todsäufer* [2] belonging to the brewery that made it, and proceeded to warn him solemnly that drinking his own goods would wreck his kidneys and bring him to an early grave. To my astonishment, the *Todsäufer* admitted it freely, but explained that he

---

[2] A *Todsäufer* (literally, dead-drinker) was, and is a sort of brewer's customers' man. He is commonly called a collector, but his duties go far beyond collecting the bills owed to breweries by saloonkeepers. He is supposed to stand a general treat in the bar whenever he calls, to go to all weddings, birthday parties and funerals in the families of saloonkeepers, and to cultivate their wives and children with frequent presents. When a saloonkeeper himself dies the *Todsäufer* is the principal mourner *ex officio,* and is expected to weep copiously. He is also one of the brewery's political agents, and must handle all the license difficulties of his clients. He belongs to all the clubs and societies that will admit him, including always, if there is one, the town press-club.

owed $2000 to a building association on a house he had bought, and wanted to work off the debt before returning to his former and less remunerative trade of soft-drink drummer. My father thereupon offered him a job as a cigar salesman, but they couldn't come to terms. He must have actually died soon afterward, for I remember my father citing him as a tragic example of what men will do and suffer for money.

But the pedagogues appeared to stand the Darley Park beer very well, and indeed plainly liked it. As father after father dropped in, and schooner after schooner was dispatched, the gogues apparently gave glowing accounts of the diligence and scholarship of their pupils, for it was not uncommon for a father, coming out for air, to give his boy an extra ten cents. Mr. Fox, a man of quasi-military bearing, usually swayed ever so gently as the session in the bar ended, and he made his way to the pavilion for the closing ceremonies of the day. As for Mr. Paul, he emerged mopping his face solemnly with his cologne-scented handkerchief, and burping surreptitiously under it. I never detected any such signs in Mr. Willie, but that was probably because he was something of an *eleganto*, and always called for small beers. His hair was plastered down with plenty of soap, and not a strand of it was ever out of place. The old professor, being a Suabian, was immune to all the ordinary effects of alcohol. Toward the close of the ceremonies in the pavilion he always fell into a doze, but he did the same thing every afternoon of his life, whether he had been consuming malt liquor or well water.

The ceremonies themselves tended to be banal, for everybody was tired by then. They began with some songs by the massed pupils, accompanied by Miss Bertha on the excursion-boat piano, and they moved through the classical répertoire of recitations. I was once chosen to do " The Wreck of the Hesperus," but blew up in the second stanza. Elocution, indeed, has always been a closed art to me, for I have never been able to memorize even the shortest piece, whether in prose or verse. At the time of my first and only appearance as an actor on the public stage (it was after I had left F. Knapp's Institute) I forgot both of my two lines. My brother Charlie was called for to pinch hit for me when " The Wreck of the Hesperus " went phooey, but he did not respond, and a quick and quiet search found him hiding under the pavilion. There was always a little girl with a piano solo, but she was invariably drowned out by a freight-train of the Pennsylvania Railroad, which ran only a few blocks away.

If there were any politicoes present, which was usually the case, they arose to expound the issues of the hour. General Ferdinand C. Latrobe, Mayor of Baltimore for seven terms, always showed up, and always made a speech. Inasmuch as the pro-

fessor was a German, the general devoted himself
courteously to whooping up the unparalleled scientific, aesthetic and moral gifts of the German
people, and to revealing all over again the fact that
he was partly of German blood himself, despite
his French-sounding name. He made exactly simi-
lar speeches at all gatherings of predominantly
non-Anglo-Saxon Baltimoreans, omitting only the
Aframericans and the Chinese. In his later years
(I had by then become a newspaper reporter) I
heard him claim not only Irish, Scotch, Welsh,
Dutch and other such relatively plausible bloods,
but also Polish, Bohemian, Italian, Lithuanian,
Swedish, Danish, Greek, Spanish and even Jewish.
Once I actually heard him hint that he was remotely an Armenian. Unable by the current *mores*
to boast of African ancestry, he consoled his colored
customers by speaking in high terms of Abraham
Lincoln, whom he described as a Republican with
a Democratic heart. The best he could do for the
Chinese, who were then very few in Baltimore, was
to quote some passages from the Analects of Con-
fucius, which he had studied through the medium
of a secretary.

When the last politico shut down the professor
called off the proceedings, and we all started home.
My father drove the family buggy, and I sat between him and my mother, with my brother roost-
ing on a hassock on the floor. We kept to the horse-
car tracks as much as possible, for the cobblestones

of Baltimore, in those days, were world-famous for their roughness. Whenever we had to turn out on them my brother bounced off his hassock, and had to be derricked back. He and I were pretty well used up by the time we got home, and after a meager supper were ordered to bed. We slept as profoundly as convicts in the death-house, for it was not until the next morning that the chigger-bites picked up in the brickyard began to make themselves manifest. Half the boys scratched violently for three or four days thereafter, but none of the girls. The old professor always dropped in to point the moral. The boys, being naturally vicious, had disobeyed orders and explored the brickyard, which was a resort of noxious insects and human desperadoes, but the girls, being virtuous and law-abiding, had stayed on the right side of the fence. Hence their immunity.

There were plenty of other gala days during the school year, but none so stupendous as the day of the annual picnic, save maybe the day of the circus parade. All parades in Baltimore passed within hearing of F. Knapp's Institute, for the City Hall was only across the street, and its portico was the customary reviewing-stand. The most brutal punishment that could be imagined by a Knapp boy, or indeed any Baltimore schoolboy, was to be confined to barracks when a circus parade was under way. So far as I can recall, it never actually happened in our school, though it was often threatened.

We always turned out in command of Mr. Fox and
Mr. Paul, each of them armed with a rattan, and
the cops made room for us along the curb. If any
of the loafers who hung about the City Hall refused to move, the cops fell upon them with fists
and night-sticks, at the same time denouncing them
as low characters, fit only for penal servitude.

I remember of these circus parades only the
patient tramp of the elephants, the loudness of the
music, and the unearthly beauty of the lady bare-
back-riders, with their yellow wigs, dazzling span-
gles and pink tights. They seemed to us boys to
be even more beautiful than Miss Bertha and Miss
Elvina, who were our everyday paragons of female loveliness. The parade consumed most of the
morning, and those boys whose fathers were taking
them to the actual circus also escaped for the afternoon. They returned next day full of astounding
tales and in a low state of health, for pink lemonade
in that era was actually pink, and four or five
glasses of it left the gall-bladder considerably fevered. There was a memorable year when two cir-
cuses came to town, and another when the circus
was followed by Buffalo Bill's Wild West Show.
We admired Buffalo Bill and shivered at the sight
of his bloodthirsty Indians, but the general feeling
was that the circus was better. Certainly the lady
sharpshooters and Indian squaws had nothing on
the bareback riders.

Now and then the old professor and his staff

would shepherd the whole student body to some other public show, usually of a painfully cultural character. I remember clearly only one such expedition. It was an exhibit of Mexican arts and handicrafts at a hall in Charles street. The squat pottery, gaudy blankets, crude jewelry and other such stuff left me cold; indeed, I dislike all Mexican fancy-goods to this day, and regard even the masterpieces of Diego Rivera as trash. But I remember very brilliantly a sort of side-show, for it consisted of two human skeletons, the first I had ever seen. One was the skeleton of a peon who had been shot by a bandit, with the bullet hole plainly visible in the center of his forehead. The other was the skeleton of the bandit who had shot him, with one of the cervical vertebrae dislocated to show the effect of the rope that had punished the crime.

These ghastly relics were displayed in two long boxes covered with black cloth, and set up at an angle of sixty degrees. My brother and I, at first sight of them, turned quickly and slunk away, but things that are horrible are always fascinating to boys, and so we came back every now and then for another look, and by the end of the afternoon we had got massive eyefuls. That night (we slept together) we pulled the quilt over our heads and dreamed dreadful dreams of shootings, stabbings, scalpings, hangings, graveyards and dissecting-rooms, with herds of bleeding ghosts all over the place. I have encountered a great many skeletons since, and got upon easy terms with some of them, but whenever I shut my eyes and ponder upon mortality I always see the poor bones of those forlorn and anonymous Mexicans, bounced into Heaven in a far country and so long ago.

The crown and consummation of the year at Knapp's was the annual exhibition in June, following soon after the picnic. For this sombre event the largest schoolroom was chosen, and chairs for the parents of the pupils were arranged on the two sides of the teacher's desk. The programme followed classical models, stretching back, I suppose, to the times of Tiglath-pileser. First the whole school would sing, with Miss Bertha at the organ and the old professor leading with his violin; then the prizes (always books) won by diligent and docile pupils would be presented to them by Mr. Fox, who was an eminent Freemason and hence accustomed to public speaking; and then Mr. Willie would call up, one by one, all those who were not downright idiotic, and show off their learning. Some recited, some spelled hard words, some bounded Caroline county, Maryland, or Ohio, or Spain, some parsed all the components of such sentences as " The dog ate the bone," and some read in high-pitched, staccato, somewhat panicky voices out of the McGuffey Readers.

My own contribution to this symposium never took the form of a recitation, for, as I have said, I was born incapable of remembering anything longer than a limerick. Once, in term, Mr. Paul gave me a German poem of two brief stanzas to memorize, and I made such heavy weather of trying to get it that my father had to rescue me with a note to the old professor, desiring him to instruct Mr. Paul to lay off such infernal nonsense. (In those days, parents who patronized private schools had some voice in what their children were taught. On another occasion my father was full of indignation when I brought home the news that Mr. Paul believed and was teaching that the first *a* in *national* should be pronounced exactly like the first *a* in *nation*. Indeed, he was so upset that he made a call on the old professor the next morning, and was closeted with him for an hour. Mr. Paul, so far as I know, never formally recanted, but he at least went so far as to avoid the word thereafter.)

My own contribution to the annual exhibition usually took the form of a mathematical demonstration at the blackboard, say the multiplication of 75.876593 by 1129.654, or the division of 17/39ths by 71/163rds. I had no interest whatever in figures, but my father was a violent fan for them, so it gave him a great kick if I came out with an error of no more than plus-or-minus ten per cent., and when we got home he handed me a nickel, which in those days would buy a grab-bag containing at least half a pound of broken taffy and a ring or stickpin set with a large ruby.

My cousin Pauline, who was a very good reader, went through McGuffey at high speed, and my brother Charlie usually gave a more or less creditable performance at spelling, especially when the words lined out happened to be of less than two syllables. The other boys and girls displayed their various gifts one by one, and so the long morning wore on, with Mr. Willie sweating away doggedly, the boys scraping their feet on the floor and squirming in their chairs, and the parents (save when their own progeny were up) yawning dismally and rubbing themselves. As for the old professor, he invariably fell into a quiet doze, with his gold-rimmed spectacles shoved up on his forehead. When the City Hall bell struck twelve and the noon whistles began to blow he awoke suddenly and half rose to his feet.

" Villie," he would say, " daash ish genook."

At all events, that is how it sounded to me, and how I recall it today. He was, as I have noted, a Suabian, and reverted to the dialect of his native *Dorf* whenever his faculties were dimmed. Mr. Willie understood him to say " Das ist genug," which, in English, is " That's enough," and so the proceedings terminated.

The boys always piled out leaping and howling like early Christian martyrs delivered by angels from the stake, for next day was the beginning of the Summer vacation.

IV

THE BALTIMORE OF

𝔱𝔥𝔢 𝔈𝔦𝔤𝔥𝔱𝔦𝔢𝔰

THE CITY into which I was born in 1880 had a
reputation all over for what the English, in their
real-estate advertising, are fond of calling the
amenities. So far as I have been able to discover
by a labored search of contemporary travel-books,
no literary tourist, however waspish he may have
been about Washington, Niagara Falls, the prai-
ries of the West, or even Boston and New York,
ever gave Baltimore a bad notice. They all agreed,
often with lubricious gloats and gurgles, (*a*) that
its indigenous victualry was unsurpassed in the
Republic, (*b*) that its native Caucasian females
of all ages up to thirty-five were of incomparable
pulchritude, and as amiable as they were lovely,
and (*c*) that its home-life was spacious, charming,

full of creature comforts, and highly conducive to the facile and orderly propagation of the species.

There was some truth in all these articles, but not, I regret to have to add, too much. Perhaps the one that came closest to meeting scientific tests was the first. Baltimore lay very near the immense protein factory of Chesapeake Bay, and out of the bay it ate divinely. I well recall the time when prime hard crabs of the channel species, blue in color, at least eight inches in length along the shell, and with snow-white meat almost as firm as soap, were hawked in Hollins street of Summer mornings at ten cents a dozen. The supply seemed to be almost unlimited, even in the polluted waters of the Patapsco river, which stretched up fourteen miles from the bay to engulf the slops of the Baltimore canneries and fertilizer factories. Any poor man could go down to the banks of the river, armed with no more than a length of stout cord, a home-made net on a pole, and a chunk of cat's meat, and come home in a couple of hours with enough crabs to feed his family for two days. Soft crabs, of course, were scarcer and harder to snare, and hence higher in price, but not much. More than once, hiding behind my mother's apron, I helped her to buy them at the door for two-and-a-twelfth cents apiece. And there blazes in my memory like a comet the day when she came home from Hollins market complaining with strange and bitter indignation that the fishmongers there — including old Harris, her favorite — had begun to *sell* shad roe. Hitherto, stretching back to the first settlement of Baltimore Town, they had always thrown it in with the fish. Worse, she reported that they had now entered upon an illegal combination to lift the price of the standard shad of twenty inches — enough for the average family, and to spare — from forty cents to half a dollar. When my father came home for lunch and heard this incredible news, he predicted formally that the Republic would never survive the Nineteenth Century.

Terrapin was not common eating in those days, any more than it is in these, but that was mainly because few women liked it, just as few like it today. It was then assumed that their distaste was due to the fact that its consumption involved a considerable lavage with fortified wines, but they still show no honest enthusiasm for it, though Prohibition converted many of them into very adept and eager boozers. It was not, in my infancy, within the reach of the proletariat, but it was certainly not beyond the bourgeoisie. My mother, until well past the turn of the century, used to buy pint jars of the picked meat in Hollins market, with plenty of rich, golden eggs scattered through it, for a dollar a jar. For the same price it was possible to obtain *two* wild ducks of respectable if not royal species — and the open season ran gloriously from the instant the first birds wandered in from Labrador to the time the last stragglers set sail for Brazil.

So far as I can remember, my mother never bought any of these ducks, but that was only because the guns, dogs and eagle eye of my uncle Henry, who lived next door, kept us oversupplied all Winter.

Garden-truck was correspondingly cheap, and so was fruit in season. Out of season we seldom saw it at all. Oranges, which cost sixty cents a dozen, came in at Christmas, and not before. We had to wait until May for strawberries, asparagus, fresh peas, carrots, and even radishes. But when the huge, fragrant strawberries of Anne Arundel county (pronounced Ann'ran'l) appeared at last they went for only five cents a box. All Spring the streets swarmed with hucksters selling such things: they called themselves, not hucksters, but Arabs (with the first *a* as in *day*), and announced their wares with loud, raucous, unintelligible cries, much worn down by phonetic decay. In Winter the principal howling was done by colored men selling shucked oysters out of huge cans. In the dark backward and abysm of time their cry must have been simply " Oysters! ", but generations of Aframerican larynxes had debased it to " Awneeeeeee! ", with the final *e*'s prolonged until the vendor got out of breath. He always wore a blue-and-white checked apron, and that apron was also the uniform of the colored butlers of the Baltimore gentry when engaged upon their morning work — sweeping the sidewalk, scouring the white marble front steps, polishing up the handle of the big front door, and bragging about their white folks to their colleagues to port and starboard.

Oysters were not too much esteemed in the Baltimore of my youth, nor are they in the Baltimore of today. They were eaten, of course, but not often, for serving them raw at the table was beyond the usual domestic technic of the time, and it was difficult to cook them in any fashion that made them consonant with contemporary ideas of elegance. Fried, they were fit only to be devoured at church oyster-suppers, or gobbled in oyster-bays by drunks wandering home from scenes of revelry. The more celebrated oyster-houses of Baltimore — for example, Kelly's in Eutaw street — were patronized largely by such lamentable characters. It was their playful custom to challenge foolish-looking strangers to wash down a dozen raw Chincoteagues with half a tumbler of Maryland rye: the town belief was that this combination was so deleterious as to be equal to the kick of a mule. If the stranger survived, they tried to inveigle him into eating another dozen with sugar sprinkled on them: this dose was supposed to be almost certainly fatal. I grew up believing that the only man in history who had ever actually swallowed it and lived was John L. Sullivan.

There is a saying in Baltimore that crabs may be prepared in fifty ways and that all of them are good. The range of oyster dishes is much narrower, and they are much less attractive. Fried oysters I have just mentioned. Stewed, they are undoubtedly edible, but only in the sorry sense that oatmeal or boiled rice is edible. Certainly no Baltimorean not insane would argue that an oyster stew has any of the noble qualities of the two great crab soups — shore style (with vegetables) and bisque (with cream). Both of these masterpieces were on tap in the old Rennert Hotel when I lunched there daily (years after the term of the present narrative) and both were magnificent. The Rennert also offered an oyster pot-pie that had its points, but the late Jeff Davis, manager of the hotel (and the last public virtuoso of Maryland cookery), once confessed to me that its flavor was really due to a sly use of garlic. Such concoctions as panned and scalloped oysters have never been eaten in my time by connoisseurs, and oyster fritters (always called flitters in Baltimore) are to be had only at free-for-all oyster-roasts and along the wharves. A roasted oyster, if it be hauled off the fire at the exact instant the shell opens, is not to be sniffed at, but getting it down is a troublesome business, for the shell is too hot to be handled without mittens. Despite this inconvenience, there are still oyster-roasts in Baltimore on Winter Sunday afternoons, and since the collapse of Prohibition they have been drawing pretty good houses. When the Elks give one they hire a militia armory, lay in a thousand kegs of beer, engage 200 waiters, and prepare for a mob. But the mob is not attracted by the oysters alone; it comes mainly to eat hot-dogs, barbecued beef and sauerkraut and to wash down these lowly victuals with the beer.

The greatest crab cook of the days I remember was Tom McNulty, originally a whiskey drummer but in the end sheriff of Baltimore, and the most venerated oyster cook was a cop named Fred. Tom's specialty was made by spearing a slice of bacon on a large fork, jamming a soft crab down on it, holding the two over a charcoal brazier until the bacon had melted over the crab, and then slapping both upon a slice of hot toast. This titbit had its points, I assure you, and I never think of it without deploring Tom's too early translation to bliss eternal. Fred devoted himself mainly to oyster flitters. The other cops rolled and snuffled in his masterpieces like cats in catnip, but I never could see much virtue in them. It was always my impression, perhaps in error, that he fried them in curve grease borrowed from the street railways. He was an old-time Model T flat-foot, not much taller than a fire-plug, but as big around the middle as a load of hay. At the end of a busy afternoon he would be spattered from head to foot with blobs of flitter batter and wild grease.

It was the opinion of my father, as I have recorded, that all the Baltimore beers were poisonous, but he nevertheless kept a supply of them in the house for visiting plumbers, tinners, cellar-inspectors, tax-assessors and so on, and for Class D social callers. I find by his bill file that he paid $1.20 for a case of twenty-four bottles. His own favorite malt liquor was Anheuser-Busch, but he also made occasional experiments with the other brands that were then beginning to find a national market: some of them to survive to this day, but the most perished under Prohibition. His same bill file shows that on December 27, 1883, he paid Courtney, Fairall & Company, then the favorite fancy grocers of Baltimore, $4 for a gallon of Monticello whiskey. It retails now for from $3 to $3.50 a *quart*. In those days it was always straight, for the old-time Baltimoreans regarded blends with great suspicion, though many of the widely-advertised brands of Maryland rye were of that character. They drank straight whiskey straight, disdaining both diluents and chasers. I don't recall ever seeing my father drink a high-ball; the thing must have existed in his day, for he lived on to 1899, but he probably regarded its use as unmanly and ignoble. Before every meal, including breakfast, he ducked into the cupboard in the diningroom and poured out a substantial hooker of rye, and when he emerged he was always sucking in a great whiff of air to cool off his tonsils. He regarded this appetizer as necessary to his well-being. He said that it was the best medicine he had ever found for toning up his stomach.

How the stomachs of Baltimore survived at all in those days is a pathological mystery. The

standard evening meal tended to be light, but the
other two were terrific. The répertoire for breakfast, beside all the known varieties of pancake and
porridge, included such things as ham and eggs,
broiled mackerel, fried smelts, beef hash, pork
chops, country sausage, and even — God help us
all! — what would now be called Welsh rabbit.
My father, save when we were in the country,
usually came home for lunch, and on Saturdays,
with no school, my brother Charlie and I sat in.
Our favorite Winter lunch was typical of the time.
Its main dishes were a huge platter of Norfolk
spots or other pan-fish, and a Himalaya of corn-
cakes. Along with this combination went succo-
tash, buttered beets, baked potatoes, string beans,
and other such hearty vegetables. When oranges
and bananas were obtainable they followed for
dessert — sliced, and with a heavy dressing of
grated cocoanut. The calorie content of two or
three helpings of such powerful aliments probably
ran to 3000. We'd all be somewhat subdued afterward, and my father always stretched out on the
dining-room lounge for a nap. In the evening he
seldom had much appetite, and would usually complain that cooking was fast going downhill in
Baltimore, in accord with the general decay of
human society. Worse, he would warn Charlie and
me against eating too much, and often he undertook to ration us. We beat this sanitary policing
by laying in a sufficiency in the kitchen before

sitting down to table. As a reserve against emergencies we kept a supply of ginger snaps, mushroom crackers, all-day suckers, dried apricots and solferino taffy in a cigar-box in our bedroom. In fear that it might spoil, or that mice might sneak up from the cellar to raid it, we devoured this stock at frequent intervals, and it had to be renewed.

The Baltimoreans of those days were complacent beyond the ordinary, and agreed with their envious visitors that life in their town was swell. I can't recall ever hearing anyone complain of the fact that there was a great epidemic of typhoid fever every Summer, and a wave of malaria every Autumn, and more than a scattering of smallpox, especially among the colored folk in the alleys, every Winter. Spring, indeed, was the only season free from serious pestilence, and in Spring the communal laying off of heavy woolen underwear was always followed by an epidemic of colds. Our house in Hollins street, as I first remember it, was heated by Latrobe stoves, the invention of a Baltimore engineer. They had mica windows (always called isinglass) that made a cheery glow, but though it was warm enough within the range of that glow on even the coldest Winter days, their flues had little heat to spare for the rooms upstairs. My brother and I slept in Canton-flannel nightdrawers with feathers above us and underneath, but that didn't help us much on January mornings

when all the windows were so heavily frosted that
we couldn't see outside. My father put in a steam-
heating plant toward the end of the eighties — the
first ever seen in Hollins street —, but such things
were rare until well into the new century. The
favorite central heating device for many years was
a hot-air furnace that was even more inefficient
than the Latrobe stove. The only heat in our bathroom was supplied from the kitchen, which meant
that there was none at all until the hired girl began
to function below. Thus my brother and I were
never harassed by suggestions of morning baths, at
least in Winter. Whenever it was decided that we
had reached an intolerable degree of grime, and
measures were taken to hound us to the bathroom,
we went into the vast old zinc-lined tub together,
and beguiled the pains of getting clean by taking
toy boats along. Once we also took a couple of
goldfish, but the soap killed them almost instantly.

At intervals of not more than a month in Winter
a water-pipe froze and burst, and the whole house
was cold and clammy until the plumbers got
through their slow-moving hocus-pocus. Nothing,
in those days, seemed to work. All the house ma-
chinery was constantly out of order. The roof
sprang a leak at least three times a year, and I
recall a day when the cellar was flooded by a broken
water-main in Hollins street, and my brother and
I had a grand time navigating it in wooden wash-
tubs. No one, up to that time, had ever thought

of outfitting windows with fly-screens. Flies over-
ran and devoured us in Summer, immense swarms
of mosquitoes were often blown in from the swamps
to the southwest, and a miscellany of fantastic
moths, gnats, June-bugs, beetles, and other insects, some of them of formidable size and pug-
nacity, buzzed around the gas-lights at night.

We slept under mosquito canopies, but they were
of flimsy netting and there were always holes in
them, so that when a mosquito or fly once got in
he had us all to himself, and made the most of it.
It was not uncommon, in Summer, for a bat to
follow the procession. When this happened my
brother and I turned out with brooms, baseball bats
and other weapons, and pursued the hunt to a kill.
The carcass was always nailed to the backyard
fence the next morning, with the wings stretched
out as far as possible, and boys would come from
blocks around to measure and admire it. Whenever an insect of unfamiliar species showed up we
tried to capture it, and if we succeeded we kept it
alive in a pill-box or baking-powder can. Our
favorite among pill-boxes was the one that held
Wright's Indian Vegetable Pills (which my father
swallowed every time he got into a low state), for
it was made of thin sheets of wood veneer, and was
thus more durable than the druggists' usual cardboard boxes.

Every public place in Baltimore was so furiously
beset by bugs of all sorts that communal gather-

ings were impossible on hot nights. The very cops
on the street corners spent a large part of their
time slapping mosquitoes and catching flies. Our
pony Frank had a fly-net, but it operated only
when he was in motion; in his leisure he was as
badly used as the cops. When arc-lights began
to light the streets, along about 1885, they attracted so many beetles of gigantic size that their
glare was actually obscured. These beetles at once
acquired the name of electric-light bugs, and it
was believed that the arc carbons produced them
by a kind of spontaneous generation, and that their
bite was as dangerous as that of a tarantula. But
no Baltimorean would ever admit categorically that
this Congo-like plague of flying things, taking one
day with another, was really serious, or indeed a
plague at all. Many a time I have seen my mother
leap up from the dinner-table to engage the swarming flies with an improvised punkah, and heard her
rejoice and give humble thanks simultaneously that
Baltimore was not the sinkhole that Washington
was.

These flies gave no concern to my brother Charlie
and me; they seemed to be innocuous and even
friendly compared to the chiggers, bumble-bees
and hornets that occasionally beset us. Indeed,
they were a source of pleasant recreation to us,
for very often, on hot Summer evenings, we would
retire to the kitchen, stretch out flat on our backs
on the table, and pop away at them with sling-

shots as they roosted in dense clumps upon the ceiling. Our favorite projectile was a square of lemon-peel, roasted by the hired girl. Thus prepared, it was tough enough to shoot straight and kill certainly, but when it bounced back it did not hurt us. The hired girl, when she was in an amiable mood, prepared us enough of these missiles for an hour's brisk shooting, and in the morning she had the Red Cross job of sweeping the dead flies off the ceiling. Sometimes there were hundreds of them, lying dead in sticky windrows. When there were horse-flies from the back alley among them, which was not infrequently, they leaked red mammalian blood, which was an extra satisfaction to us. The stables that lined the far side of the alley were vast hatcheries of such flies, some of which reached a gigantic size. When we caught one we pulled off its wings and watched it try idiotically to escape on foot, or removed its legs and listened while it buzzed in a loud and futile manner. The theory taught in those days was that creatures below the warm-blooded level had no feelings whatever, and in fact rather enjoyed being mutilated. Thus it was an innocent and instructive matter to cut a worm into two halves, and watch them wriggle off in opposite directions. Once my brother and I caught a turtle, chopped off its head, and were amazed to see it march away headless. That experience, in truth, was so astonishing as to be alarming, and we never monkeyed with turtles thereafter. But we got a good deal of pleasure, first and last, out of chasing and butchering toads, though we were always careful to avoid taking them in our hands, for the juice of their kidneys was supposed to cause warts.

At the first smell of hot weather there was a tremendous revolution in Hollins street. All the Brussels carpets in the house were jimmied up and replaced by sleazy Chinese matting, all the hair-cloth furniture was covered with linen covers, and every picture, mirror, gas bracket and Rogers group was draped in fly netting. The carpets were wheelbarrowed out to Steuart's hill by professional carpet beaters of the African race, and there flogged and flayed until the heaviest lick yielded no more dust. Before the mattings could be laid all the floors had to be scrubbed, and every picture and mirror had to be taken down and polished. Also, the lace curtains had to come down, and the ivory-colored Holland shades that hung in Winter had to be changed to blue ones, to filter out the Summer sun. The lace curtains were always laundered before being put away — a formidable operation involving stretching them on huge frameworks set up on trestles in the backyard. All this uproar was repeated in reverse at the ides of September. The mattings came up, the carpets went down, the furniture was stripped of its covers, the pictures, mirrors and gas brackets lost their netting, and the blue Holland shades were displaced by the ivory

ones. It always turned out, of course, that the
flies of Summer had got through the nettings with
ease, and left every picture peppered with their
calling cards. The large pier mirror between the
two windows of the parlor usually got a double
dose, and it took the hired girl half a day to ren-
ovate it, climbing up and down a ladder in the
clumsy manner of a policeman getting over a fence,
and dropping soap, washrags, hairpins and other
gear on the floor.

The legend seems to prevail that there were no
sewers in Baltimore until after the World War,
but that is something of an exaggeration. Our
house in Hollins street was connected with a private sewer down the alley in the rear as early as
I have any recollection of it, and so were many
other houses, especially in the newer parts of the
town. But I should add that we also had a powder-
room in the backyard for the accommodation of
laundresses, whitewashers and other visiting members of the domestic faculty, and that there was
a shallow sink under it that inspired my brother
and me with considerable dread. Every now and
then some child in West Baltimore fell into such
a sink, and had to be hauled out, besmeared and
howling, by the cops. The one in our yard was
pumped out and fumigated every Spring by a
gang of colored men who arrived on a wagon that
was called an O.E.A. — *i.e.*, odorless excavating
apparatus. They discharged this social-minded

duty with great fervor and dispatch, and achieved non-odoriferousness, in the innocent Aframerican way, by burning buckets of rosin and tar. The whole neighborhood choked on the black, greasy, pungent smoke for hours afterward. It was thought to be an effective preventive of cholera, smallpox and tuberculosis.

All the sewers of Baltimore, whether private or public, emptied into the Back Basin in those days, just as all those of Manhattan empty into the North and East rivers to this day. But I should add that there was a difference, for the North and East rivers have swift tidal currents, whereas the Back Basin, distant 170 miles from the Chesapeake capes, had only the most lethargic. As a result it began to acquire a powerful aroma every Spring, and by August smelled like a billion polecats. This stench radiated all over downtown Baltimore, though in Hollins street we hardly ever detected it. Perhaps that was due to the fact that West Baltimore had rival perfumes of its own — for example, the emanation from the Wilkins hair factory in the Frederick road, a mile or so from Union Square. When a breeze from the southwest, bouncing its way over the Wilkins factory, reached Hollins street the effect was almost that of poison gas. It happened only seldom, but when it happened it was surely memorable. The householders of the vicinage always swarmed down to the City Hall the next day and raised blue hell, but they never got anything save promises. In fact, it was not until the Wilkinses went into the red and shut down their factory that the abomination abated — and its place was then taken, for an unhappy year or two, by the degenerate cosmic rays projected from a glue factory lying in the same general direction. No one, so far as I know, ever argued that these mephitic blasts were salubrious, but it is a sober fact that town opinion held that the bouquet of the Back Basin was. In proof thereof it was pointed out that the clerks who sweated all Summer in the little coops of offices along the Light street and Pratt street wharves were so remarkably long-lived that many of them appeared to be at least 100 years old, and that the colored stevedores who loaded and unloaded the Bay packets were the strongest, toughest, drunkenest and most thieving in the whole port.

The Baltimore of the eighties was a noisy town, for the impact of iron wagon tires on hard cobblestone was almost like that of a hammer on an anvil. To be sure, there was a dirt road down the middle of every street, kept in repair by the accumulated sweepings of the sidewalks, but this cushioned track was patronized only by hay-wagons from the country and like occasional traffic: milk-men, grocery deliverymen and other such regulars kept to the areas where the cobbles were naked, and so made a fearful clatter. In every way, in fact, city life was much noiser then than it is now. Children at play were not incarcerated in playgrounds and policed by hired ma'ms, but roved the open streets, and most of their games involved singing or yelling. At Christmas time they began to blow horns at least a week before the great day, and kept it up until all the horns were disabled, and in Summer they began celebrating the Fourth far back in June and were still exploding fire-crackers at the end of July. Nearly every house had a dog in it, and nearly all the dogs barked more or less continuously from 4 a.m. until after midnight. It was still lawful to keep chickens in backyards, and many householders did so. All within ear range of Hollins street appeared to divide them as to sex in the proportion of a hundred crowing roosters to one clucking hen. My grandfather Mencken once laid in a coop of Guineas, unquestionably the noisiest species of *Aves* known to science. But his wife, my step-grandmother, had got in a colored clergyman to steal them before the neighbors arrived with the police.

In retired by-streets grass grew between the cobblestones to almost incredible heights, and it was not uncommon for colored rag-and-bone men to pasture their undernourished horses on it. On the steep hill making eastward from the Washington Monument, in the very heart of Baltimore, some comedian once sowed wheat, and it kept on coming up for years thereafter. Every Spring the Baltimore newspapers would report on the prospects of the crop, and visitors to the city were taken to see it. Most Baltimoreans of that era, in fact, took a fierce, defiant pride in the bucolic aspects of their city. They would boast that it was the only great seaport on earth in which dandelions grew in the streets in Spring. They believed that all such vegetation was healthful, and kept down chills and fever. I myself once had proof that the excess of litter in the streets was not without its value to mankind. I was riding the pony Frank when a wild thought suddenly seized him, and he bucked me out of the saddle in the best manner of a Buffalo Bill bronco. Unfortunately, my left foot was stuck in the stirrup, and so I was dragged behind him as he galloped off. He had gone at least a block before a couple of colored boys stopped him. If the cobblestones of Stricker street had been bare I'd not be with you today. As it was, I got no worse damage than a series of harsh scourings running from my neck to my heels. The colored boys took me to Reveille's livery-stable, and stopped the bloodshed with large gobs of spider web. It was the hemostatic of choice in Baltimore when I was young. If, perchance, it spread a little tetanus, then the Baltimoreans blamed the mercies of God.

V

Rural Delights

THOUGH the bourgeoisie of Baltimore, in the days
I write of, always denied fiercely that the town
was an inferno in Summer, they nevertheless
cleared out whenever they could — and usually
they could. The nether moiety of them — mainly
bachelors and young married couples — went to
boarding houses in the hills that fenced in the town
to westward and northward, the middle section
rented cottages in the same cool and sanitary re-
gions, and the relatively well-heeled bought or
built Summer homes of their own. Some of these
Summer homes still stand as monuments to the
unearthly taste of the Chester A. Arthur or Cast
Iron era, though most of them have lost the towers
and cupolas that were once their chief flaunts of
elegance, and nearly all the jig-saw rails and braces
of their wide-flung porches have been replaced by
less elaborate millinery.

People now live in them the year round, shuttling in and out of town by motor-car. Efficient oil-heaters keep them snug in Winter, and the telephone and radio bring them all the great boons and usufructs of our Christian civilization. In the days I write of they were vastly more remote; in fact, they were so remote that the women and children in them, having once undergone the ordeal of being moved out, stayed put for the rest of the Summer. The head of each house, of course, had to come to town every day to look after his business, for it was not usual, at that time, for males with any sense of responsibility to take holidays, but no one ever mistook this round trip for a pleasure jaunt; on the contrary, it was regarded as heroic, and mentioned with praise. The only feasible way to get to our first Summer retreat in Howard county, Maryland, was by Baltimore & Ohio train to the ancient village of Ellicott City, and then up a steep zigzag road in the village hack. My father and my uncle Henry, whose family shared the house with us, made the round trip every day, but its second half always left them hot, dusty and worn-out, and I doubt that they could have endured it if the ground rules had not allowed them a couple of mint juleps when they finally reached the front porch. The luxurious day-coaches that now distinguish the Baltimore & Ohio were unheard of in those primitive days. The Main Line local to Ellicott City was made up of creaky wooden cars that had all seen heroic service in the Civil War, and in the fifteen-mile run (it took nearly an hour) they shipped enough cinders to set all their passengers to strangling.

From our house in Hollins street to Ellicott City was but ten miles by the old National pike, but the road had no surface save bare rock and there were four or five toll-gates and six or seven immense hills along the way, so no one ever drove it if the business could be avoided. One of the hills was so steep and so full of hair-pin bends that it was called the Devil's Elbow. A hay-wagon coming up would take half a day to cover the mile and a half from bottom to top, and sometimes a Conestoga wagon from Western Maryland (there were still plenty of them left in the eighties) got stuck altogether, and had to be rescued by the plow-horses of the adjacent farmers. At intervals of a mile or so along the road there were old-time coaching inns, and they were still doing a brisk trade in 25-cent country dinners and 5-cent whiskey.

The one nearest to town, kept by a German named Adam Dietrich, actually survived until the great catastrophe of Prohibition. Its ancient wagon-yard hugged the townward side of Loudon Park Cemetery, and in my youth it was believed that all experienced hack horses, on starting home from a funeral, turned in automatically to give the pallbearers a whack at old Adam's beer, which sold for five cents, came in glasses as large as gas masks, and carried a crab-cake or two fried oysters as *lagniappe*. It was no fun in those days to go to a funeral in Loudon Park. The outward trip, at the solemn pace funerals then affected, took a full hour. But the trip homeward, once the pallbearers had wiped their mustaches, was naturally much quicker, for most of it was downhill and the hack horses knew that oats were ahead. The hay-wagon drivers who made the long and arduous trek from Howard and Frederick counties did not patronize Adam, but preferred the specialists in 5-cent whiskey. Having imbibed, they would take their seats on boards which jutted out from the sides of their lumbering wagons, between the fore and hind wheels, and from that perch they undertook to work the brakes. Very often a jolt knocked one of them off, and the hind wheels converted him into an angel, or into the two halves of an angel. For many years this mishap was one of the principal causes of death among Maryland farmers, and it was not until hay-wagons began to disappear that anyone thought of putting the driver's seat in a safer place.

The house above Ellicott City was a double one, with a hall down the middle. We occupied one side, and the family of my uncle Henry had the other. It had been built by a German named Reus, a wine-grower from the Rhineland, and he had chosen the site because the hillside that swept down to the upper Patapsco, there a placid country stream, seemed perfect for vineyards. In the eighties his terraces were still visible, but their vines were in a sad state of decay, for Mr. Reus had discovered too late that Americans were not wine drinkers. He was now dead, and the place, which was still called the Vineyard, was owned by his widow, whose elder son had married my father's half-sister. She had two more sons, somewhat older than my brother Charlie and I, but still young enough to be polite to us. They were very pleasant fellows, and the two Summers that we spent with them were full of delight. When the big house was rented they lived with their mother and a sister in a tenant-house, and on the place there was also a farmhouse inhabited by a German *Bauer* named Darsch, of whom more anon. From the big house there was a superb view of the valley of the Patapsco — a winding gorge with wooded heights on both sides. Many years later, standing on the hill at Richmond in England and enjoying the famous prospect of the Thames, I was struck by the fact that it was completely familiar. Suddenly I recalled that the view from the Vineyard was almost precisely the same, though on a smaller scale.

The impact of such lovely country upon a city boy barely eight years old was really stupendous. Nothing in this life has ever given me a more thrilling series of surprises and felicities. Everything was new to me, and not only new but romantic, for the most I had learned of green things was what was to be discovered in our backyard in Hollins street, and here was everything from wide and smiling fields to deep, dense woods of ancient trees, and from the turbulent and exciting life of the barnyard to the hidden peace of woodland brooks. The whole panorama of nature seemed to take on a new and larger scale. The sky stretched further in every direction, and was full of stately, piled up clouds that I had never seen before, and on every side there were trees and flowers that were as strange to me as the flora of the Coal Age. When a thunder-storm rolled over the hills it was incomparably grander and more violent than any city storm. The clouds were blacker and towered higher, the thunder was louder, and the lightning was ten times as blinding. I made acquaintance with cows, pigs and all the fowl of the barnyard. I followed, like a spectator at a play, the immemorial drama of plowing, harrowing, planting and reaping. Guided by the Reus boys, who had been born on the place, I learned the names of dozens of strange trees and stranger birds. With them I roved the woods day after day, enchanted by the huge aisles between the oaks, the spookish, Grimms' Fairy Tale thickets, and the cool and singing little streams. There was something new every minute, and that something was always amazing and beautiful.

I recall with special vividness the charm of early morning in the country. We all turned out at an hour that would have seemed unearthly in the city, for my father and my uncle had to stagger down the crooked road to Ellicott City and catch the eight o'clock train for Baltimore. After breakfast, and sometimes before, I would go for a walk in the fields, still wet with the dew. They radiated a fragrance that far surpassed that of Mr. Paul's cologne water, and even that of the Jockey Club and New-Mown Hay of our hired girls. I'd lie on my belly watching the grasshoppers, crickets and other such saucy fellows at work around the roots of the grass — and picking up a supply of chiggers that was renewed daily, and kept me scratching all Summer. I also liked the hot calm of July and August afternoons. The whole country would pass into a sort of cataleptic state, with no sound breaking the silence save the drone of bees along the hedge-rows and the far-off clang of the blacksmith's hammer down in the village. The cows, clearing out of the fields, drowsed under the trees, the barnyard fowl dozed in the shadows of straw-stack and manure-pile, and the wild birds all seemed to vanish. Darsch the farmer was always busy somewhere along the slope, but he was a silent man, and seldom spoke to the laborious son at his side, or even to his horse.

There was a brook down in the woods, called the Sucker branch, that seemed to me to encompass the whole substance and diameter of romantic adventure. My brother and I waded in it, dammed it,

80

leaped over it, and searched under its stones for crayfish and worms. It rose in a distant field, ran down through the deepest part of the Vineyard woods, and disappeared toward the Patapsco in a thicket so dense and forbidding that my brother and I never ventured into it. Where the path from the house came to the brook there were the ruins of an old grist-mill, dating back to the first years of the century and maybe even beyond, but with its dam and the better part of its wooden wheel still surviving. Under the wheel there was a little pool that seemed infinitely deep to my brother and me: we would heave stones into it, and were always sure that we could never hear them strike the bottom. My father and uncle once undertook, on a Summer afternoon, to go swimming in it, but it was too small to give them elbow-room, and they quickly clambered out, shivering with the cold of the spring water. The Reus boys preferred a swimming-hole in the Patapsco itself, at the foot of the long hill stretching down from our house. They reported it to be full of bottomless pits and treacherous undertows, and refused loftily to let my brother and me come along.

The trees along the brook belonged to the original forest, and some of them were immense. Great vines clung to their trunks, and between them was a jungle of saplings and shrubs. There we made acquaintance with brambles and poison oak, and learned to detect the tracks of possums, coons and

foxes, though we never saw any in the flesh. The
Reus boys, inspired by our willingness to learn,
also showed us the tracks of wolves, mountain lions,
bears, and even tigers and elephants, but here we
remained skeptical. This region was our Wild
West, our Darkest Africa, our Ultima Thule. It
even had its anthropophagus — a half-grown yahoo who was supposed to hunt little boys over the
countryside, and to inflict mysterious indignities
upon them when captured. What these indignities
were we could never make out, and the Reus boys
also appeared to be uncertain, but whenever there
was a noise in the underbrush across Sucker branch
one of them would shriek the yahoo's name, and
all of us would make for home at a gallop. Our
cousin John Henry was always a member of these
expeditions. He was somewhat older than my
brother Charlie and somewhat younger than I, and
he was commonly called Little Harry to distinguish
him from me, though in later years he grew tall
enough to look over my head.

I had caught butterflies in the backyard at Hollins street, but at the Vineyard they were enor-
mously more numerous. My mother made me a new
net, and in few weeks I had a fine collection, all of
them poniarded to cards with pins. My brother
and I also captured a great many lizards, and often
came home of a late afternoon with a bird fallen
from the nest, or a can of minnows from the brook,
or a grasshopper leaking his tobacco-juice all over

our hands, or maybe the skull of a rabbit come to
death and dissolution in the woods. The Reus boys
taught us many of the ancient arts and crafts of
country boys — how to make whistles of willow
twigs, how to climb trees, how to detect poison-oak,
how to cut off a chicken's head, and so on. They
even tried to teach us how to milk a cow, but the
switching of the creature's tail disturbed us so
much that we were unable to concentrate. One day
they announced proudly that they were squiring
the family cow to a farm up Merrick's lane for a
necessary biological purpose, and we pleaded to be
taken along. They were willing enough and prom-
ised an instructive exhibition, but the project was
overruled by higher authority.

My uncle Henry, unable to go out for ducks in
Summer, kept his eagle eye in trim by shooting
such chickens as were needed for the table. He
would go down to the barnyard on Sunday morning, draw a bead upon a strutting cockerel, and lift
off its head with the ease of a laryngologist fetching an adenoid. We boys greatly admired his technic, and so did Darsch the farmer. At dawn one
Sunday morning there was a loud explosion in the
direction of the barnyard, followed by a series of
grisly, despairing yells, as of an archbishop collared by Satan. My father and uncle turned out in
their night-shirts, and made for the scene with slip-
pers flapping. They returned in a few moments
with Darsch, and my mother and aunt spent the

next half hour bandaging him with strips of bed-sheet. Never in this life have I seen a more luxuri-ant hemorrhage, though I have sat at the ringside through many a high-toned exhibition of scientific boxing. It appeared that Darsch, panting to emu-late my uncle, had unearthed a fowling-piece brought from Germany in 1857, loaded it to the muzzle, and loosed it at an old rooster. When the barrel exploded the rooster suffered nothing worse than shock, but Darsch himself was dreadfully chewed up. But it is almost impossible to kill a German *Bauer* with anything short of siege artil-lery, and in a week he was back at the plow and see-ing out of both eyes.

Some time after this, on a Sunday afternoon, while my father and his brother were sitting on the verandah drinking mint juleps, Darsch passed along the roadway in front of the big house, driv-ing a calf. My uncle stopped him to inquire how his wounds were getting on, and then offered him the hospitality of a julep. The drink was a new one to Darsch, who had been to Baltimore only twice in nine years, and it appeared at once that he re-garded it with approbation. Indeed, he not only liked it, but said so with unprecedented loquacity, and was soon chattering in a care-free and aimless manner, with swinging gestures. This exhilaration suggested something to my uncle, who was a man, like my father, of predominantly anti-social hu-mor. Reaching for an old-time tin shaker that

stood on the table, he poured three or four fingers
of rye into it, and then offered to give Darsch's
julep another shake. This, he explained, was a
necessary process, designed to keep the julep from
going flat. Darsch handed up his glass, got it back
reinforced, took a long pull of it, and began bab-
bling louder and faster than ever before. His calf
wandered off, but he did not notice it. The second
time my uncle made it five or six fingers, and the
third time he emptied what was left of the bottle.
Suddenly Darsch drained the glass with a great
gulp, mint and all, leaped high into the air, let
off a single explosive whoop, and started down the
roadway at a gallop. My uncle and father set out
after him, hoping to capture and calm him before
he could do himself any harm, but he was too fast
for them, and by the time they got to the barnyard
he was disappearing through the door of the old
bank-barn. They found him presently in the stable
below, threshing around in the litter behind the
cow. He had taken a header through the hatch-
way. They hauled him home and his wife put him
to bed, and the next day he was down with what was
described as malaria. I recall my uncle observing
afterward that it was an agreeable and instructive
episode, but that it had pretty well emptied a prime
bottle of Maryland rye, and was thus rather expensive.

Housekeeping at the Vineyard must have been
something of an ordeal for my mother and my aunt,

who fed their flocks separately. The best cook-stoves available were poor things that burned kerosene, and they were set out in a sort of arbor behind the house. Down in the village there was a butcher whose family had carried on in one of the old stone houses along the main (and only) street for the better part of a century, but I can recall no baker, and all the bread we ate was baked at home. Vegetables and fruits, such as they were, came from Darsch's market-garden, and fowl came from his barnyard. There must have been ice in the house, for I can't imagine my father drinking warm beer without alarming symptoms, and he and his brother often made mint juleps, especially when company took the long trail out from the city of a Sunday. But there were times when ice ran short, for I recall a Sunday afternoon when, after an overdose of Seckel pears, filched from Darsch's sclerotic trees, I developed a case of 1000-volt cholera morbus, and a colored boy had to be dispatched to the village on horseback to fetch a cake. When he arrived he had it in a gunnysack lashed to his horse. My father cracked it with a hatchet that he found in the cellar, cutting himself two or three times, and my mother fed it to me with a kitchen spoon. It seemed to work, for by Tuesday I was back at the Seckel pears.

The road down to the village was steep and rough, and the trip up was full of tribulation. It started off the main street at what must have been

at least a ten per cent. grade, passed the county
jail (bowered in flowers, and always showing a sad
blackamoor or two at its barred windows), skirted
a curious old house called the Château (it had
towers and battlements, and clung to a steep crag
overhanging the Patapsco), went by the columned
portico of the Patapsco Female Institute, and finally brought up at our gate. One day my mother
sent me down to the village for a can of lard and
a sack of flour, and on my painful way home I was
overtaken by a colored man driving a large, empty
wagon. I accepted his offer of a lift with sincere
thanks, and climbed in with my burden. Unhappily, he had but lately delivered a load of coal,
and his wagon was still black with its remains, so
when his horses started up the rough road and the
wagon began to jolt and bounce, the dust almost
smothered me. I got home with my face and hands
black, my clothes ruined, the lard covered with a
foul, bituminous scum, and the flour turned to a
depressing gray. I was washed with kitchen soap,
arrayed in a fresh outfit, and sent back to the village for another cargo, and this time I toted it
home on foot.

We were at the Vineyard only two Summers, but
it made so powerful an impression on me that I remember every detail of the place to this day — the
wonderful adventures in the woods and along the
brook, the fascinating life of beasts and birds,
the daily miracles of the farm, and above all, the

gay songs of the Reus boys of an evening, to the accompaniment of their sister Carrie's pre-Beethoven piano. If I am able today to distinguish between an oak tree and a locust, a goose and a duck, a potato vine and a tomato plant, it is because I acquired those valuable knacks on that happy hill. Some time ago my brother August and I drove up to it on a Sunday morning, and found Carrie and her husband living in the big house. The main terraces of the vineyard had been converted into roads, the roads were lined with bungalows, and in the field that I roved for butterflies there were more bungalows and worse ones, but the woods down by the brook had not changed at all, save that the trees were now almost as large in fact as they seemed to me as a boy. The old barnyard was also still there, with a sow and her pigs snuffling about. But Darsch the farmer was gone, and so was his diligent son, and the last Seckelpear tree had long since yielded to human progress.

Early in 1892, at the close of the period covered by this record, my father bought a country house of his own at Mt. Washington, to the north of Baltimore, and at the same time my uncle Henry bought one at Relay, half way to Ellicott City. Mt. Washington was then a remote and beautiful place, and in Spring and Autumn I went to school in the city by train, but it was already mainly given over to the Summer homes of city people, and in a little while it began to attract the malig-

nant notice of real-estate developers. We lived
there every Summer until my father's death, but
Baltimore was creeping out block by block, year
by year. First a trolley line penetrated to Roland
Park, half a mile or more away, and then another
thrust itself along the Falls road, only a few hundred feet from our house. Today that southern
part of Mt. Washington is only a shabby suburb
of the city, with a filling-station where a one-room
country school used to be, and traffic lights at
every corner.

Nevertheless, a part of it has been fortuitously
preserved, and remains today substantially as it
was in 1892. This is a stretch of perhaps half a
mile of wild woodland, running up a steep hill from
the east bank of Jones' falls, south of Belvedere
avenue. The land there is too steep to encourage
realtors, and so it continues almost untouched.
Even hikers from the city avoid it, for the old
mill-road that used to lead into it has long since
washed away, and there are no other paths. My
brother Charlie and I roved it for many happy
Summers, setting traps for rabbits in the woods
(and never catching any), fishing and gigging eels
in the stream, and trying to dam it at every shallow. An old carp of huge size lived in a pool under
the Belvedere avenue bridge, and we used to spend
hours throwing stones at him as he basked just
under the surface, and never hitting him. He was
finally fetched by a wicked boy who lifted a stick

of dynamite from a trolley construction camp, and let him have it from the bridge. The roar brought a rush of game wardens from all directions, but by that time we were safe in the woods. The carp either made off for Europe or was blown to bits, for no sign of him was ever seen thereafter.

This bridge, which still stands, was also the scene of my own first experience as a target. The line of the Northern Central Railway ran along the west bank of Jones' falls, and the freight trains that came down from the north began to slow up there for the entrance to the Baltimore yards. The same wicked boy who assassinated the carp invented the game of dropping horse apples and other such waggish missiles upon the brakemen who rode on top of the box-cars, working the old hand brakes. The trick was to fire the shot just as the car emerged below the bridge, and then hide behind the heavy wooden stringpiece. Unfortunately, the brakemen, in their dudgeon and alarm, mistook the horse apples for rocks, and conceived the theory that they were being beset by homicidal tramps. On a memorable afternoon one of them was waiting for us, and as the first apples fell he yanked out his revolver and let go. I can still hear the whistle of that lead. Some of it came so near to my head that I could actually feel its heat.

VI

THE

Head of the House

My grandfather Mencken, in the days when I first became aware of him, was approaching sixty, and hence seemed to me to be a very old man. But there was certainly nothing decrepit about him, even though a broken leg dating from the Civil War era had left him with a slight limp, for he threw back his shoulders in a quasi-military fashion, he had a piercing eye of a peculiarly vivid blue, and he presented to the world what I can only describe as a generally confident and even somewhat cocky aspect. His bald head rose in a Shakespearean dome, and the hair that survived over his ears was brushed forward stiffly. His cheeks were shaven down to the neck, but he wore a mustache of no particular kind, and allowed his beard to sprout and hang down within the meridians of longitude marked off by his eyes. Whiskers of such irrational design were not uncommon in that age, which was immensely more hairy than the present glorious day. Many of the extant generals of the Civil War had sets of them, and so did many German forty-eighters. My grandfather, in a way of speaking, was a forty-eighter himself, for he shoved off for these shores from his native Saxony at almost the precise moment the German Vorparlament met at Frankfort-on-Main. But that was as far as his connection with democratic idealism ever went. In his later life he used to hint that he had left Germany, not to embrace the boons of democracy in this great Republic, but to escape a threatened overdose at home. In world affairs he was a faithful customer of Bismarck, and in his capacity of patriotic American he inclined toward the ironically misnamed Democratic party, which had fought a long war to save slavery and was still generally disreputable. His two sons, who were high tariff Republicans, finally managed, I believe, to induce him to vote against Grover Cleveland in 1884, but my father told me years later that they viewed his politics with some distrust to the end of his days.

I recall him best on his visitations to our house in Hollins street, which, though not very frequent, were carried out with considerable ceremonial. He lived in Fayette street, only a few blocks away, and

usually arrived on foot. When the stomp-stomp
of his tremendous shillelagh of a cane was heard,
and he heaved into sight in his long-tailed black
coat, his Gladstonian collar and his old-fashioned
black cravat, a hush fell upon the house, my mother
and father put on their best party manners, and
my brother Charlie and I were given a last nerv-
ous inspection and cautioned to be good on penalty of the knout. Arrived, he deposited his hat
on the floor beside his chair, mopped his dome medi-
tatively, and let it be known that he was ready for
the business of the day, whatever it might turn out
to be, and however difficult and onerous. It covered,
first and last, an immense range, running from
infant feeding and the choice of wallpaper at one
extreme to marriage settlements and the intrica-
cies of dogmatic theology at the other. No man
on this earth ever believed more innocently and
passionately in the importance of the family as
the basic unit of human society, or had a higher
sense of duty to his own. As undisputed head of the
American branch of the Menckenii he took jurisdiction over all its thirty members — his two sons,
his three daughters, his two daughters-in-law, his
three sons-in-law, and his twenty grandchildren
— with his wife, my step-grandmother, thrown in
as a sort of friendly alien. There was never, so far
as I could learn afterward, any serious challenge
of his authority, nor, I must add, did he ever exercise it in a harsh and offensive manner. He

simply assumed as a matter of course — indeed, as an axiom so self-evident that the human mind could not conceive a caveat to it — that he was charged by virtue of his status and office with a long list of responsibilities, and he met them in the amiable and assured fashion of a man who knew his work in the world, and was ready to do it though the heavens fell.

My mother, in the years after his death, always defended the justice of his decisions, or, at all events, their strict legality, though more than once, by her own account, they went counter to her own judgment and desire. There was, for example, the matter of the christening of my younger brother, born in 1889. For some reason that I never learned she wanted to call him Albert, and for months that was actually his studio or stable name. Even my father, who was prejudiced against the name because the only Albert he knew was a dead-beat who owed him a bill of $135, nevertheless acquiesced, and all the cups, rattles, knitted jackets, belly-bands and velvet caps that came in for the baby were so engraved or embroidered. But my father yet hesitated strangely to send for a clergyman and have the business over, and one day the reason therefor appeared. It was a beautiful Sunday in early Spring and my grandfather chose it to set up his Court of King's Bench in the Summer-house in our backyard. Without any time-consuming preliminaries, he announced simply that the baby would have to be called August — plain August and nothing else, with no compromise on a second name that might convert him eventually into A. Albert, A. Bernard, A. Clarence . . . . . . or A. Zoroaster. August had been the name of his own father, and was the name of his first-born son, my father. It was a proud and (to his ears) mellifluous name, ancient in the Mencken family and going back, in one form or other, to the dawn of civilization. Since this erstwhile Albert was my mother's fourth child, and in all human probability would be her last, it was of paramount necessity, as a matter of family decency and decorum, that he should be August. And August he was, and is.

Why the name hadn't been given to me I don't know, and the fact that it wasn't shows a touch of the mysterious, for I was the *Stammhalter* and hence the object of my grandfather's special concern and solicitude. As the eldest son of his eldest son I'd someday enjoy, in the course of nature, the high dignities of head of the family, and it goes without saying that he must have given a great deal of consideration to my labeling. His reasons for deciding that I was to be named after his second son, my uncle Henry, I have never been able to discover, and for many years I wondered what source had provided my incongruous middle name of Louis. Then I learned that my grandfather's first wife and my own grandmother, Harriet McClellan, had borne and lost a son in 1862, and died herself a few months later, and that this ill-starred and forgotten infant had been named Louis after one of her uncles. The old man never ceased to mourn his poor Harriet. They had married when she was but sixteen, and had been happy together in years of hard struggle. My mother once told me that he used to make surreptitious afternoon visits to Hollins street in his declining years, to talk about his lost love. His undying thought of her greatly touched my mother, and was probably mainly responsible for the affection and respect that she always seemed to have for him. His judicial decisions as head of the house had more than once gone against her, but she was nevertheless staunchly for him, and liked to tell me about him.

One of his judgments I recall very clearly, though it must have been handed down not later than 1886. It had to do with the hairdressing of my brother Charlie and me. We had been patronizing a neighborhood barber of the name of Lehnert, and we liked him very much, for he cut our hair in not more than three minutes by the clock, and always gave us a horse-doctor's dose of highly perfumed hair-oil. When we got back from his atelier we let the admiring hired girl smell our heads, which continued to radiate a suffocating scent for days· afterward. But my grandfather objected to Lehnert's free and far from well-considered use of the clippers, and one day issued an order that he was to be notified the next time our hair needed cutting. When the time came word was duly sent to him, and he appeared in Hollins street the following Sunday morning. My father vanished discreetly but my mother stood by for the operation, which was carried out in the side-yard. What I chiefly recall of it is that Charlie and I sat in a kitchen chair and were swathed in a bed-sheet, and that it seemed to us to take a dreadfully long while. Lehnert could have clipped a whole herd of boys in the same time. When the job was done at last my mother professed politely to admire the result, but there was very little enthusiasm in her tone. The next day my father took us both downtown, and had my grandfather's zigzag shear marks smoothed out by the head barber at the Eutaw House, a majestic man of color who claimed to have serviced not only all the principal generals of the Civil War, but also every Governor of Maryland back to colonial days. But when the time came to return to Lehnert for another clip he was warned to follow the model before him, and this he always did thereafter, to the relief and satisfaction of all concerned.

My grandfather, as I have said, wore a Gladstonian collar and a stock-like cravat of archaic design. Both had disappeared from the marts of commerce before my time, but my aunt Pauline had plans and specifications for them, and so enjoyed the honor of making them. She was the *châtelaine* of my grandfather's big house in Fay-

ette street, for his wife, my step-grandmother, was
in indifferent health. Aunt Pauline was already
married, with two children of her own, but she
never forgot her filial duty to her father, nor did
he. When he arrived home for dinner, which was
at about 2 p.m., the soup had to be ready to go on
the table at the precise instant he hung up his
hat in the hall. He had copious and complicated
ideas about cooking and household management,
as he had about medicine, law, moral theology,
economics, interior decoration and the use of the
spheres, and his public spirit, though it was not
strong, nevertheless forbade him to keep them to
himself. In his backyard in Fayette street he carried on extensive horticultural experiments, virtually all of which, I believe, failed. What I chiefly
remember of them is his recurrent reports that
cats had rolled in and ruined his strawberries, or
that a storm had blown down his lima-beans, or
that some other act of God had wrecked his effort
to produce a strain of tobacco resistant to worms,
high winds, and the irrational fluctuations of the
market. But he seems to have had some luck with
the *Curcurbitaceae*, for every year he presented all
his daughters and daughters-in-law with gourds
for use in darning stockings. Inasmuch as these
gourds, though very light, had surfaces as hard as
iron, they did not wear out, and so my mother,
who never threw anything away if room could be
found for it in the house, accumulated a large bat-

tery. Sometimes, when she was out shopping, my brother Charlie and I fought with them in the cellar, for when one of them collided with a human skull it made a loud, hollow, satisfying report, and yet did not cause death or even unconsciousness.

There is a document in the family archives, headed grandly " Halte im Gedächtniss Jesum Christum! ", which certifies that my grandfather submitted to the rite of confirmation as a Christian of the Protestant sub-species in the church at Borna, Saxony, on March 20, 1842, but he had apparently lost his confidence in Jahveh by the time I became acquainted with him. Indeed, it would not be going too far to say that he was an outright infidel, though he always got on well with the rev. clergy, and permitted his three daughters to commune freely with the Protestant Episcopal Church, the American agency of his first wife's Church of England. It was in his character of skeptic that he subscribed toward the Baltimore crematorium in 1889, and ordered his two sons to subscribe too — so far as I know, the only example of overt social-mindedness that he ever showed. He belonged to no organization save a lodge of Free-masons, and held himself diligently aloof from the German societies that swarmed in Baltimore in the eighties. Their singing he regarded as a public disturbance, and their *Turnerei* as insane. Most of the German business men of Baltimore, in those days, had come from the Hansa towns, and as a

Saxon he was compelled to disdain them as *Platt-deutschen,* though his own remote forbears had been traders in Oldenburg. I somehow gathered the impression, even as a boy, that he was a rather lonely man, and my mother told me years later that she was of the same opinion. Left a widower at thirty-four, with four small children to care for and his roots in America still shaky, he had seen some hard and bitter years, and they had left their marks upon him. He showed none of the expansive amiability of his two sons, but was extremely reserved.

By the time I knew him his days of struggle were over and he was in easy waters, but he still kept a good deal to himself, and when he took me of an afternoon, as a small boy, on one of his headlong buggy-rides, he seldom paid a visit to anyone save the Xaverian Brothers at St. Mary's Industrial School, a bastile for problem boys about two miles from Hollins street. These holy men tried to teach their charges trades, and one of the trades they offered was that of the cigarmaker. My grandfather, who dealt in Pennsylvania leaf tobacco, sold them their raw materials, and my father and uncle undertook to market their output — in the end, an impossible matter, for the cheroots that the boys made were as hard as so many railroad spikes, and no one could smoke them. When my grandfather called upon the Xaverians the tobacco business was quickly disposed of, and he and they sat down to drink beer and debate theology. These discussions, as I recall them, seemed to last for hours, and while they were going on I had to sit in a gloomy hallway hung with gory religious paintings — saints being burned, broken on the wheel and disemboweled, the Flood drowning scores of cows, horses, camels and sheep, the Crucifixion against a background of hair-raising lightnings, and so on. I was too young, of course, to follow the argument; moreover, it was often carried on in German. Nevertheless, I gathered that it neither resulted in agreement nor left any hard feelings. The Xaverians must have put in two or three years trying to rescue my grandfather from his lamentable heresies, but they made no more impression upon him than if they had addressed a clothing-store dummy, though it was plain that he respected and enjoyed their effort. On his part, he failed just as dismally to seduce them from their oaths of chastity, poverty and obedience. I met some of them years afterward, and found that they still remembered him with affection, though he had turned their pastoral teeth.

The buggy that he used for his movements about town was an extraordinarily stout vehicle, and it had need to be, for when he got under way he paid no attention to the fact that the cobblestones of Baltimore were very rough. Where we went when I was aboard I didn't always know, for the top was always up and we elder grandchildren rode standing in the space between the seat and the back curtain. Sometimes he would jam in four or five of us, with a couple of juniors on the seat beside him and two or three more on hassocks on the floor. When, in his wild career over the cobbles, he struck one of the stepping-stones that used to run across the roadway at street corners, we all took a leap into the air, and came down somewhat mixed up. But somehow it never hurt us, and in the end we got so used to it that we rather liked it. In the last years of his life, after my brother Charlie and I had acquired a pony, my grandfather would drive out with us of an afternoon — he in his caterpillar-tread buggy and we in our cart. Once, proceeding out the Franklin road, we came in sight of a tollgate, and he ordered us to drive ahead of him. When the tollkeeper asked for his money we were to point to the buggy following, and say that the old man in it would pay for us. We did so as ordered, but when he came up he denied that he knew us. By that time, of course, we were out of the tollkeeper's reach. The old man thought it was a swell joke, and told my father and uncle about it as if expecting applause, but they failed to be amused. The next time we drove out the Franklin road the tollkeeper charged ten cents instead of five, and he kept on charging us ten cents instead of five until his professional wounds were healed.

My grandfather made frequent trips to Pennsylvania to buy tobacco, and was full of anecdotes of the singular innocence of the Pennsylvania Germans, whose ghastly dialect he had picked up. His favorite tale concerned a yokel of Lancaster county from whom he had bought a crop of tobacco for future delivery, offering a three-months' note in payment. The yokel declined the note on the ground that he needed nothing to help his memory: he would be on hand without fail when the time came to settle. " Keep it yourself," he said, " so you won't forget to pay me." My grandfather traded with these ill-assimilated *Bauern* for many years in complete amity, and had a high regard for them. He sold their tobacco all over. Some of it actually went to Key West, which was then assumed by most Americans to be foreign territory, using only Havana leaf in its celebrated cigars. In deference to the visitors who sometimes dropped in at the factories, the Pennsylvania leaf sent to them was repacked in empty Havana tobacco bales. My grandfather, as a moral theologian, admitted that there was something irregular about this transaction, but he consoled himself by saying that Key West was full of swindlers escaped from Cuba and points south, and that it was impossible to do any business with them at all without yielding something to their peculiar ethics.

The house in Fayette street was a wonderland

to us youngsters of Hollins street, for grandchildren are always indulged more than children,
and we had privileges in it that were unknown at
home. I have described in Chapter I a pillow-
fight that almost wrecked it. We always made a
formal call on Christmas morning — my brother
Charlie and I representing the Augustine line of
the family, and my cousins Pauline and John
Henry representing the Henrician. Ostensibly, of
course, our mission was to offer our duty to our
grandparents, but actually, we glowed with other
expectations. They were never disappointed. The
parlor in Fayette street had a much higher ceiling
than those in Hollins street, and so the Christmas
tree that flamed and coruscated there was larger
and more splendid. At its foot were piles of toys,
and among them there was always an express-
wagon — to haul the other things home. One year
this wagon was for my cousin John Henry, the
next it was for Charlie, the next it was for me, and
so *da capo*. After taking aboard a suitable refreshment of *Pfeffernüsse*, *Springele*, *Lebkuchen*
and other carbohydrates, and stuffing our pockets
with almonds, butternuts, walnuts, candy and
fruit, we loaded our cargo and started home at a
run, yelling and cavorting along the way. Christmas in those days was a gaudy festival, and my
Grandmother Mencken (or maybe it was my Aunt
Pauline) had a singular facility for choosing good
Christmas presents. Down to the middle of my

teens she always managed to find something for me that really delighted me, and many of the books that provided my earliest reading were her selections — including the " Chatterbox " that took me through my first full-length story. But of this, more hereafter.

VII

MEMORIALS OF

𝕲𝖔𝖗𝖒𝖆𝖓𝖉𝖎𝖟𝖎𝖓𝖌

My brother Charlie and I, in the days of our
nonage, were allowed officially to eat all that we
could hold but twice a year. The first of our two
debauches came in the early Spring, the occasion
being the annual picnic of F. Knapp's Institute, already described in Chapter III; the second was
at Christmas, beginning for the same on the morning of the great day itself and continuing doggedly
until our gizzards gave out at last, and Dr. Z. K.
Wiley, the family doctor, arrived to look at our
tongues and ply us with *oleum ricini*.

Our running time, in the average year, was
about thirty-six hours, with eight hours out for
uneasy sleep, making a net of twenty-eight. When
we came leaping downstairs in our flannel night-

drawers on Christmas morning there was not only
a blazing tree to dazzle us, and a pile of gifts to
surprise us (of course only in theory, for we knew
the cupboard where such things were kept, and
always investigated it in advance and at length),
but also a table loaded with candies, cakes, raisins,
citrons and other refreshments of the season, on
all of which, and to any amount we could endure,
we were free to work our wicked will.

At other times things of that sort were doled out
to us in a very cautious and almost niggardly way,
for the medical science of the era taught that an
excess of sweets would ruin the teeth. But at
Christmas, under the prevailing booziness and
goodwill to men, this danger was ignored, and we
were permitted to proceed *ad libitum*, not only at
home, but also on our morning visit to our Grandfather Mencken's house in Fayette street. Thus
we worked away all of Christmas day, keeping our
pockets full and grabbing another load every time
we came within arm-reach of the reserves. When we
were ordered to bed at last, for a night of pathological dreams, we went only reluctantly, and immediately after breakfast on Christmas Monday
we resumed operations. It was in the early evening
of that day that Dr. Wiley drove up in his buggy,
hitched his horse to the ring in the marble horse-
block out front, and came in to do his duty.

He was a tall, spare Georgian with a close-
cropped head and a military goatee. He had been

a surgeon in the Confederate army, and was thus
appreciably older than my father, who was a boy
of seven when the Civil War began, but the two
were nevertheless very good friends, and whenever
the doctor made one of his regular calls he and my
father investigated the demijohns parked in the
dining-room cupboard, and discussed at length the
evils of the times. The doctor was a humane and
understanding man, and so he never introduced
the subject of succoring my brother and me until
we had had a dozen or more last whacks at the stuff
on the table. Then he would suddenly fix us with
his cold gray eye, call for a tablespoon, and proceed
to view our tongues. His verdict, of course, was
always the same. Indeed, my mother invariably
anticipated it by fetching the castor-oil bottle
while he pondered it. Two horrible doses from the
same spoon, and we were packed off to bed. Christmas was over, though the tree still stood, and some
of the toys were yet unbroken. We never had much
appetite the day following.

Dr. Wiley had a low opinion of the Yankees,
and was full of anecdotes of their treachery in the
war. His accounts of surgical practice in the Confederate army were so gruesome that my mother
always retired when he introduced them, but my
brother and I enjoyed them, as boys always enjoy
tales that raise the hair. But his best stories had
to do with his professional exploits as dean of one
of the Baltimore medical colleges in the seventies.

There was then no Anatomy Act in Maryland, and in consequence the students suffered a dearth of cadavers. The only way to get a supply was to lift them from colored graveyards, and in this scientific *Arbeit* Dr. Wiley, by virtue of his office, necessarily had some hand, though not, of course, as an actual field worker.

He liked to tell how he had figured out a way to beat the Baltimore cops when they took to searching wagons driving in the Annapolis road late at night. His scheme, he said, was to prop up the carcass between the two students who manned every wagon. When a cop heaved in sight, they would steady the late lamented, and if he wobbled nevertheless they would explain to the cop that he was a friend in his cups. The Baltimore police, of course, were eager to stretch every probability in favor of the young doctors, and so they usually overlooked the singularity of a pair of Caucasians taking so much trouble with a drunken Aframerican and the even greater unusualness of an Aframerican going on a jag in his best Sunday clothes and a white choker collar.

Whether or not Dr. Wiley really invented this device to liberate anatomy from the imbecility of the law I don't know: it was claimed, as I learned much later, by every dean of a Baltimore medical school, and in those days there were eight or ten of them. But he liked to tell the story, and my brother and I never got tired of it, though our delight in it was always punished by fearful dreams. We greatly admired the doctor, despite the fact that his standard treatment for a sore throat was mopping it with *tinctura ferri chloridi*, which had a taste like a mixture of stove polish and tabasco. I am informed that medicine has made considerable progress since his day, but all the same he had a great deal of natural talent for his trade, and his clinical experience was so enormous that he was seldom at a loss.

Twice, with scarlet fever in the house, he pulled the patients through, and somehow managed to quarantine the rest of us. Of the four Mencken children, he eased three into this slough of misery, all of them sound and howling, and from time to time he dealt successfully with such universal pests as chicken-pox, measles, whooping-cough, quinsy and cholera morbus. He cured me, in my teens, of malaria, and his instruction that the milk used in the house be boiled probably saved us all from typhoid. When he performed the rite of vaccination there was a scar like a volcanic crater to show for it. In her old age my mother gave him at least five per cent. of the credit for the fact that all her children had reached maturity with straight limbs, powerful digestions, and no cross-eyes.

His order that the household milk be boiled was a source of minor but continuous gustatory delight to my brother and me. The milk was brought in the morning by a milkman who had it in a huge can

with a shiny brass spigot, and when he rang his
bell the hired girl went out to his wagon, and
fetched it in in a pitcher. In its raw state it foamed
like beer, and was full of cow hairs, small twigs and
other such adulterations. She got rid of them by
straining it through a cloth, and then boiled it in
a large saucepan. The smell of the boiling always
reached my brother and me, and we waited impa-
tiently until it was over. Then the hired girl
poured the milk back into the pitcher, and made a
mark with a knife across the bottom of the saucepan, which was covered with a gummy precipitate,
brown underneath and reeking with incomparable
flavors. One side of the mark was my brother's
territory, and the other was mine. We fell to with
spoons, and had the saucepan clean in a minute.

In those days ice-cream was still something of a
novelty in the world, and the nearest store that
sold it, an old-fashioned confectioner's, was six or
eight blocks from Hollins street. Thus getting it
in was a nuisance, and sometimes also a vanity, for
on a hot Summer day it would melt on the way.
My father accordingly bought a freezer, and announced grandly that we could now feast like Bel-
shazzar whenever the mood was on us. But that
was as far as he ever went in the matter, for his
gusto for physical labor was even less than his skill
at the mechanic arts, so he always avoided diligently the usual chores of a householder. This left
the operation of the freezer to the hired girl, with

such help as my mother and my brother and I could give her. It was not much. The first time we tackled the job it took nearly an hour, and all of us were worn out. Worse, the ice-cream came out of the machine in large, irregular hunks, frozen solid in their middles and slushy at their edges. Yet worse, some of the crushed rock-salt that was mixed with the ice had got into the cream.

My father ordered it condemned as probably poisonous, but my brother and I followed it back to the kitchen, and devoured it there during the afternoon. Dr. Wiley came that night, looked at our tongues as usual, and prescribed his standard remedy. For a month or so thereafter nothing was heard about the ice-cream freezer, but then it began to appear that the hired girl had been experimenting with it on the sly, and mastering its technic. One Sunday the first fruits of her researches came upon the table — a very passable imitation of boughten ice-cream, with large segments of peach (including slivers of kernel) imbedded in it. After that we had ice-cream every Sunday, and then twice a week, and then three times, and then almost every day ; indeed, we had it so often that even my brother and I began to sicken of it, and to this day I always think of it as next door in unappetizingness to chain-store bread and fruit salad, and seldom eat it save in politeness.

The only member of the family who never got enough was the pony Frank, who had been ac-

quired in 1890 or thereabout, and lived in a tiny
stable at the lower end of the backyard. One Sunday he broke out of his imprisonment and trotted
up to the sideyard that ran along the dining-room.
The window being open, he stuck in his head in his
usual blarneying manner and began to sniff. It
occurred to someone that he smelled the ice-cream,
and a gob of it in a kitchen pan was set on the sill,
to see what he would make of it. He downed it with
happy snuffles, and whinnied for more. After that
he got his share whenever ice-cream was on the bill-
of-fare, and eventually he was eating as much as
all the rest of us put together. My father made an
end to this by issuing a formal injunction, supported by an oral opinion. Feeding ice-cream to
horses, he declared, was as insane a waste of money
as shooting at clay pigeons or contributing to
foreign missions. Frank repined somewhat, but
was placated with an occasional half-peck of raw
carrots, which he liked even better than ice-cream.
So, in fact, did I — and so I do now.

There was another delicacy that delighted my
brother and me almost as much as the rubbery
lining of the milk saucepan, but we could enjoy it,
unfortunately, only in Summer, when we were in
the country. It consisted of stewed blackberries,
spread while still warm on home-made bread, also
still warm. To this day I can taste it at the moments when an aging man's memory searches
through his lost youth for bursts of complete felic-

ity. It had a heavenly flavor, and an even more
heavenly smell. My brother and I would start out
of an afternoon with a couple of lard pails and
pluck the berries along the edge of some nearby
wood. If there was a shortage of ripe ones we'd
turn to the adjacent fields and hunt for dewberries.
The job cost us a good many chigger bites and now
and then a bee sting, but who cared?

When the cans were full we hurried back to the
house, and emptied them on a newspaper spread
out on the kitchen table. The hired girl would then
go through the crop, rejecting the contaminating
gravel, twigs, dead grasshoppers and wild flowers,
and when the cleaning was done it would be raked
into a saucepan along with a handful of sugar. The
stewing took only a little while, but it seemed pretty
long to my brother and me. When it was finished
the fragrant berries were spread upon large slices
of the home-made bread, and we fell to. The hired
girl had strict orders to give us no more than two
slices apiece, but we had ways of blackmailing her.
One was to agree to return the copy of the *Fireside
Companion* that we had lifted and hidden as a
device of pressure politics. Another was to promise
to pull harder the next time she had a day off, and
needed help with the lacing of her stays. The hired
girls of those days were built like airplane-carriers,
but always bought corsets designed for Marguerite
Gautier. I recall one, of Irish extraction and
heavily muscle-bound, who squeezed and pulled

114

herself into such brief compass that she fainted dead away, and had to be revived with a stiff shot of Monticello. The whiskey made her dizzy and set her to weeping, and in a little while she had a full-fledged and alarming attack of what were then called hystics.

This gobbling of stewed blackberries was policed only defectively, but nevertheless it was policed. The house statutes, as I have said, limited us to two slices of bread, and there was a rider to the effect that they must not be too thick. If law enforcement was knowingly slack — and I have no doubt that my mother knew of and condoned our violations, for hired girls always blabbed — it was because there was a theory in those days that all stewed fruits were good for children. In the raw state even apples were regarded with suspicion, but when stewed they took on all the virtues of spinach, rhubarb and sulphur-and-molasses. At F. Knapp's Institute the boarding pupils were fed apple-butter every day, not only because it was cheap, but also because it was supposed to tone up the system, inure them to the perfect Baltimore climate, and prevent boils.

But my brother and I had no fancy for stewed apples, nor for stewed pears, peaches, cherries, plums, apricots, bananas, grapes, pineapples, oranges or what not. Our sole passion was for stewed blackberries (including, of course, dewberries, which are their brothers) ; we even excluded stewed raspberries, huckleberries and strawberries. But for all raw fruits, since they were regarded as deleterious, we naturally had a great liking, and stuffed them down at every chance. On the hilltop above Ellicott City where we spent two Summers there were the remains of a large orchard. The fruit had not been sprayed for thirty years, and was thus in a state of extreme senescence. I recall especially that the Seckel (always pronounced *sickle*) pears had skins of the thickness and consistency of tin-foil, and were almost coal black. We were warned that they were dangerous to life and limb, and had even floored hogs, but the warning only urged us to follow the suicidal pattern of boys by eating more and more. Nothing happened save an occasional bellyache, sometimes rising to the virulence of cholera morbus. We ate until the compulsion wore off, and then simply stopped.

Many other eatables, in those days, were thought to be injurious to the young, or even fatal. One of them was cheese. When a boy was allowed to eat it at all it was a sign that he was almost well enough along to be intrusted with horses, edged tools and firearms, and even so he was always introduced to it by slow stages, with many cautious halts. His first dose was a very thin slice, and he was watched carefully for symptoms of spasms. If he appeared to turn a shade pale he was at once given a jigger of ipecac and put to bed, with the blankets piled a foot high, Winter or Summer.

My brother and I had little confidence in such
notions, and one day we made off with a heel of
cheese that had been laid aside by the hired girl
for her mouse-traps. We divided it evenly and ate
it boldly, defying Jahveh, Dr. Wiley or anyone
else it might concern to do his worst. Once more,
nothing much happened. The taste was dreadful
— indeed, so dreadful that we pitied the poor mice.
But apart from a few sharp twinges in the gas-
tric region, maybe of psychic origin, we suffered
no damage.

Pork was another article of diet that was thought
in that age to be unfriendly to the young. We
were never permitted to eat it at night, for at night
all foods, including even such generally salubrious
things as raw carrots, were believed to take on
virulence. My brother and I, ever eager for scientific experiment, dispatched at least a pound of cold
roast pork one night when our parents were at the
theatre, and suffered no evil that we could detect
with the crude methods then available. If we slept
a little uneasily, it was probably only conscience,
for even boys of six and eight are afflicted by that
curse of mankind. Another night we ate the better
part of a prime *Cervelatwurst,* and heard the hired
girl accused the next morning of feeding it to a
suitor who had waited on her before our raid. She
was stupid beyond the general, and defended herself by declaring that she had given him only four
or five ham sandwiches, half a pie, a cup of coffee,

and six bottles of Class D Baltimore beer. Under cover of the ensuing uproar we slipped off to school.

Thus we gradually accumulated a profound distrust of the dietetic science of the day, and ate anything we could collar, and in any amount, whenever constabulary backs were turned. There were plenty of days when, though we radiated innocence, we actually got down almost as many calories as we were allowed on the glorious day of F. Knapp's annual picnic. But such licentiousness, of course, gradually diminished as we gathered years and wisdom, and we got a boost along the road every time Dr. Wiley dropped in to do his dismal duty. It was not really the castor oil that alarmed us, for every boy of ordinary vanity, in those days, liked to boast that he could swallow it in any quantity, and without gagging. What scared us was the doctor's inspection of our tongues — always long drawn out, and done in sinister silence. We trembled lest he discover signs of sore throat, and get out his dreadful bottle of chloride of iron and his ancient and scratchy mop.

VIII

THE TRAINING OF A

Gangster

The Baltimore of the eighties had lately got over an evil (but proud) name for what the insurance policies call civil commotion. Down to the Civil War and even beyond its gangs were of such enterprise and ferocity that many connoisseurs ranked them as the professional equals, if not actually the superiors, of the gangs of New York, Marseilles and Port Said. It was nothing for them to kidnap a police sergeant, scuttle a tugboat in the harbor, or set fire to a church, an orphan asylum or a brewery. Once a mob made up of the massed gangs of the town broke into the jail and undertook to butcher a party of military gentlemen who had sought refuge there after a vain effort to save an unpopular newspaper from pillage. One of these gentlemen, a doddering veteran of the Revolution named General James M. Lingan, was done to death with great barbarity, and another, General Light Horse Harry Lee, father of the immortal Robert E. Lee, was so badly used that he was never the same again.

At the opening of the Civil War, as every school-boy knows, another Baltimore mob attacked a Massachusetts regiment passing through the city on its way to save democracy at Bull Run, and gave it such a lacing that what it got in that battle three months later seemed almost voluptuous by comparison. This was in April, 1861. Before the end of the year the town proletariat had switched from the Confederate theology to the Federal, and devoted itself to tarring and feathering Southern sympathizers, and wrecking their houses. The war over, it continued its idealistic exercises until the seventies, and at the time I was born Baltimore was still often called Mob Town, though by then the honorific had begun to be only retrospective.

Thus it was necessary for every self-respecting boy of my generation to belong to a gang. No one, in fact, ever asked him if he wanted to join or not join; he was simply taken in when he came to the right ripeness, which was normally between the ages of eight and nine. There was, of course, some difference between the gangs of the proletariat and those of the more tender bourgeoisie. The former tried to preserve, at least to some extent, the grand tradition. They had quarters in empty houses or stable lofts, smoked clay pipes, rushed the can, carried lethal weapons, and devoted themselves largely to stoning cops and breaking into and looting the freight cars of the Baltimore & Ohio Railroad. The latter were a great deal milder and more elegant. They carried only clubs, and then only in times of danger; they never got any further along the road to debauchery than reading dimenovels and smoking cigarettes; and the only thing they ever stole (save, of course, ash-barrels and garbage-boxes on election night) was an occasional half-peck of apples, potatoes or turnips. These victuals were snatched on the run from the baskets that corner-grocers then set outside their stores, along with bundles of brooms, stacks of wooden kitchen-pails, and hog carcasses hanging from hooks.

I attained, by the age of eight, to a considerable proficiency in this larceny, and so did my brother Charlie. Our victim was usually Mr. Thiernau, a stout, bustling, sideburned man who operated a grocery-and-meat store at Gilmor and Baltimore streets, less than a block from our back gate. He wore invariably what was then the uniform of his calling — a long white apron stained with blood, a Cardigan jacket, and large cuffs made of some sort of straw. Around the little finger of his left hand ran a signet ring, and behind his right ear he carried his pencil. So far as I can remember, he never made any attempt to pursue the boys who looted him; in truth, I suspect that his baskets were set out as a kind of accommodation to them, with the aim of gaining their favor. Not infrequently they were delegated to buy supplies for their mothers, and on such occasions they always chose Mr. Thiernau's store, not that of the Knoops across the street. The Knoops, two brothers and a cousin, appear to have leaned toward Levirate ideas, for when the cousin died one of the brothers married his widow. They were Germans of large girth, gloomy aloofness and high commercial acumen, and they accumulated among them a considerable estate, but they never exposed anything that was edible on the sidewalk, and so the boys of the neighborhood were against them. Even Mr. Thiernau, I believe, kept his best vegetables to be sold inside his store, not stolen in front of it.

One day, after my brother Charlie and I had made a fine haul of sweet potatoes, my father came home unexpectedly and caught us roasting them on a fire in the backyard. He demanded to know where we had got them from, and our guilty looks betrayed us. He thereupon made a great uproar, declaring that he would drown us, ship us to the Indian country or even hand us over to the child-stealers rather than see us grow up criminals. I put all the blame on Charlie, for he had actually made the snatch while I bossed the job and watched, and

my father ordered him to return the potatoes to
Mr. Thiernau at once, half burned as they were.
Charlie set off boo-hooing, threw the potatoes into
a garbage-box in the alley, and came home prepared to report that Mr. Thiernau had taken them
back with polite thanks. But he delayed on the way
to watch the Thiernau colored driver unload a
cargo of dead hogs, and by the time he returned
my father had apparently forgotten the matter,
for we heard no more from him about it. We discovered the next day, however, that the hired girl
had orders to supply us with potatoes whenever
the roasting fever was on us, and for a week or so
we patronized her. But her stock never seemed to
have the right flavor, though it came from the same
Thiernau's, and we eventually resumed our larcen-
ies. They were terminated a year or so later by
Mr. Thiernau's sudden death, which was a great
shock to us, and naturally turned us to moral con-
siderations and made us uneasily Hell-minded.

The Hollins street gang functioned as a unit
only on occasions of public ceremonial — for in-
stance, at election time. It began lifting boxes and
barrels for the election night bonfire two or three
weeks before the great day, usually under command
of a large, roomy boy named Barrel Fairbanks,
and they were commonly stored in the stable behind his house. If we managed to collar a paint
barrel it was a feat that cheered us, for paint barrels burned with a fierce flame and made a great

deal of smoke. The grocerymen and feed dealers of the neighborhood, knowing that we were on the prowl, tried to save their good boxes and barrels by setting out their decrepit ones, and we always accepted the suggested arrangement. It was only when there was a real famine in fuel that we resorted to taking back gates off their hinges, and even then we confined ourselves to gates that were ready to fall off of their own motion.

The first election night bonfire that I remember was built on the evening of that day in November, 1888, which saw the stuffings of Cleveland and Thurman knocked out of them by Harrison and Morton. The returns were published from the portico of a Democratic ward club at Lombard and Stricker streets, across Union Square from our house, and the fire was kindled at the crossing of Hollins and Stricker streets. As the sad news dribbled along the Democrats fell into a low state of mind, and some of them actually went home before the kegs of beer that they had laid in were empty; but my father rejoiced, for as a high-tariff Republican he was bound in conscience to regard Cleveland as a fiend in human form. I recall him coming down to the corner to see and applaud the fire, which blazed higher than the houses along Hollins street. The cops offered no objection to it, though in those days they were all Democrats, for the flames did no damage to the solid Baltimore cobblestones that underlay them, and if they singed a few trees it was only God's will. When the cobbles yielded to asphalt, long after I was a grown man, election-night bonfires were prohibited.

I recall one election night when the tough boys from the region of the Baltimore & Ohio repair-shops, having had bad luck in collecting material for their own fire, made an attempt to raid ours. They arrived just as it was kindled. They were armed with clubs, and made their attack from two sides, yelling like Indians. We of Hollins street were ordinarily no match for these ruffians, but that night there was an audience looking on, so we fought fiercely, and finally managed to drive them off. Some of them, retreating, carried off blazing boxes, but not many. I got a clout across the arm that night, and nursed it proudly for a week. I was in hopes that Dr. Wiley would order the arm into a sling, but when he dropped in the next day he could find nothing save a large blue bruise. When he began to show signs of taking a routine look at my tongue, I slipped away quickly, pleading an important engagement.

Every Baltimore boy, in those days, had to be a partisan of some engine company, or, as the phrase ran, to go for it. The Hollins street boys went for No. 14, whose house was in Hollins street three blocks west of Union Square. Whenever an alarm came in a large bell on the roof of the engine-house broadcast it, and every boy within earshot reached into his hip-pocket for his directory of alarm-boxes. Such directories were given out as advertisements by druggists, horseshoers, saloon-keepers and so on, and every boy began to tote one as soon as he could read. If the fire was nearby, or seemed to be close to a livery-stable, a home for the aged, or any other establishment promising lively entertainment, all hands dropped whatever was afoot and set off for it at a gallop. It was usually out by the time we reached the scene, but sometimes we had better luck. Once we saw a blaze in a slaughter-house, with a drove of squealing hogs cremated in a pen, and another time we were entranced by a fire in the steeple of a Baptist church. Unhappily, this last ended as a dud, for the firemen quickly climbed up their high ladders and put it out.

The duties of a boy who went for an engine were not onerous. The main thing was simply to go for it. At an actual fire he could not distinguish between his own firemen and those of some other and altogether abhorrent company, for they all wore the same scoop-tailed helmets and the same black rubber coats. But he was expected nevertheless to go for them through thick and thin. If, venturing into a strange neighborhood, he was halted by the local pickets and asked to say what engine he went for, he always answered proudly and truthfully, even though the truth might cost him a black eye. I never heard of a boy failing to observe this obligation of honor. Even the scoundrels who went for No. 10, when we caught one of them in our territory, never tried to deceive us. The most they would do would be to retreat ten paces before letting off their clan cry. We would then proceed, as in duty bound, to hang them out, which is to say, to chase them off the soil of our Fatherland.

The frontiers of the various gangs in West Baltimore were known to all the boys denizened there, and it was not common for a boy to leave his own territory. If he did so, it was at the risk of being hung out, or maybe beaten. But fights between adjoining gangs were relatively rare, for the cops kept watch along the borders, and all hands avoided them diligently. Once the Hollins street gang, engaged in exploring Franklin Square, which was three blocks from Union Square, encountered a gang that went for No. 8 engine, and a battle was joined. But it had gone on for no more than a few minutes when a cop came lumbering up Calhoun street, and both armies at once fled northward, which is to say, into No. 8 territory. The No. 8 boys, though they were officially obliged to do us in at every chance, concealed us in their alleys until the cop gave up the chase, for in the presence of the common enemy gang differences sank to the level of the academic. Any boy in flight from a cop was sure of sanctuary anywhere. In fact, a favorite way of making a necessary journey through

127

hostile lines was to do it at a run, yelling " Cheese it! The cops! " Boys respected this outcry even when they knew it was fraudulent.

There was in West Baltimore a neutral territory that all gangs save the ruffians from the region of the B. & O. shops respected — and they seldom invaded it, for they had better hunting-grounds nearer their base. It was a series of open lots beginning at Fulton avenue and Baltimore street, three blocks from Union Square, and running westward until it was lost in a wilderness of lime-kilns, slaughter-houses and cemeteries. From east to west it must have been a mile long, and from south to north half a mile wide. It is now covered with long rows of the red brick, marble trimmed two-story houses that are so typical of Baltimore, but in my nonage it was wild country, with room enough for half a dozen baseball diamonds, not to mention huge thickets of Jimson weeds, nigger-lice, and other such nefarious flora. The lower end, at Fulton avenue, was much frequented by the colored men who made their livings beating carpets. They would erect poles, string them with washlines, hang the carpets, and then flog them by the hour, raising great clouds of dust. A little further to the westward other colored men pursued the art and mystery of the sod-cutter. They would load their rolled-up sods on wheelbarrows and push them down into the city, to refresh and adorn the back-yards of the resident bourgeoisie.

We Hollins street boys spent many a pleasant afternoon roving and exploring this territory, which had the name of Steuart's Hill. We liked to watch the operation of the lime-kilns, all of them burning oyster shells, and the work of the carpet-beaters and sod-cutters. But best of all we liked to visit the slaughter-houses at the far western end. There was a whole row of them, and their revolting slops drained down into a deep gully that we called the Canyon. This Canyon was the Wild West of West Baltimore, and the center of all its romance. Whenever a boy came to the age when it became incumbent on him to defy God, the laws of the land and his father by smoking his first cigarette, he went out there for the operation. It was commonly a considerable ceremony, with a ring of older boys observing and advising. If the neophyte got sick he was laid out on one of the lower shelves of the Canyon until he recovered. If he began crying for his mother he was pelted with nigger-lice and clods of lime.

The Canyon was also a favorite resort of boys who read dime novels. This practice was regarded with horror by the best moral opinion of the time, and a boy who indulged it openly was given up as lost beyond hope. The best thing expected of him was that he would run away from home and go west to fight the Indians; the worst was that he would end on the gallows. In the more elderly years of my infancy I tried a few dime novels, trembling like

a virgin boarding an airship for Hollywood, but I
found them so dull that I could scarcely get
through them. There were other boys, however,
who appeared to be able to bear them, and even to
like them, and these addicts often took them out
to the Canyon to read in peace. No cops ever
showed themselves in that vicinity, which was probably, in fact, outside the city limits of Baltimore.
It was an Alsatia without laws, and tolerated every
sort of hellment. I have seen a dozen boys stretched
on the grass within a circumference of fifty feet,
all of them smoking cigarettes and reading dime
novels. It was a scene of inspiring debauchery,
even to the most craven spectator.

One afternoon, having been left behind when the
Hollins street gang made a trip to the Canyon, I
set out alone to overtake it. Just west of Fulton
avenue, which is to say, in full sight of householders
and passers-by along Baltimore street, I was held
up with perfect technic by three boys of a strange
gang. One of them aimed a cap pistol at my head
and ordered me to stick up my hands, and the other
two proceeded to frisk me. They found a pocket-
knife, a couple of sea-shells, three or four nails, two
cigarette pictures, a dozen chewing-tobacco tags, a
cork, a slate pencil, an almost fossil handkerchief,
and three cents in cash. I remember as clearly as if
it were yesterday their debate over the three cents.
They were sorely tempted, for it appeared that
they were flat broke, and needed money badly. But

in the end they decided primly that taking it would be stealing. The other things they took without qualm, for that was only hooking.

When they turned me loose at last I ran all the way to the Canyon, and sounded the alarm. The gentlemen of the Hollins street gang were pleasantly engaged in throwing stones into a pool of hog blood that had formed beneath the scuppers of one of the slaughter-houses, but when they heard my story they started for the scene of the outrage at once, scooping up rocks on the way. They got there, of course, too late to capture the bandits, but they patrolled the vicinity for the rest of the afternoon, and revisited it every day for a couple of weeks, hoping to make a collar, and get me back my handkerchief, nails, slate pencil, and chewing-tobacco tags. I may say at once that they were never recovered, nor did I ever see the robbers again. They must have come from some remote part of West Baltimore. Or perhaps they were prisoners escaped from the House of Refuge.

This bastile was a mile westward, on the banks of Gwynn's Falls. It was a harsh granite building surrounded by sepulchral trees, and all the boys of West Baltimore feared it mightily. Its population consisted of boys who had become so onery that their own fathers resigned them to the cops. The general belief was that a rascal who once entered its gates was as good as lost to the world. If he ever got out at all, which was supposed to be very unusual, the cops were waiting to grab him again, and thereafter he made quick progress to the scaffold. I knew only one boy who ever actually sat in its dungeons. He was a lout of fourteen whose father kept an oyster-bay in Frederick avenue. The passion of love having seized him prematurely, he got into a fight over a girl, and stabbed the other fellow with an oyster-knife. I well recall the day the cops dragged him through Union Square to the watch-house in Calhoun street, and then hurried back to haul his victim to the University of Maryland hospital in a grocery-wagon.

This affair caused a great sensation in Hollins street, for it was the introduction of many of us to the hazards and terrors of amour. We crowded around the watch-house a day or two later, waiting to hear the result of the cutthroat's trial, and slunk away in silence when a colored malefactor we knew came out and reported that he had been doomed to the House of Refuge, or, as we always called it, the Ref. We assumed as a matter of course that he had been sentenced for life. If he ever got out I didn't hear of it, and for all I can tell you he may be there yet, though the Ref was long ago transformed into a storehouse for the Baltimore sewer department. No member of the Hollins street gang ever entered its door. We had our faults, as I freely admit, but the immemorial timorousness of the bourgeoisie restrained us from downright felony. Two of the boys I chased cats with in 1888 drank themselves to death in their later years, two others went into politics, one became a champion bicycle racer, three became millionaires, and one actually died an English baronet, but none, to my knowledge, ever got to the death-house, or even to the stonepile.

In those days the nicknames of boys ran according to an almost invariable pattern, though all boys, of course, did not have them. The example of Barrel Fairbanks I have mentioned: he was too fat to be called simply Fats and not quite fat enough to be worthy the satirical designation of Skinny, so he took the middle label of Barrel. Any boy who happened to be lame was called Hop, anyone who had lost an eye was One-eye, and anyone who wore glasses (which was then very unusual) was Four-eyes. If a boy had a head of uncommon shape he was always called Eggy. The victims of such cruel nicknames never, so far as I can recall, objected to them; on the contrary, they appeared to be proud of their distinctions. Many nicknames were derived from the professions of their bearers' fathers. Thus the eldest son of a doctor was always Doc, and if a boy's father had the title of Captain — whether ship captain, fire captain, police captain, or military captain, it was all one — he was himself known as Cap. The eldest sons of all policemen above the grade of patrolmen took their father's titles as a matter of course. A block or two up Hollins street lived a sergeant whose son was called

Sarge, and when the father was promoted to a lieutenancy the son became Loot. In case a boy's father had the military title of Major, which was not
unusual in those days, for West Baltimore swarmed
with householders who had been officers in the Civil
War, he was called Major himself. I never knew
a boy whose father was a colonel or general, but
those to be found elsewhere in Baltimore undoubtedly followed the rule. The eldest sons of pedagogues were all called Professor, and if a boy's
father was a professional gambler (there was such
a boy in Hollins street) he was apt to be called
either Colonel or Sport. Younger sons did not
share in these hereditary honors, which went by
primogeniture. The nicknames they bore, if they
had any at all, were based upon their own peculiarities.

The latter-day custom of calling boys by their
full given names was quite unknown. Every
Charles was Charlie, every William was Willie,
every Robert was Bob, every Richard was Dick and
every Michael was Mike. I never heard a boy
called Bill: the form was always Willie or Will.
Bill was reserved for adults of the lower ranks, for
example, ashcart drivers. My own stable-name, as
I have noted, was Harry, and my immediate relatives so hail me to this day. My father's brother
Henry, whose house was next door to ours in Hollins street, was Uncle Hen to us until the time of
the World War, when the changing fashion con-

verted him into the more decorous Uncle Henry. I had two uncles with the same given name of John: one was Uncle John to me and the other was Uncle Johnnie, though Uncle Johnnie was the elder. I had an uncle named William, but I still call him Uncle Will, though his son, more than forty years his junior, rates the formal William. My father was Gus to his wife and all his friends, though his sisters called him August, and his underlings called him Mr. August. My mother's given name was Anna, but my father always called her Annie, and she was Aunt Annie to the cousins next door. One of the rules of the time was that a boy named Albert was always called Buck, never Al. Only a boy with an unusual given name escaped these *Koseformen*. The name of Theodore, for example, which was seldom encountered in the pre-Roosevelt era, was never supplanted by Teddy or Ted, but always remained Theodore. There was a boy in Hollins street named Seymour, and he remained Seymour until he broke his leg, when he became Hop. But most boys were Eddie, Johnnie, Bob, Dick or Willie.

The humor of the young bourgeoisie males of Baltimore, in those days, was predominantly skatological, and there was no sign of the revolting sexual obsession that Freudians talk of. The favorite jocosities had to do with horse apples, O.E.A. wagons and small boys who lost control of their sphincters at parties or in Sunday-school;

when we began to spend our Summers in the country my brother and I also learned the comic possibilities of cow flops. Even in the city a popular ginger-and-cocoanut cake, round in contour and selling for a cent, was called a cow flop, and little girls were supposed to avoid it, at least in the presence of boys. Colored girls were fair game for any prowling white boy, but there was never anything carnal about hunting them; they were pursued simply because it was believed that a nigger-louse burr, entangled in their hair (we always kept stocks at hand in the season), could not be removed without shaving their heads. Otherwise, the relations between the races were very friendly, and it was not at all unusual for a colored boy from the alley behind Hollins street to be invited to join a game of one-two-three, or a raid on Mr. Thiernau's potatoes and turnips. Many of the cooks in our block were colored women, though our own were always Caucasians down to 1900 or thereabout. All surplus victuals and discarded clothes were handed as a matter of course to the neighboring blackamoors, and they were got in for all sorts of minor jobs. There have been no race riots in Baltimore to this day, though I am by no means easy about the future, for a great many anthropoid blacks from the South have come to town since the city dole began to rise above what they could hope to earn at home, and soon or late some effort may be made to chase

them back. But if that time ever comes the up-
rising will probably be led, not by native Baltimoreans, but by the Anglo-Saxon baboons from the
West Virginia mountains who have flocked in for
the same reason, and are now competing with the
blacks for the poorer sort of jobs.

The Baltimore Negroes of the eighties had not
yet emerged into the once-fine neighborhoods they
now inhabit; they still lived, in the main, in alleys,
or in obscure side-streets. We boys believed in all
the traditional Southern lore about them — for
example, that the bite of one with blue gums was
poisonous, that those of very light skin were treacherous and dangerous, that their passion for water-
melon was at least as powerful as a cat's for catnip,
and that no conceivable blow on the head could
crack their skulls, whereas even a light tap on the
shin would disable them. Mr. Thiernau once set
me to tussling with a colored boy in his store, and I
made desperate efforts to reach his shins with my
heel, but he was too agile for me, and so he got the
better of the bout. When I reached home my
mother sniffed at me suspiciously, and then ordered
me to take a bath and change my clothes from the
skin out. The alley behind our house had some
colored residents who had lived there for many
years, but most of its inhabitants came and went
rather frequently, with the rent-collector assisting
them. He always appeared on Saturday evening,

and if the rent was not ready he turned out his tenant at once, without bothering to resort to legal means. The furniture that he thus set out on the sidewalk was often in a fantastic state of dilapidation, but it always included some of the objects of art that poor blackamoors of that era esteemed — a blue glass cup with the handle off, a couple of hand-painted but excessively nicked dinner-plates, a china shepherdess without a head, and so on. These things had come out of trash-cans, but they were fondly cherished. Behind the alley in the rear of our house, cutting off the Negro cabins from the houses in Baltimore street, ran a blind and very narrow sub-alley, perhaps not more than three feet wide. It was considered a good joke to inveigle a strange boy into it, for it was full of fleas. There were many such blind alleys in West Baltimore. One of them, running off Gilmor street, a block or so from our house, was called Child-stealers' alley, and we avoided it whenever possible. It was supposed to be the den of a monster who stole little children and carried them off to unknown but undoubtedly dreadful dooms. Such criminals were never spoken of as kidnappers, but always as child-stealers. So far as I can recall, none of them ever actually stole a child; indeed, none was ever seen in the flesh. But they were feared nevertheless.

Like all other boys, my brother Charlie and I were always in a condition of extreme insolvency. My mother had read an article in an early issue of

the *Ladies' Home Journal* [1] arguing that children
should not be given money freely but required to
earn it, and this became the rule of the house. My
brother and I alternated in shining our father's
Congress gaiters of a morning, and received five
cents for each shine, then the standard price in
Baltimore. For other chores we were paid on the
same scale, and in good weeks our joint income
reached sixty or seventy cents, and sometimes even
a dollar. But it was never enough, so we supple-
mented it by various forms of graft and embezzlement. When my mother sent me to Hollins market
with two or three dollars in hand and a list of supplies to be bought, I always knocked down at least
a nickel. My brother and I also got a little revenue
from Sunday-school collection money, for when we
were given dimes we put in only nickels, and when
we were given nickels we put in only pennies. All
the male scholars save a few milksops followed the
same system. The teachers must have been aware
of it, but they never did anything about it. We
picked up more money by walking to and from
school — a round trip of at least three miles —
and pocketing the three-cent fare each way. Sometimes, when a car was crowded we managed to elude
the conductor, and so rode without paying. On
some cars there was no conductor, and the driver

---

[1] She had subscribed for it from its first issue, and continued to do so until her death in 1925. Once, when she somehow let her subscription lapse, she got a letter from Edward
W. Bok, the editor, urging her not to desert him.

had to see to the fares. Inasmuch as he couldn't leave his horses, there were channels running down the sides of the car to carry to him the coins inserted by passengers. When a dozen boys got on a car together, it was usually possible for at least half of them to dodge paying fare. The driver always made a pother, but every boy swore that it was his money that had rolled down. The ensuing debate could be easily protracted until we were at our destination.

When all such devices failed, and Charlie and I faced actual bankruptcy, we had to resort to more desperate measures. Here, unhappily, we were cribbed, cabined and confined by the notions of dignity that prevailed among the West Baltimore bourgeoisie. We somehow understood without being told that it would be unseemly for us to run errands for Mr. Thiernau, or to carry the marketing of strange ladies returning home from Hollins market, or to shovel snow off sidewalks in Winter, or to help hostlers with their horses, or carriage-washers at their work. But there was one labor that, for some reason or other, was considered more or less elegant, though it was strictly forbidden by all parents, and that was selling newspapers. In 1889 or thereabout my brother Charlie and I undertook it in the hope of accumulating quickly enough funds to buy a cat-and-rat rifle. We had an air-rifle, but wanted a cat-and-rat rifle, which used real cartridges, and our father's harsh and

profane prohibition of it only made us want it the
more. So we hoofed down to the alley behind the
old *Evening World* office in Calvert street — a
good mile and a half from Hollins street — and
laid in six *Worlds* at half a cent apiece. Leaping
on horse-cars and howling " Paper! Paper! " was
a grand adventure, but we soon found that a great
many tougher, louder and more experienced boys
were ahead of us, and when we counted up our
profits at the end of two or three hours of hard
work, and found that we had made but six cents
between us, we decided that selling papers was far
from what it had been cracked up to be. Inciden-
tally, we never got that cat-and-rat rifle.

School took in in those days early in September,
and ran on until the end of June. There were very
few holidays save the Saturdays and Sundays,
and boys had to depend for their major escapes
from learning upon the appearance of measles or
chicken-pox in the house. But there was one day
that was always kept in Baltimore, and that was
September 12, the anniversary of the Battle of
North Point. This historic action was fought at
the junction of the Chesapeake Bay and the Patapsco river in 1814, and as a result of it Baltimore
escaped being burned by the British, as Washington was. Moreover, it produced two imperishable
heroes in the shape of a pair of Baltimore boys,
Wells and McComas, who hid in a tree and assassinated the British commander, General Robert

141

Ross. Yet more, Francis Scott Key, jugged on a British ship in Baltimore harbor, wrote " The Star-Spangled Banner " while the accompanying bombardment of Fort McHenry was going on. Thus September 12 was always celebrated in Baltimore, and all the boys got a day off from school, which was to me a matter of special rejoicing, for the day was my birthday. The last doddering veterans of the War of 1812 are dead now, and there is no longer a Defenders' Day parade, but September 12 remains a legal holiday in Maryland, and my birthday is still marked by blasts of patriotic rhetoric and artillery.

IX

𝕮𝖔𝖕𝖘

AND THEIR WAYS

THE FIRST policeman I ever became acutely aware
of on this earth was one Cookie, a short, panting fellow with the sagittal section of an archbishop. I
was about six years old at the time, and along with
my brother Charlie I was watching and admiring
some older boys playing at par, which was the Baltimore name for leap-frog. This was on a hot Summer afternoon and at the corner of Hollins and
Gilmor streets, not more than a hundred feet from
our own front door. Suddenly one of the par-play-
ers stopped his play, turned pale, shook with a kind
of palsy, pointed like a setter, and exclaimed
" Cookie! " in a shrill, hysterical voice. The rest
picked up the enemy at once. He was plodding
along Gilmor street in the shadow of the high wall

of the House of the Good Shepherd, stretching a whole block down to Lombard street.

The next thing I recall is being dragged along at a speed of what seemed to be at least a mile a minute by the obese Barrel Fairbanks, with my brother tagging behind in tow of a boy named Socks Cromwell. Why we were in such haste I didn't gather at the minute, for I was yet unaware of the dreadful nefariousness of the police. Infants of six were still ignorant in such matters. They gaped at cops as innocently as they gaped at letter-carriers, garbage-men and organ-grinders' monkeys. But now my brother and I had been accepted as licensed followers, though still very far from members, of the Hollins street gang, and the facts quickly soaked into us when its lawful leaders ordered a halt in Booth alley behind our house, to catch breath and consider strategy.

Some were in favor of running on to Reveille's livery-stable, two blocks away, and hiding in the hay. Others proposed making a long detour around Reveille's and laying a course by forced draft out Fayette street to Steuart's Hill. There were objections to both plans. The Reveille brothers were hospitable to boys whose fathers stabled buggies in their establishment (which let in my brother and me), but for boys in general they had only a sour welcome, and none at all for boys in gangs. As for Steuart's Hill, it was at least six blocks away by the route suggested, and most of that route was uphill. Moreover, the Hill was likely to be swarming, on a Summer afternoon, with boys from strange gangs, and if they were in a mood of aggression they might break the truce usually prevailing there, and make short work of the Hollins street gang, burdened, as it was, by such raw and loutish troops as my brother and I.

All this may sound like a long council, but it actually took no more than half a minute. Finally, some smart fellow suggested that we send a spy to the end of the alley to find out if Cookie was still lumbering down on us. No one volunteered for that office, so the smart fellow had to undertake it himself. He sneaked up to Gilmor street along the back-fences, according to the approved technic for scouts in the Indian country, and peeped cautiously around the stable at the corner. Returning in a moment, his caution gone, he reported that Cookie had anchored in a cool spot along the convent wall, and was engaged in mopping his bald head and biting off a chew of tobacco. The hunt was thus over, for Cookie's ordinary jurisdiction did not extend to Booth alley, and he would follow boys there, it appeared, only in the heat of pursuit. No such heat was visible.

But the time and place seemed opportune for the older boys to instruct my brother and me in the tricks and deviltries of cops, and this they did at length. It was never safe, they explained, to let a cop come within reach. There was no telling what infamy he might be up to. For one thing, he might grab a more or less innocent boy, accuse him of breaking a window-pane in a house six blocks away, and proceed to do justice upon him on the spot, with the thin leather thong that flowed from the end of every cop's espantoon, enabling him to swing it ostentatiously as he patrolled his beat. For another thing, he might rush upon boys playing catty and break up the game in sheer ill-nature, with no excuse save the labored one that a flying catty had hit a baby carriage, and scared the infant half to death. For a third thing, he was an incurable tattle-tale, and delighted in writing down the names of boys detected in chasing cats, or throwing nigger-lice at colored girls, or blowing spitballs at the Salvation Army, and then blabbing on them to their fathers.

In brief, a cop was a congenitally iniquitous character, an enemy to society, a master of all the slimy devices of espionage and betrayal. He was against all the manly sports of boys of normal mind and high metabolism. If they started a ball-game in the street he would take his stand behind a tree a block away, watching for some violation of his arbitrary and incomprehensible regulations, and spoiling all the fun. He objected to the harmless pulling of girls' pigtails, to making bonfires in alleys, to setting dogs to fighting in Union Square, to catching goldfish in the pond there, to overturning and emptying ash-boxes, to stealing rides on trucks or horse-cars, to hunting sparrows with air-rifles, to making game of cripples and idiots, to throwing horse-apples at aged or drunken men, to walking along the tops of backyard fences, to prodding mules with sticks, to pulling doorbells on Hallowe'en, to making sliding-places in the gutters in Winter, to scaring little girls with false-faces, to nailing up backyard gates, to putting on white pillow-slips after dark and terrorizing pious colored people, to yelling " Rats! " at Chinese laundrymen, to upsetting the wooden Indians in front of cigar-stores.

Himself an habitual snitcher of peanuts and Johnny-bread from poor Italians, he prohibited lifting a few cheap turnips or carrots from the baskets outside the stores of rich grocerymen. When there was a funeral and boys collected on the sidewalk to see the pallbearers in their plug hats, he spoiled it by heaving into sight, and setting the whole gang to flight. When there was a fire, he made watching it hazardous, and no fun. No boy of any sense would approach voluntarily within half a block of a cop. If one came ambling down the street the sidewalk would clear as swiftly as if he had been Sitting Bull himself. A boy who had occasion to enter a livery-stable always peeped first, to make sure that no cop was there before him. A boy who turned a corner and came face-to-face with one took to flight at once, yelling " Cheese it! " to warn all other boys. Even girls felt uneasy when they saw a blue uniform, though cops never molested them. But from the moment a boy made the first faltering step toward manhood they had it in for him, and he had it in for them.

The one thing to be said in favor of these ruffianly kill-joys was that they were heavy on their feet, and hence easy to out-run. There may have been lean and high-geared cops in other communities, but I never heard of one in the West Baltimore I grew up in. They all wore extraordinarily thick and uncomfortable-looking uniforms, in Summer as in Winter, squeaky shoes with soles as solid as slabs of oak, and domed helmets that always fell off when they attempted to run, scattering lead-pencils, peanuts, red bandana handkerchiefs and chewing-tobacco, and maybe a few cigars, oranges or bananas. A cop in pursuit of a boy had to hold on to his helmet with one hand, and with the other clutch his revolver, lest it go off in the holster flopping from his stern and shoot him in the leg. Any boy in the full possession of his faculties could beat such a mud-scow in a fair race. Even Barrel Fairbanks, fat as he was, could do it. It was only the boy collared by stratagem — always dirty — who was ever actually captured and switched.

So far as I can recall, this switching, when it was done, never brought out any hullabaloo from the victim's parents. His father continued to speak to the cop amicably, and his mother continued to threaten him with the cop when he failed to wash behind his ears. Even the boys themselves did not object to the switching *per se;* all they complained of was being switched by the object of their common contempt and execration — an insult rather than an injury. In those Mousterian days no one had yet formulated the theory that a few licks across the backside would convert a normal boy into a psychopathic personality, bursting with Freudian complexes and a rage against society. It was still universally considered that an occasional rataplan cleansed him of false ideas and softened his native boorishness. School-teachers whaled very freely, and with no more thought of tort than a dentist pulling a tooth, and so did parents. On a window-sill in the kitchen of our house in Hollins street lay a wooden ruler that certainly gathered no cobwebs. Once, having tasted it three times in a single morning, my brother Charlie sneaked it away and buried it in the yard, but the next day there was another in its place, and no questions asked.

I remember well the first time a cop actually came into the house: it must have been a year or so after our initiation into the infamy of Cookie. The time was a Sunday morning, an unusual one for callers, and when the doorbell rang Charlie and I peeped out of a third-story window to see who was there. When we saw the blue uniform we were almost paralyzed with fright — but not quite enough to keep us from piling into a cupboard in the rear room, pulling the door shut, and holding it tight. We stayed there until the bell rang for lunch, and even then we came down the stairs very gingerly, peeping over the banister to make sure that the monster had left. We gathered from my father's talk to my mother that he was one Lieutenant Smith, apparently a cop of great puissance. But we couldn't make out what he had come for, and we were too scared to ask. It was a great relief when we gathered that it was not for us.

Rather curiously, the most ferocious cop I ever knew was more tolerant of boys than the general, and enjoyed a kind of repute among them that was almost, though certainly not quite good. He was a huge Irishman of the name of Murphy, and he wore the heavy black mustache that went in those days with the allied sciences of copping and bartending. Murphy, I suspect, really wanted to be friends with the boys, but they never let him get near enough to them to show it. When we were playing ball in the street, he would come round the corner with a sort of ingratiating tread, much different from his standard plodding, and stand there rather wistfully as we yelled " Cheese it ! " and galloped away.

Murphy reserved all his Berserker fury for the Aframericans who lived in Vincent alley, two blocks away. Our own dark neighbors in Booth alley were of a peaceful disposition, and the few ructions back there were almost always caused by visitors, but in Vincent alley the wars continued round the calendar, and were especially bloody on Saturday nights. I mean bloody in its literal sense. There were not many ladies of the Vincent alley set who had not been slashed more than once by the bucks they adored and supported, and I can recall no buck who had not had an ear bitten off, or a nostril slit, or a nose mashed. The alley began to buzz at 6 p.m. on Saturday, when such of its male inhabitants as worked at all came home with their pay, and by 8 o'clock Murphy was hard at it dragging the wounded out of its tenements and clubbing the felonious into insensibility.

There were in those days no patrol-wagons in Baltimore: a cop who made an arrest had to tool his prisoner to the nearest watch-house on foot, with such incidental help as he could get from friendly dray-drivers. Many's the time I have watched Murphy slide, shove and yank a frantic colored lady down the long path which ran obliquely (and still runs) through Union Square, with a huge gallery of white and black fans crowding after. The screams and contortions of such viragoes entertained us boys as neatly as a fire, and we learned a lot about anatomy and physiology from their remarks. Murphy never used his espantoon on females if he could help it, and when he couldn't he always bounced them gently — a tap just sufficient to cause a transient dizziness. He reserved his masterstrokes for males. One stupendous crack, and it was all over. If his customer revived before they got to the police-station it was so unusual as to amount to a marvel. When he applied himself seriously to a bad nigger there was one bad nigger less for a minimum of thirty days.

As I have said, this was before there were any patrol-wagons in Baltimore, or, at all events, in West Baltimore. When they came in at last, in the twilight of the eighties, Murphy seemed to lose form. It was only half a block from the hell-mouth of Vincent alley to the nearest box, and dragging his prisoners so short a distance, with help so quickly and easily obtainable, sapped his old pride of craftsmanship. More than once I observed him at the box looking baffled and foolish. When the wagon backed up he heaved his blackamoor aboard with a kind of resigned contempt, and barely spoke to the driver and footman. He belonged to the post-Civil War school of bare-hand cops, and was a fit match for Killer Williams of New York, though he never rose to any rank in his profession. In the end, if my recollection serves me, he was put on trial before the police commissioners on the charge of giving a bad nigger a clout of unnecessary violence. As I recall it, he was acquitted with honor, but the notion that anyone could imagine hitting a bad nigger too hard was beyond his comprehension, and he withdrew from the force. Baltimore, by 1890, was already fast degenerating, and so was civilization.

There were not only no patrol-wagons in service

in Murphy's heyday, but also no ambulances. The cops had to get the sick and injured to hospital as best they could, and more often than not their best consisted only in commandeering a one-horse truck or ash-cart. In the case of patients emanating from Vincent alley that made no great difficulty, for no colored West Baltimorean of that era, so long as he retained his wits, would let the cops or anyone else take him to hospital. The word always meant to him the old University of Maryland Hospital at Lombard and Greene streets, and every Aframerican knew that it swarmed with medical students who never had enough cadavers to supply their hellish orgies, and were not above replenishing their stock by sticking a knife into a patient's back, or holding his nose and forcing a drink out of the black bottle down his throat.

The ordinary wounded of Vincent alley were patched up at a drug-store nearby, or by one of the sporty doctors who hung about the neighborhood livery-stables. If their injuries turned out to be beyond the science of these quacks, getting them to hospital was a laborious business — that is, in case they were conscious, and hence able to resist. Their struggles against being arrested were, in the main, only formal, and it took only a stroke or two of Murphy's wand to subdue them, but going to hospital was something else again. Not infrequently, in fact, it couldn't be managed without beating them into a coma, even with three or four

cops and half a dozen civilian volunteers on the job.
Once a patient was on his way, his neighbors gave
him up as dead, and his lady friend began looking
for a new admirer. There were, of course, aberrant
cases of Aframericans, even in Vincent alley, who
had been dragged to Lombard and Greene streets
and yet returned, but they were very rare and carried a spookish and suspicious aura. Indeed, any
blackamoor who had so survived was avoided by
his fellows thereafter. He was one who had come
unscathed from a charnel-house, and there were
certainly reasonable grounds for surmising that
he had escaped only by entering into some more
or less diabolical pact with the doctors. No one
wanted him about. He made everyone uncomfortable.

I must have been at least ten or eleven years old
before my fear of cops began to abate. It was probably laid at last by two circumstances. The first
was the fact that a young cop named Tom O'Don-
nell made a headline in the Baltimore *Sunpaper* one
morning by excavating a burglar from the cellar
of my father's warehouse in Paca street. Tom went
in after the fellow alone, bare-handed and in complete darkness, and after he had emerged with his
prisoner and dragged him to the nearest watch-
house it was discovered that he had collared a desperate cop-hater with a long string of assaults and
mayhems behind him. My father and his brother
and the other business men of the vicinity there-

upon waited on the police commissioners and demanded that Tom be promoted for his courage, and he was presently made a detective. He served in that office until only the other day, and I still see him on the streets occasionally, his eye continuing to oscillate for pickpockets, for an old cop never stops copping so long as he is on his legs. I got to know him very well in my days as a newspaper reporter, and spared no rhetoric when he made another dramatic collar, which was often. My father's high, astounding praise of him convinced my brother and me that there must be occasional cops who were not enemies of society, just as there were occasional Sunday-school teachers who were not idiots. It was disillusion and hence painful, but there was also some relief in it.

But what really shook us was the appearance in the next block of Hollins street of a boy who actually had a policeman for a father. It seemed wholly fantastic, but the evidence could not be gainsaid, for the boy admitted it himself, and we used to see his father coming home of an evening, exactly like any other father. He was a sergeant when he moved into Hollins street, but was presently promoted to a lieutenancy, and his son was thus known to us as Loot. We all liked him, and in his presence talk about the iniquity of cops had to be avoided. Gradually it fell off even when he wasn't present, and especially it fell off after he had invited us to his house to see his new steam-engine, and his father, in mufti, came down to the cellar and undertook to show us how to work it. He failed completely, as fathers always failed, and we began to realize that he was a human being almost like any other, at least when not in uniform. When the family moved away there was some recrudescence of cop-hating, but all the old steam was out of it.

Today the fear of cops seems to have departed teetotally from American boys, at least on the level of the bourgeoisie. I have seen innocents of eight or nine go up to one boldly, and speak to him as if he were anyone else. Some time ago the uplifters in Baltimore actually organized a school for Boy Scouts with cops as teachers, and it did a big trade until the cops themselves revolted. What happened was that those told off to instruct the Scouts in the rules of traffic, first aid, the operation of fire-alarm boxes, etiquette toward the aged and blind, the elements of criminal law and other such branches got so much kidding from their fellows that they were covered with shame, and in the end the police commissioner let out the academy *sine die*, and restored its faculty to more he duties.

X

LARVAL STAGE OF A

𝕭𝖔𝖔𝖐𝖜𝖔𝖗𝖒

THE FIRST long story I ever read was " The Moose Hunters," a tale of the adventures of four half-grown boys in the woods of Maine, published in *Chatterbox* for 1887. *Chatterbox*, which now seems to be pretty well forgotten, was an English annual that had a large sale, in those days, in the American colonies, and " The Moose Hunters " seems to have been printed as a sort of sop or compliment to that trade, just as an English novelist of today lards his narrative with such cheery native bait as " waal, pardner," " you betcha " and " geminy-crickets." The rest of the 1887 issue was made up of intensely English stuff ; indeed, it was so English that, reading it and looking at the woodcuts, I sucked in an immense mass of useless information about English history and the English scene, so that to this day I know more about Henry VIII and Lincoln Cathedral than I know about Millard Fillmore or the Mormon Temple at Salt Lake City.

" The Moose Hunters," which ran to the length of a full-length juvenile, was not printed in one gob, but spread through *Chatterbox* in instalments. This was an excellent device, for literary fans in the youngest brackets do their reading slowly and painfully, and like to come up frequently for air. But writing down to them is something else again, and that error the anonymous author of " The Moose Hunters " avoided diligently. Instead, he wrote in the best journalese of the era, and treated his sixteen-year-old heroes precisely as if they were grown men. So I liked his story very much, and stuck to it until, in a series of perhaps twenty sessions, I had got it down.

This was in the Summer of 1888 and during hot weather, for I remember sitting with the volume on the high marble front steps of our house in Hollins street, in the quiet of approaching dusk, and hearing my mother's warnings that reading by failing light would ruin my eyes. The neighborhood apprentices to gang life went howling up and down the sidewalk, trying to lure me into their games of follow-your-leader and run-sheep-run, but I was not to be lured, for I had discovered a new realm of being and a new and powerful enchantment. What was follow-your-leader to fighting savage Canucks on the Little Magalloway river, and what was chasing imaginary sheep to shooting real meese? I was near the end of the story, with the Canucks all beaten off and two carcasses of gigantic meese hanging to trees, before the author made it clear to me that the word *moose* had no plural, but remained unchanged *ad infinitum*.

Such discoveries give a boy a considerable thrill, and augment his sense of dignity. It is no light matter, at eight, to penetrate suddenly to the difference between *to, two* and *too*, or to that between *run* in baseball and *run* in topographical science, or *cats* and *Katz*. The effect is massive and profound, and at least comparable to that which flows, in later life, out of filling a royal flush or debauching the wife of a major-general of cavalry. I must have made some effort to read *Chatterbox* at the time my Grandmother Mencken gave it to me, which was at Christmas, 1887, but for a while it was no go. I could spell out the shorter pieces at the bottoms of columns, but the longer stories were only jumbles of strange and baffling words. But then, as if by miracle, I found suddenly that I could read them, so I tackled " The Moose Hunters " at once, and stuck to it to the end. There were still, of course, many hard words, but they were no longer insurmountable obstacles. If I staggered and stumbled somewhat, I nevertheless hung on, and by the Fourth of July, 1888, I had blooded my first book.

An interval of rough hunting followed in Hollins street and the adjacent alleys, with imaginary Indians, robbers and sheep and very real tomcats as the quarry. Also, I was introduced to chewing tobacco by the garbageman, who passed me his plug as I lay on the roof of the ash-shed at the end of the backyard, watching him at his public-spirited work. If he expected me to roll off the roof, clutching at my midriff, he was fooled, for I managed to hold on until he was out of sight, and I was only faintly dizzy even then. Again, I applied myself diligently to practising leap-frog with my brother Charlie, and to mastering the rules of top-spinning, catty and one-two-three. I recall well how it impressed me to learn that, by boys' law, every new top had to have a license burned into it with a red-hot nail, and that no strange boy on the prowl for loot, however black-hearted, would venture to grab a top so marked. That discovery gave me a sense of the majesty of the law which still sustains me, and I always take off my hat when I meet a judge — if, of course, it is in any place where a judge is not afraid to have his office known.

But pretty soon I was again feeling the powerful suction of beautiful letters — so strange, so thrilling, and so curiously suggestive of the later suction of amour — , and before Christmas I was sweating through the translation of Grimms' Fairy Tales that had been bestowed upon me, " for industry and good deportment," at the closing exercises of F. Knapp's Institute on June 28. This volume had been put into lame, almost pathological English by a lady translator, and my struggles with it awoke in me the first faint gutterings of the critical faculty. Just what was wrong with it I couldn't, of course, make out, for my gifts had not yet flowered, but I was acutely and unhappily conscious that it was much harder going than " The Moose Hunters," and after a month or so of unpleasantly wrestling with it I put it on the shelf. There it remained for more than fifty years. Indeed, it was not until the appearance of " Snow White " as a movie that I took it down and tried it again, and gagged at it again.

That second experiment convinced me that the fault, back in 1888, must have been that of either the brothers Grimm or their lady translator, but I should add that there was also some apparent resistant within my own psyche. I was born, in truth, without any natural taste for fairy tales, or, indeed, for any other writing of a fanciful and unearthly character. The fact explains, I suppose, my lifelong distrust of poetry, and may help to account for my inability to memorize even a few stanzas of it at school. It probably failed to stick in my mind simply because my mind rejected it as nonsense — sometimes, to be sure, very jingly and juicy nonsense, but still only nonsense. No doubt the same infirmity was responsible for the feebleness of my appetite for the hortatory and incredible juvenile fiction fashionable in my nonage —

the endless works of Oliver Optic, Horatio Alger, Harry Castlemon and so on. I tried this fiction more than once, for some of the boys I knew admired it vastly, but I always ran aground in it. So far as I can recall, I never read a single volume of it to the end, and most of it finished me in a few pages.

What I disliked about it I couldn't have told you then, and I can account for my aversion even now only on the theory that I appear to have come into the world with a highly literal mind, geared well enough to take in overt (and usually unpleasant) facts, but very ill adapted to engulfing the pearls of the imagination. All such pearls tend to get entangled in my mental *vibrissae*, and the effort to engulf them is as disagreeable to me as listening to a sermon or reading an editorial in a second-rate (or even first-rate) newspaper. I was a grown man, and far gone in sin, before I ever brought myself to tackle "Alice in Wonderland," and even then I made some big skips, and wondered sadly how and why such feeble jocosity had got so high a reputation. I am willing to grant that it must be a masterpiece, as my betters allege — but not to *my* taste, not for *me*. To the present moment I can't tell you what is in any of the other juvenile best-sellers of my youth, of moral and sociological hallucination all compact, just as I can't tell you what is in the Bhagavad-Gita (which Will Levington Comfort urged me to read in 1912 or thereabout), or in the works of Martin Tupper, or in the report of Vassar Female College for 1865. I tried dime-novels once, encouraged by a boy who aspired to be a train-robber, but they only made me laugh. At a later time, discovering the pseudo-scientific marvels of Jules Verne, I read his whole canon, and I recall also sweating through a serial in a boys' weekly called *Golden Days*, but this last dealt likewise with *savants* and their prodigies, and was no more a juvenile, as juveniles were then understood, than " Ten Thousand Leagues Under the Sea."

But before you set me down a prig, let me tell you the rest of it. That rest of it is my discovery of " Huckleberry Finn," probably the most stupendous event of my whole life. The time was the early part of 1889, and I wandered into Paradise by a kind of accident. Itching to exercise my newly acquired art of reading, and with " The Moose Hunters " exhausted and Grimms' Fairy Tales playing me false, I began exploring the house for print. The Baltimore *Sunpaper* and *Evening News*, which came in daily, stumped me sadly, for they were full of political diatribes in the fashion of the time, and I knew no more about politics than a chimpanzee. My mother's long file of *Godey's Lady's Book* and her new but growing file of the *Ladies' Home Journal* were worse, for they dealt gloomily with cooking, etiquette, the policing of children, and the design and construction of mil-

linery, all of them sciences that still baffle me. Nor
was there any pabulum for me in the hired girl's
dog's-eared files of *Bow Bells* and the *Fireside
Companion*, the first with its ghastly woodcuts of
English milkmaids in bustles skedaddling from
concupiscent baronets in frock-coats and cork-
screw mustaches. So I gradually oscillated, almost
in despair, toward the old-fashioned secretary in
the sitting-room, the upper works of which were
full of dismal volumes in the black cloth and gilt
stamping of the era. I had often eyed them from
afar, wondering how long it would be before I
would be ripe enough to explore them. Now I
climbed up on a chair, and began to take them
down.

They had been assembled by my father, whose
taste for literature in its purer states was of a generally low order of visibility. Had he lived into the
days of my practice as a literary critic, I daresay
he would have been affected almost as unpleasantly
as if I had turned out a clergyman, or a circus
clown, or a labor leader. He read every evening
after dinner, but it was chiefly newspapers that he
read, for the era was one of red-hot politics, and
he was convinced that the country was going to
Hell. Now and then he took up a book, but I found
out long afterward that it was usually some pam-
phlet on the insoluble issues of the hour, say
" Looking Backward," or " If Christ Came to Chicago," or " Life Among the Mormons." These

- *164*

works disquieted him, and he naturally withheld them from his innocent first-born. Moreover, he was still unaware that I could read — that is, fluently, glibly, as a pleasure rather than a chore, in the manner of grown-ups.

Nevertheless, he had managed somehow to bring together a far from contemptible collection of books, ranging from a set of Chambers' Encyclopedia in five volumes, bound in leather like the Revised Statutes, down to " Atlantis: the Antediluvian World," by Ignatius Donnelly, and " Around the World in the Yacht *Sunbeam*." It included a two-volume folio of Shakespeare in embossed morocco, with fifty-odd steel plates, that had been taken to the field in the Civil War by " William H. Abercrombie, 1st Lieut. Company H, 6th Regiment, Md. Vol. Inftr.," and showed a corresponding dilapidation. Who this gallant officer was I don't know, or whether he survived the carnage, or how his cherished text of the Bard ever fell into my father's hands. Also, there were Dickens in three thick volumes, George Eliot in three more, and William Carleton's Irish novels in a third three. Again, there were " Our Living World," by the Rev. J. G. Wood; " A History of the War For the Union," by E. A. Duyckinck; " Our Country," by Benson J. Lossing, LL.D., and " A Pictorial History of the World's Great Nations From the Earliest Dates to the Present Time," by Charlotte M. Yonge — all of them likewise in threes, folio, with lavish illustrations on steel, stone and wood, and smelling heavily of the book-agent. Finally, there were forty or fifty miscellaneous books, among them, as I recall, " Peculiarities of American Cities," by Captain Willard Glazier; " Our Native Land," by George T. Ferris; " A Compendium of Forms," by one Glaskell; " Adventures Among Cannibals " (with horrible pictures of missionaries being roasted, boiled and fried), " Uncle Remus," " Ben Hur," " Peck's Bad Boy," " The Adventures of Baron Münchhausen," " One Thousand Proofs That the Earth Is Not a Globe " (by a forgotten Baltimore advanced thinker named Carpenter), and a deadly-looking " History of Freemasonry in Maryland," by Brother Edward T. Schultz, 32°, in five coal-black volumes.

I leave the best to the last. All of the above, on my first exploration, repelled and alarmed me; indeed, I have never read some of them to this day. But among them, thumbing round, I found a series of eight or ten volumes cheek by jowl, and it appeared on investigation that the whole lot had been written by a man named Mark Twain. I had heard my father mention this gentleman once or twice in talking to my mother, but I had no idea who he was or what he had done: he might have been, for all I knew, a bartender, a baseball-player, or one of the boozy politicoes my father was always meeting in Washington. But here was evidence that he was a man who wrote books, and I noted at once that the pictures in those books were not of the usual funereal character, but light, loose and lively. So I proceeded with my inquiry, and in a little while I had taken down one of them, a green quarto, sneaked it to my bedroom, and stretched out on my bed to look into it. It was, as smarties will have guessed by now, " Huckleberry Finn."

If I undertook to tell you the effect it had upon me my talk would sound frantic, and even delirious. Its impact was genuinely terrific. I had not gone further than the first incomparable chapter before I realized, child though I was, that I had entered a domain of new and gorgeous wonders, and thereafter I pressed on steadily to the last word. My gait, of course, was still slow, but it became steadily faster as I proceeded. As the blurbs on the slip-covers of murder mysteries say, I simply couldn't put the book down. After dinner that evening, braving a possible uproar, I took it into the family sitting-room, and resumed it while my father searched the *Evening News* hopefully for reports of the arrest, clubbing and hanging of labor leaders. Anon, he noticed what I was at, and demanded to know the name of the book I was reading. When I held up the green volume his comment was " Well, I'll be durned! "

I sensed instantly that there was no reproof in this, but a kind of shy rejoicing. Then he told me that he had once been a great reader of Mark Twain himself — in his younger days. He had got hold of all the volumes as they came out — " The Innocents " in 1869, when he was still a boy himself; " Roughing It " in 1872, " The Gilded Age " in 1873, " Tom Sawyer " in 1876, " A Tramp Abroad " in 1880, the year of my birth, and so on down to date. (All these far from pristine firsts are still in the Biblioteca Menckeniana in Hollins street, minus a few that were lent to neighbor boys and never returned, and had to be replaced.) My father read them in the halcyon days before children, labor troubles and Grover Cleveland had begun to frazzle him, and he still got them down from the shelf on quiet evenings, after the first-named were packed off to bed. But a man of advancing years and cares had to consider also the sorrows of the world, and so he read in Mark less than aforetime.

As for me, I proceeded to take the whole canon at a gulp — and presently gagged distressfully. " Huckleberry Finn," of course, was as transparent to a boy of eight as to a man of eighty, and almost as pungent and exhilarating, but there were passages in " A Tramp Abroad " that baffled me, and many more in " The Innocents," and a whole swarm in " The Gilded Age." I well recall wrestling with the woodcut by W. F. Brown on page 113 of the " Tramp." It shows five little German girls swinging on a heavy chain stretched between two stone posts on a street in Heilbronn, and the legend under it is " Generations of Bare Feet." That legend is silly, for all the girls have shoes on, but what puzzled me about it was something quite different. It was a confusion between the word *generation* and the word *federation*, which latter was often in my father's speech in those days, for the American Federation of Labor had got under way only a few years before, and was just beginning in earnest to harass and alarm employers. Why I didn't consult the dictionary (or my mother, or my father himself) I simply can't tell you. At eight or nine, I suppose, intelligence is no more than a small spot of light on the floor of a large and murky room. So instead of seeking help I passed on, wondering idiotically what possible relation there could be between a gang of little girls in pigtails and the Haymarket anarchists, and it was six or seven years later before the " Tramp " became clear to me, and began to delight me.

It then had the curious effect of generating in me both a great interest in Germany and a vast contempt for the German language. I was already aware, of course, that the Mencken family was of German origin, for my Grandfather Mencken, in his care for me as *Stammhalter*, did not neglect to describe eloquently its past glories at the German universities, and to expound its connections to the most remote degrees. But my father, who was only half German, had no apparent interest in either the German land or its people, and when he spoke of the latter at all, which was not often, it was usually in sniffish terms. He never visited Germany, and never signified any desire to do so, though I recall my mother suggesting, more than once, that a trip there would be swell. It was " A Tramp Abroad " that made me German-conscious, and I still believe that it is the best guide-book to Germany ever written. Today, of course, it is archaic, but it was still reliable down to 1910, when I made my own first trip. The uproarious essay on " The Awful German Language," which appears at the end of it as an appendix, worked the other way. That is to say, it confirmed my growing feeling, born of my struggles with the conjugations and declensions taught at F. Knapp's Institute, that German was an irrational and even insane tongue, and not worth the sufferings of a freeborn American. These diverse impressions have continued with me ever since. I am still convinced that Germany, in the intervals of peace, is the most pleasant country to travel in ever heard of, and I am still convinced that the German language is of a generally preposterous and malignant character.

" Huck," of course, was my favorite, and I read it over and over. In fact, I read it regularly not less than annually down to my forties, and only a few months ago I hauled it out and read it once more — and found it as magnificent as ever. Only one other book, down to the beginning of my teens, ever beset me with a force even remotely comparable to its smash, and that was a volume called

" Boys' Useful Pastimes," by " Prof. Robert Griffith, A.M., principal of Newton High School." This was given to me by my Grandmother Mencken at Christmas, 1889, and it remained my constant companion for at least six years. The sub-title describes its contents: " Pleasant and profitable amusement for spare hours, comprising chapters on the use and care of tools, and detailed instructions by means of which boys can make with their own hands a large number of toys, household ornaments, scientific appliances, and many pretty, amusing and necessary articles for the playground, the house and out-of-doors." Manual training was still a novelty in those days, and I suspect that the professor was no master of it, for many of his plans and specifications were completely unintelligible to me, and also to all the neighborhood boys who dropped in to help and advise. I doubt, indeed, that any human being on earth, short of an astrophysicist, could have made anything of his directions for building boat models. But in other cases he was relatively explicit and understandable, and my brother Charlie and I, after long efforts, managed to make a steam-engine (or, more accurately, a steam-mill) according to his recipe. The boiler was a baking-powder tin, and the steam, issuing out of a small hole in the top, operated a sort of fan or mill-wheel. How we provided heat to make steam I forget, but I remember clearly that my mother considered the process dangerous, and ordered us to take the engine out of the cellar and keep it in the backyard.

I had no more mechanical skill than a cow, but I also managed to make various other things that the professor described, including a what-not for the parlor (my mother professed to admire it, but never put it into service), a rabbit-trap (set in the backyard, it never caught anything, not even a cat), and a fancy table ornamented with twigs from the pear tree arranged in more or less geometrical designs. " Boys' Useful Pastimes " was printed by A. L. Burt on stout paper, and remains extant to this day — a rather remarkable fact, for other boys often borrowed it, and sometimes they kept it on their work-benches for a long while, and thumbed it diligently. One of those boys was Johnnie Sponsler, whose father kept a store in the Frederick road, very near Hollins street. Johnnie was vastly interested in electricity, as indeed were most other boys of the time, for such things as electric lights, motors, telephones and doorbells were just coming in. He thus made hard use of Professor Griffith's Part VII, which was headed " Scientific Apparatus and Experiments," and included directions for making a static machine, and for electroplating door-keys. He later abandoned the sciences for the postal service, and is now, I believe, retired. " Boys' Useful Pastimes," and my apparent interest in it, may have been responsible for my father's decision to transfer me from F.

Knapp's Institute to the Baltimore Polytechnic in 1892. If so, it did me an evil service in the end, for my native incapacity for mechanics made my studies at the Polytechnic a sheer waste of time, though I managed somehow to pass the examinations, even in such abysmal subjects as steam engineering.

The influence of " Huck Finn " was immensely more powerful and durable. It not only reinforced my native aversion to the common run of boys' books; it also set me upon a systematic exploration of all the volumes in the old secretary, and before I finished with them I had looked into every one of them, including even Brother Schultz's sombre history of Freemasonry in Maryland. How many were actually intelligible to a boy of eight, nine, ten? I should say about a fourth. I managed to get through most of Dickens, but only by dint of hard labor, and it was not until I discovered Thackeray, at fourteen, that the English novel really began to lift me. George Eliot floored me as effectively as a text in Hittite, and to the present day I have never read " Adam Bede " or " Daniel Deronda " or " The Mill on the Floss," or developed any desire to do so. So far as I am concerned, they will remain mere names to the end of the chapter, and as hollow and insignificant as the names of Gog and Magog.

But I plowed through Chambers' Encyclopedia relentlessly, beginning with the shortest articles

173

and gradually working my way into the longer
ones. The kitchen-midden of irrelevant and incredible information that still burdens me had its
origins in those pages, and I almost wore them out
acquiring it. I read, too, the whole of Lossing,
nearly all of Charlotte M. Yonge, and even some
of Duyckinck, perhaps the dullest historian ever
catalogued by faunal naturalists on this or any
other earth. My brother Charlie and I enjoyed
" Our Living World " chiefly because of the colored
pictures, but I also read long stretches of it, and
astonished my father by calling off the names of
nearly all the wild beasts when the circus visited
Baltimore in 1889. Finally, I recall reading both
" Life Among the Mormons " and " One Thousand Proofs That the Earth Is Not a Globe."

Thus launched upon the career of a bookworm,
I presently began to reach out right and left for
more fodder. When the Enoch Pratt Free Library
of Baltimore opened a branch in Hollins street, in
March, 1886, I was still a shade too young to be
excited, but I had a card before I was nine, and
began an almost daily harrying of the virgins at
the delivery desk. In 1888 my father subscribed
to *Once-a-Week*, the predecessor of *Collier's*, and a
little while later there began to come with it a long
series of cheap reprints of contemporary classics,
running from Tennyson's poems to Justin M'Carthy's " History of Our Own Times "; and simultaneously there appeared from parts unknown a simi-

lar series of cheap reprints of scientific papers, including some of Herbert Spencer. I read them all, sometimes with shivers of puzzlement and sometimes with delight, but always calling for more. I began to inhabit a world that was two-thirds letterpress and only one-third trees, fields, streets and people. I acquired round shoulders, spindly shanks, and a despondent view of humanity. I read everything that I could find in English, taking in some of it but boggling most of it.

This madness ran on until I reached adolescence, and began to distinguish between one necktie and another, and to notice the curiously divergent shapes, dispositions and aromas of girls. Then, gradually, I began to let up.

But to this day I am still what might be called a reader, and have a high regard for authors.

XI

FIRST STEPS IN

Divinity

In the days of my earliest memories my father had an acquaintance named Mr. Garrigues, a highly respectable man of French origin who operated a men's hat-store in West Baltimore, not far from our home in Hollins street. This hat-store of his, though it drove an excellent trade, occupied him only on week-days; on Sundays he threw himself, rather curiously for a man of his race, into superintending the Sunday-school of a little Methodist chapel in nearby Wilkens avenue. Early one Winter evening he dropped in while my brother Charlie and I were playing Indians up and down the front staircase, and proposed to my father that we be articled to his Sunday-school. I recall, of course, nothing of his argument, though my brother and

I naturally eavesdropped; I remember only that it
lasted but a few minutes, and that the very next
Sunday afternoon Mr. Garrigues came to the
house in a high silk hat, and conducted us to his
seminary.

It was not until years afterward that I learned
why my father had succumbed so quickly, or indeed
at all. I understood by that time that he was what
Christendom abhors as an infidel, and I took the
liberty of expressing some wonder that he had been
willing, in that character, to expose his two innocent sons to the snares of the Wesleyan divinity.
He hemmed and hawed a little, but finally let go
the truth. What moved him, he confessed, was
simply his overmastering impulse to give over the
Sunday afternoons of Winter to quiet snoozing.
This had been feasible so long as my brother and I
were puling infants and could be packed off for
naps ourselves, but as we increased in years and
malicious animal magnetism and began to prefer
leaping and howling up and down stairs, it became
impossible for him to get any sleep. So he was a
set-up for Mr. Garrigues, and succumbed without
firing a shot. " The risk," he went on to explain,
" was much less than you seem to think. Garrigues
and his Methodists had you less than two hours a
week, and I had you all the rest of the time. I'd
have been a hell of a theologian to let them nail
you."

I recall very little of his counter-revolutionary

propaganda, and all that little took the form of a sort of satirical cross-examination, deliberately contrived to be idiotic. " Have they got you to Jonah yet? Have you heard about him swallowing the whale? " And so on. I recall even less of the teaching in the Sunday-school itself, though I apparently picked up from it some knowledge of the *dramatis personae* of the Old Testament. At all events, I can't remember the time when I did not know that Moses wrote the Ten Commandments with a chisel and wore a long beard; that Noah built an ark like the one we had in our Christmas garden, and filled it with animals which, to this day, I always think of as wooden, with a leg or two missing; that Lot's wife was turned into a pillar (I heard it as *cellar*) of table salt; that the Tower of Babel was twice as high as the Baltimore shottower; that Abraham greatly pleased Jahveh by the strange device of offering to butcher and roast his own son, and that Leviticus was the father of Deuteronomy. But all this learning must have been imparted by a process resembling osmosis, for I have no recollection of any formal teaching, nor even of any teacher.

The one thing I really remember about that Sunday-school is the agreeable heartiness of the singing. It is, of course, the thing that all children enjoy most in Sunday-schools, for there they are urged to whoop their loudest in praise of God, and that license is an immense relief from the shushing

they are always hearing at home. Years later I
lived for a while beside a Christian Science establishment in which the larval scientificoes were
taught, presumably, that their occasional belly-
aches were only mortal error, but all I ever heard
of this teaching was their frequent antiphon of
cheerful song, with each singer shrilling along in
a different key. If the Bach Choir could work up
so much pressure in its pipes, the Mass in B minor
would become as popular as " Sweet Adeline." So
far as I can make out, I attended Mr. Garrigues's
hive of hymnody but two Winters, and yet I carried away from it a répertoire of Methodist shouts
and glees that sticks to me to this day, and is turned
loose every time I let three-bottle men take me for
a ride.

My favorite then, as now, was " Are You Ready
For the Judgment Day? " — a gay and even rol-
licking tune with a saving hint of brimstone in the
words. I am told by Paul Patterson, who got his
vocal training in the Abraham Lincoln Belt of
Inner Illinois, that the No. 1 hymn there in the
eighties was " Showers of Blessings," but in Baltimore, though we sang it, it was pretty far down the
list. We grouped it, in fact, with such *dolce* but
unexhilarating things as " In the Sweet By-and-
By " and " God Be With You Till We Meet
Again " — pretty stuff, to be sure, but sadly lacking in bite and zowie. The runner-up for " Are
You Ready? " was " I Went Down the Rock to

179

Hide My Face," another hymn with a very lively
swing to it, and after " the Rock " came " Stand
Up, Stand Up for Jesus," " Throw Out the Life-
line," " At the Cross," " Draw Me Nearer, Nearer,
Nearer, Blessed Lord," " What a Friend We Have
in Jesus," " Where Shall We Spend Eternity? "
" The Sweet By-and-By," and " Hallelujah, Hallelujah, Revive Us Again," which last was cabbaged by the I.W.W.'s years later, and converted
into proletarian ribaldry. We also learned the
more somber classics — " Nearer, My God, To
Thee," " Onward, Christian Soldiers," " Whiter
Than Snow," " From Greenland's Icy Mountains,"
" Rock of Ages," " There is a Green Hill Far
Away," and so on — but they were not sung often,
and my brother and I had little fancy for them. It
was not until I transferred to another Sunday-
school that I came to know such lugubrious horrors
as " There is a Fountain Filled With Blood." The
Methodists avoided everything of that kind. They
surely did not neglect Hell in their preaching, but
when they lifted up their voices in song they liked
to pretend that they were booked to escape it.

My early preference for " Are You Ready? "
was no doubt supported by the fact that it was also
a favorite among the Aframerican evangelists who
practised in the alley behind Hollins street, alarming and shaking down the resident sinners. These
evangelists did not confine themselves to Sundays,
but worked seven days a week, and it seemed to

me as a boy that there was always one of them in operation. They were both male and female. I recall clearly a female who wore a semi-ecclesiastical robe of violent purple, and had a voice so raucous that the white neighbors often begged the cops to chase her away. Whenever she was hustled out she kept on shouting warnings over her shoulder, always to the effect that the Day of Judgment was just round the corner. Her chief target was a low-down white man who lived in the alley with a colored woman, and had a large family of mulattoes. When he retreated into his house she howled at him through the window. So far as I know, she never made any impression on him, nor on his children, though his lady sometimes gave her a penny. This sinful white man, who never did any work, eventually disappeared, and the colored people reported that he had been killed in a brawl, and his body hustled to the University of Maryland dissecting-room. Of his children, one son was later reported to be hanged.

The evangelists always began their proceedings by lining out a hymn, and usually it was " Are You Ready? " It brought out all the colored people who happened to be at home, and in a few minutes white boys began to leap over the Hollins street back-fences to join the congregation. (In those days no self-respecting boy ever went through a gate. It was a point of honor to climb over the fence.) When the opening hymn reached its tenth and last stanza the evangelist would pray at length, mentioning salient sinners by name. Then there would be another hymn, and after that he would launch into his discourse. Its subject was always the same : the dreadful state of Aframerican morals in West Baltimore. It was delivered in a terrifying manner — indeed, it ran mainly to shrieks and howls — but it was seldom long, for the colored people preferred their theology in small and powerful doses. Then there would be another hymn, and the reverend would begin to show signs that a collection was impending. The moment those signs were detected nine-tenths of his audience vanished. Not infrequently, in fact, ten-tenths of it vanished, and all he could do, after mopping his brow and stuffing his handkerchief into his hat, was to shuffle on to some other alley.

We white boys always joined in the hymns, and listened to the sermons. From the latter we picked up a great deal of useful information about the geography, dimensions, temperature, social life and public works of Hell. To this day I probably know more about the matter than most ordained clergymen. The Hell we heard about was chiefly peopled, of course, by the colored damned; it was sometime later before I began to understand clearly that there was also accommodation for Caucasians. We seldom attempted to rough-house these services, though once in a while a boy whose people had family prayers and who thus hated religion would heave a dead cat over the fence or run down the alley yelling " Fire! " The colored communicants commonly gave ear with perfect gravity. Indeed, the only one who ever ventured to dispute the theology on tap was Old Wesley, the alley metaphysician, who reserved his caveats for the preaching of his brother, a divine who pastored a tar-paper tabernacle down in Calvert county, and showed up only to rowel and bedevil Wesley for living in adultery with our next-door neighbor's colored cook.

It was the dream of every alley evangelist to be called to a regular church, and sometimes that dream was realized. The call consisted in renting a room in a tumble-down house, putting in a couple of rows of benches, and finding two or three pious colored women to feed the pastor and pay the rent. There was always a sign outside giving the name of the establishment, the name of the pastor (followed by D.D.), and the order of services. These signs followed an invariable pattern, with all the *S*'s backward, and plenty of small *a*'s, *e*'s and *r*'s scattered through the capitals. Such signs are still plentiful in the poorer colored neighborhoods of Baltimore, and the old church names survive — the Watch Your Step Baptist Temple, the Sweet Violet Church of God, the Ananias Penecostal Tabernacle, and so on. One such basilica that I recall stood in the middle of a lot down near the Baltimore & Ohio tracks, surrounded by Jimson weeds and piles of rusting tin-cans. The sistren of the Ladies' Aid roved the vicinity, cadging contributions from white passers-by. Whenever my father and his brother passed of a Sunday morning on their way to George Zipprian's beer-garden across the tracks they gave up ten cents apiece to the first collector who flagged them. They always made her jab a hat-pin through her collection-card in their presence, professing to fear that otherwise she might bilk the pastor.

We were not permitted to enter any of these tabernacles, for they were supposed to swarm with ticks, fleas, spiders, lice, thousand-legs and other *Arthropoda*. But we were free to attend the street-corner hullabaloos of the Salvation Army, which was then a novelty in the United States, and almost as good as a circus. Here our training in Wesleyan hymnody stood us in good stead, for the hymns the Army howled were the same that we had howled ourselves in Mr. Garrigues's chapel. We let go with all brakes off, and greatly enjoyed the ensuing confessions of the saved. There was one old man who admitted such appalling crimes that we never got enough of him, and it was a sad day when he failed to appear, and one of the corner loafers intimated that he had been hauled off to a lunatic asylum. When the beautiful Amazons of God began circulating in the crowd with their tambourines we took to our heels, for we believed in conscience that salvation should be free.

Mr. Garrigues died suddenly in 1888, and my father thereupon shifted us to another and much larger Sunday-school, run by the English Lutherans in Lombard street. It met, unfortunately, on Sunday mornings, so he had to suffer some interruption of his afternoon nap, but as we grew older and more decorous that objection faded out. We liked it very much during the first few years, for the superintendent, Mr. Harman, was a Methodist at heart and often lined out the rousing hymns that we knew and esteemed. We also greatly enjoyed the cornet-playing of the treasurer, whose name I recall as Mr. Mentzer. He was an elegant fellow in a silky mustache, a white choker collar and an immaculate cutaway, and when he lifted his cornet to his lips it was with a very graceful flourish — at all events, it seemed so to us. As he let go *fortissimo* the whole Sunday-school seemed to heave, and the stained-glass rattled in the church upstairs. In the singing that went with his blasts of tone ordinary yelling was not enough; a boy of any spirit had to scream. More than once I came home hoarse, and was put to gargling with pain-killer.

The pastor of the church in those days was the Rev. Sylvanus Stall, D.D., a tall, gaunt Pennsylvanian with a sandy beard and melancholy voice. I find on investigation that he was precisely forty years old in 1887, but he seemed to my brother and me to be as ancient as Abraham. He looked at first glance like a standard-model Class B Protestant ecclesiastic, but there was much more to him than met the eye. One Sunday morning in 1889 or thereabout he showed up in Sunday-school with a strange contraption under his arm. Rapping for order, he announced that it was a newly invented machine that could talk like a human being, and not only talk but even sing. Then he instructed us to sing his favorite hymn, which was " God Be With You Till We Meet Again." We bawled it dutifully, and he explained that the machine would now bawl it back. " But not," he went on, " as loudly as you did. Listen carefully, and you will hear it clearly enough. The sound of the machine is very faint, but it is also very penetrating." So he turned it on, and we heard a phonograph for the first time. Ah, that it had been the last!

A little while later the good doctor quit pastoring to take the editorship of a church paper, with dashes into book-writing on the side. His first two or three books had such depressing titles as " Methods of Church Work," " Five-Minute Object Sermons " and " Bible Selections For Daily Devotion," and appear to have scored only successes of esteem. But in 1897, long after I had escaped his former Sunday-school and almost forgotten him, he brought out a little volume called " What a Young Boy Ought to Know," and thereafter he began rolling up money with such velocity that when he died in 1915 he was probably the richest

Lutheran pastor, at least in the earned brackets, that the Republic has ever seen. For that little volume founded the great science of sex hygiene, which eventually developed into a major American industry, with thousands of practitioners and a technic become as complicated as that of bridge or chess.

He wrote all its official texts for male seekers — "What a Young Man Ought to Know," "What a Young Husband Ought to Know," "What a Man of Forty-five Ought to Know," and so on — and he inspired, copy-read and published all its texts for females, beginning with "What a Young Girl Ought to Know" and ending, I suppose, with "What a Decent Grandmother Ought to Forget." Indeed, he held the field unchallenged until the explosion of the Freud ammunition-dump of horrors, and by that time he was so well heeled that he could afford to laugh ha-ha. He left his money, I believe, to a college for training missionaries to the sexually misinformed and underprivileged, but where it is located I don't know and don't care.

Of the theology he radiated in his Baltimore days I retain precisely nothing. There was, in fact, little expounding of doctrine in his Sunday-school; the instruction, in so far as there was any at all, was predominantly ethical, and had as its chief apparent aim the discouragement of murder, robbery, counterfeiting, embezzlement and other such serious crimes, none of which occurred in the student body in my time. Those were the cradle days of religious pedagogy, and the teachers confined themselves mainly to expounding the week's International Sunday-school Lesson, and trying to induce their pupils to memorize the Golden Text. Inasmuch as I could never memorize anything, I failed regularly. But there was no penalty for failure, and it was hardly remarked, for virtually all the other boys in my class failed too.

Tiring of this puerile futility, I began to agitate for my release at the age of ten, and finally escaped when I went into long pants. My father, it turned out, had not underestimated the potency of his evil influence: it left me an infidel as he was, and as his father had been before him. My grandfather died too soon to have much direct influence upon me, but I must have inherited something of his attitude of mind, which was one of large tolerance in theological matters. No male of the Mencken family, within the period that my memory covers, ever took religion seriously enough to be indignant about it. There were no converts from faith among us, and hence no bigots or fanatics. To this day I have a distrust of such fallen-aways, and when one of them writes in to say that some monograph of mine has aided him in throwing off the pox of Genesis my rejoicing over the news is very mild indeed.

XII

THE RUIN OF AN

𝔄𝔯𝔱𝔦𝔰𝔱

THE PIANO that introduced me to the tone-art was
a Stieff square made in Baltimore, with a shiny
black case, a music-rack that was a delirium of jig-
saw whorls, and legs and ankles of the sort that survive today only on lady politicians. It came into
the house in Hollins street on January 13, 1888,
and there it groaned and suffered for twenty years,
gradually taking on the unhealthy patina and tin-
can tone of age. How many hours I gave over to
banging it, first and last, I don't know, but certainly they must have been enough to set loose a
couple of billion decibels. When, in 1906 or thereabout, I joined a music club, and we began to play
occasionally in Hollins street, the infirmities of the
old Stieff were remarked unpleasantly by the other

members, and after a year or two of resistance I traded it in for an upright. Inasmuch as squares, by that time, had gone completely out of fashion, even on excursion boats and in houses of ill-fame, the dealer who acquired it could not find a buyer for it, and in the end he had to contribute it to a huge bonfire of unsalable instruments that the despairing piano men of the east staged at Atlantic City, to the accompaniment of considerable publicity. A few years later someone invented the trick of turning old squares into colonial desks, and there arose a sudden demand for them from antique manufacturers, with the prices soaring. The dealer spent his brief remaining days denouncing me for overreaching him, and his clamor in the saloons was largely responsible for the bad name that I still bear in Baltimore as a prince of pelf.

My first teacher was a gentleman I chiefly remember, not because of what he taught me, but because of the extraordinary luxuriance of his whiskers. Hair on the face, of course, was not unusual in the eighties; indeed, it was the rule, and I knew men with beards almost a yard long, and others who affected Burnsides, Dundrearys and even Galways. But foliage so wild and lawless as that of Mr. Maass — for such was his name — was nevertheless somewhat unusual. It was divided in the middle in such a way that it seemed to be blown apart by a gale of wind, and it swept so far to either side that it passed and concealed his narrow shoulders. He wore it, I learned, because he suffered from a weakness of the chest, and that same weakness had wrecked his career as a piano virtuoso. He was working at the time, in fact, as my father's bookkeeper, and he slipped away from his stool twice a week to fan my nascent talents and pick up an extra dollar. He was a patient and kindly man, and must have been a very fair teacher, for in hardly more than a year he got me through Ferdinand Beyer's Preliminary School for the Piano-Forte,[1] and even introduced me to some of the lesser horrors of Karl Czerny's School of Velocity.[2] But the weakness in the chest continued, and only too soon poor Mr. Maass had to give up both his teaching and his bookkeeping. A little while longer, and he was dead. I remember nothing of his funeral, and not much more of his pedagogy,

[1] I have the book yet, and lately paid a binder $7.50 to repair its dog's ears. In Grove's Dictionary of Music there is an article by the late Edward Dannreuther dismissing Beyer as "a fair pianist and tolerable musician whose reputation rests upon an enormous number of easy arrangements, transcriptions, potpourris, fantasias, divertissements, and the like, such as second-rate dilettanti and music-masters at ladies' schools are pleased to call amusing and instructive." Dannreuther's own compositions consisted, according to another writer in Grove, of "two sets of songs and one of duets." I pronounce a curse upon him in passing. He died in 1905, and is probably still in Purgatory. May he linger there for 10,000,000,000 more years!

[2] For Czerny I never developed any affection, and neither did any other male piano student of my generation. He was admired only by vinegary little girls who wore tight pigtails tied with pink ribbons, and played his infernal scales and arpeggios in a pretentious and offensive manner. So late as 1930, being in Vienna, I visited and desecrated his grave.

but I recall very well his gentle spirit and his stupendous whiskers.

On his departure I fell into the hands of a series of lady teachers, and they both wrecked my technic and debauched my taste. There were thousands of such damsels roving the American towns in the last century, radiating an influence for evil even worse than that of the contemporary white-slave traders, spiritualists and politicians. They charged a uniform price of twenty-five cents apiece for lessons, and derived their really living wages from the retailing of sheet music. Some of the music they taught me still exists in my library: " La Châtelaine," by A. Leduc; Dance Écossaise, by Fred T. Baker; the " Old Roman " march, by M. H. Rosenfeld (dedicated to " the Hon. Allen G. Thurman, the noblest Roman of them all "); " Monastery Bells," Leybach's Fifth Nocturne, the " Black Key " polka, the " Chopsticks " waltz, and other such rubbish. I achieved a considerable fluency in its performance, and at the age of ten was often put up to drive unwelcome guests out of the house.

This purpose, of course, was concealed from me, and I believed innocently that my proficiency was admired. The trick was played by my father. When some bore dropped in unexpectedly of an evening (which was no uncommon misadventure in those days, for there were no telephones) he would get out the jugs that were his tools of hospitality,

yell upstairs for me to come down, set me at the
Stieff square, and order me to play "something
lively." I thereupon launched into a programme
of marches and gallops, all of them executed with
the loud pedal held down. If I let up long enough
to attempt something soft and sneaking, he would
stop me at once, and order me to turn on the juice
again. This dreadful din went on until the guest
withdrew. I remember trying to figure out why a
rational man, entertaining his apparent friends,
should want to deafen them, but the truth did not
occur to me until long afterward. In fact, it did
not occur to me even then; I derived it from one of
my father's occasional confidences, which increased
as I grew in years and discretion.

This unwitting service as bouncer made me a
slave to the *forte* pedal, and I remain more or less
under its spell to this day, as critics have often
noted. My father was tone-deaf, and was thus not
incommoded when, in reaching for the C below the
bass clef, I hit B or D. He had been put to the fiddle in boyhood, but never got beyond the third position in Jacques-Féréol Mazas's Complete Violin
Method: the rest of the book (which is still in the
house) shows no pedagogical marks. He had two
violins, but ventured to play them only when encouraged by libation. At such times he would
tune up by performing "Yankee Doodle." If it
sounded plausible he would proceed. Some years
after his death I showed his violins to the late Al-

bert Hildebrandt, of Baltimore, a friend of mine and a renowned violin expert. He dismissed one of them as trash, but told me that the other was an excellent German imitation of a sound Cremona model. He put it in order for me, and I was later offered $200 for it. Astounded, I called a family court of inquiry, and eventually excavated the fact that my father's stepmother had bought it for him on a visit to Leipzig in the sixties. She knew no more about violins than he did, but somehow she had managed to pick up a good one.

The lady music teachers, as I have said, undermined my virtuosity and vitiated my taste, but despite their hard efforts they did not destroy either altogether. I managed somehow to become a pretty good sight-reader, and I was soon proceeding by the way of the Strauss waltzes (which still delight me) to the whole salon répertoire of the time. There was some Mozart in it, and even some Beethoven, but it ran mainly to Moskowski and his cogeners. I well recall the sensation when Paderewski's minuet in G was added to it: people lined up for the music in the music-stores as they were soon afterward lining up for the Sousa marches. My command of waltzes, polkas, schottisches, mazurkas and so on, and later on of two-steps, kept me on the piano-stool at parties, and so I managed to get through my nonage without learning to dance. I took a few belated lessons at the end of my teens, but turned out to be unteachable without recourse to complicated and costly apparatus, apparently because my center of gravity was not stable.

My real regret today, looking back over my career as a *Tonkünstler*, is that those preposterous lady Leschetizkys never gave me any instruction in elementary harmony. They avoided the subject, of course, simply because they knew nothing about it, and had, in fact, probably never heard of it. I don't recall any of them ever referring to a composition by naming its key; they always said it was " in three sharps," or " five flats," and never distinguished between major and minor. I was twelve years old before it dawned upon me that there must be ascertainable differences between chords, and it was a good while thereafter before I began to find out what those differences were. The creative frenzy of the mid-teen years prompted me to write a great many piano pieces, chiefly waltzes, but I had to harmonize them by the method of trial and error at the piano. If my inclination had run to songs this method might have made a George M. Cohan of me, or even an Irving Berlin. Perhaps fortunately, I was born with an intense distaste for vocal music, and to this day think of even the most gifted Wagnerian soprano as no more than a blimp fitted with a calliope. If a bass singer shows up at my funeral to sing " *Im tiefen Keller sitz' ich hier* " it will take the whole platoon of clergy and pallbearers to hold me down.

It was not until I was passing out of my teens

that I ever opened a *Harmonielehre* and not until several years afterward that I began to associate familiarly with competent musicians. It was then too late for me to devote any serious attention to the subject, for I was in active practice as a reporter on a newspaper, and the job kept me jumping. That was long before it had occurred to anyone that reporters would be benefitted culturally by five-day weeks and time-and-a-half for overtime. I worked six days of twelve hours each, and often had to lend a hand on my day off. There was a year during which I accumulated no less than twenty full days of overtime. The city editor gave me what I thought was a handsome compensation by raising my pay $2 a week, letting me do copyreading on the side for the experience, and adding five days to my annual vacation.

If I speak of my lack of sound musical instruction lightly, please do not be deceived. I was only dimly aware of it at the time, but it was really the great deprivation of my life. My early impulse to compose was no transient storm of puberty, explicable on purely endocrine grounds. It stuck to me through the years of maturity, and is still far from dead as I slide into the serenity of senility. When I think of anything properly describable as a beautiful idea, it is always in the form of music. Alcohol has the effect of filling my head with such ideas, and I daresay hashish would do even better. I have sketched out, in my day, at least ten sonatas

196

for piano, and there was a time when I had accumulated fifty or sixty pounds of music-paper, all of it covered with pothooks. It ran, in the main, to waltzes, always my great delight, but it also included the score of a musical comedy put on by the boys at the Baltimore Polytechnic in 1895 or thereabout — most of it, of course, snitched from other composers. This musical comedy, despite a book that was frowned on as contumacious and even a bit salacious, made a great success, and I sat at the piano as its whole orchestra.

In those days I knew nothing about orchestra music, but when the music club I have mentioned began to function I developed an interest in fiddles and flutes, and was soon writing for them. One of our first members, now long dead, was an Irishman named Joe Callahan, a charming fellow who loved music to excess, but was of such limited skill as a violinist that he could be trusted only on the open strings. I wrote many parts for him in the safe keys of C and G major, and it gave him great delight to chime in, even though he could do it only occasionally. I also wrote violin and cello obbligatos for the songs of a lady singer who joined us for a while. Once I launched into the incredible project of arranging Dvořák's " New World " symphony for piano, violin and cello, and another time I actually made such an arrangement of Beethoven's No. 1. For years I collected orchestra scores, and what is more, studied them diligently, though I am almost as tone-deaf as my father, and could never get any more out of them than a ghostly reverberation, like the sound of a brass band heard from afar on a rainy night.

Meditating on this, my lifelong libido that has never come to anything, I become aware of the eternal tragedy of man. He is born to long for things that are beyond him, as flight through the air is beyond a poor goldfish in a globe, and stardom in Hollywood must remain forever outside the experience, though not outside the dreams, of all save a few hundred of the girls in the ten-cent stores. Not many men of my unhappily meagre equipment have ever had a better chance than I to fling their egos into the face of this world. I have, in fact, made a living for many years by thrusting myself upon the attention of strangers, most of them reluctant. I have written and printed probably 10,000,000 words of English, and continue to this day to pour out more and more. It has wrung from others, some of them my superiors, probably a million words of notice, part of it pro but most of it con. In brief, my booth has been set up on a favorable pitch, and I have never lacked hearers for my ballyhoo. But all the same I shall die an inarticulate man, for my best ideas have beset me in a language I know only vaguely and speak only like a child.

The loss to humanity, of course, is not serious enough to cause any general gloom. In truth, my real reason for failing to pursue music to a bitter finish was probably not, as I have intimated, that I was too busy with other things, nor even that I was too old when my first really good chance came. It was simply that I had no talent for it. This dreadful fact gradually forced itself into my consciousness as the years passed, helped along by the satirical efforts of musical friends, and today it is so firmly embedded that though I still itch I no longer scratch. But the underlying mystery remains. Why should a man so completely devoid of fitness for the tone-art yet have so powerful an impulse to practise it, and get so much pleasure out of it? I have no answer, but I suspect that my disease is more widespread than is generally assumed. Every concert audience probably swarms with baffled Beethovens and frustrated Wagners. I used to believe and argue that any person who had a genuine love of music would undertake some effort, soon or late, to make it, but even that I now doubt, for I know men who go to concerts almost as regularly as they eat, and sit at the phonograph or the radio by the hour, and yet have so little impulse to raise a din themselves, and so little curiosity about the ways and means of doing so, that they can't so much as pick out the scale of C major at the piano. As for me, I delight in the sound of horse-hair on catgut as honestly and as vastly as a cop delights in beer, and yet I am quite unable to tune a fiddle. The mystery is only one of a thousand that bedevil man in his swift and senseless flight through the world. The gods, in the main, are vicious, but now and then they show an unmistakable touch of humor.

My inclination toward the graphic arts began earlier and ended earlier than my devotion to music, and was much feebler. There are, in the family files, crude drawings dated 1886 and 1887, and a little while later, sitting under Mr. Paul at F. Knapp's Institute, I copied a whole series of the drawing-books then in fashion, and picked up some pale skill at draftsmanship as that science was then understood by German pedagogues. But my natural lack of manual dexterity hindered me here, and I never got beyond the elements. At Christmas, 1888, some one gave me a box of water-colors, and during the years following I made various attempts to use them. Having learned by reading that paintings were commonly done on canvas, I made a small wooden frame, stretched it with muslin borrowed from my mother's rag-bag, and was astonished and baffled to find that when water-colors were applied to it they all ran together. This unhappy *Jugendwerk* still survives. Also, there is a water-color on paper, signed " H. L. Mencken, July, 1892," which not only survives, but is framed in a gilt frame, and hangs on my office wall. It shows a scene along Jones falls, near our Summer home at Mt. Washington, and is anything but bad for a boy less than twelve years old. The rocks are painted in a thoroughly bold and modern manner, and the water falling over them actually looks like water. I have often thought of entering this composition in some free-for-all exhibition of Modernist Art — with the date and signature, of course, discreetly painted out.

XIII

IN THE FOOTSTEPS OF

𝕲utenberg

On November 26, 1887 my father sent his book-keeper, Mr. Maass, to the establishment of J. F. W. Dorman, at 217 East German street, Baltimore, and there and then, by the said Maass's authorized agency, took title to a Baltimore No. 10 Self-Inker Printing Press and a font of No. 214 type. The press cost $7.50 and the font of type $1.10. These details, which I recover from the receipted bill in my father's file, are of no conceivable interest to anyone else on earth, but to me they are of a degree of concern bordering upon the super-colossal, for that press determined the whole course of my future life. If it had been a stethoscope or a copy of Dr. Ayers' Almanac I might have gone in for medicine; if it had been a Greek New Testament or a set of

baptismal grappling-irons I might have pursued
divinity. As it was, I got the smell of printer's ink
up my nose at the tender age of seven, and it has
been swirling through my sinuses ever since.

The press and type, of course, were laid in by
my father against Christmas, and were concealed
for the nonce in a cupboard at home, but my brother
Charlie and I had a good look at them before early
candlelight of November 27. We decided that they
were pretty nifty, or, as the word was then, nobby.
If Charlie, comparing them to the velocipede that
lay in wait for him, was bemused by envy, he had
only himself to blame, for he had delayed his coming into the world for twenty months after my own
arrival, and was still virtually illiterate. It was
barely three months, in fact, since he had begun to
attend the sessions of F. Knapp's Institute, and he
yet had some difficulty in distinguishing, without il-
lustrative wood-cuts, between the words *cat* and *rat*.
Compared to him, I was so far advanced in *literae
humaniores* as to be almost a savant. During the
previous Summer I had tackled and got down my
first book, and was even then engaged in exploring
the house library for another. No doubt this new
and fevered interest in beautiful letters was marked
in the household, and set afloat the notion that a
printing-press would be to my taste. Indeed, I
probably hinted as much myself.

If my mother approved, which she undoubtedly
did, she must have developed a certain regret on

Christmas Day, for my father undertook to show me how to work the press, and inasmuch as he knew no more about printing than Aristotle and had so little manual dexterity that he could not even lace a shoe, he made a ghastly mess of it. Before he gave it up as a bad job all the ink that came with the outfit had been smeared and slathered away, and at least half the type had been plugged with it or broken. I recall clearly that we ran out of white cards before noon, and had to resort to the backs of his business cards. By that time all the brass gauge-pins had been crushed, one of the steel guides that held cards against the platen was bent, and the mechanism operating the ink-roller was out of order. It was a sad caricature of a printing-press that went to the cellar at midday, when my mother ordered a halt and a clean-up.

Next morning, after my father shoved off for his office, I unearthed it and set to work to scrub the ink off it and make it go. Unfortunately, I had almost as little skill with my hands as my father, so it must have been New Year's Day, at the earliest, before I succeeded. My cash takings, that Christmas, had been excellent; in fact, I had amassed something on the order of $2. With this money I went down to Dorman's, bought a new can of ink and a large bottle of benzine, and also laid in a new font of type. With the press there had come a font of Black Letter and to it, apparently on the advice of Mr. Maass, who was an aesthete, my fa-

ther had added one of Script. My own addition
was a prosaic font of Roman, with caps only. I
now had enough faces to begin printing on a commercial scale, and early in 1888 I was ready with
the following announcement:

𝔥. 𝔏. 𝔐encken

Card Printer

**1524 HOLLINS ST.
BALTIMORE, MD.**

Up to this time I had always written my name
Henry L., or Harry, which last, as I have noted,
has been my stable-name all my life. My change to
H. L. was not due to any feeling that the form better became the dignity of a business man, but simply to the fact that my father, in the course of his
Christmas morning gaucheries, had smashed all my
Black Letter lower-case r's, and I had to cut my
coat to fit my cloth. During the ensuing months I
had some accidents of my own, and by the time I began to print billheads I had wrecked the penultimate cap *M* in my Roman font, and was forced to
abbreviate Baltimore to Balto. But I still had an
undamaged *&* in Black Letter and also a service-
able though somewhat mangey cap *C*, so I added
" & Co " to the style and designation of my house.

So far as I can remember, my father was my

only customer. His taste in typography, as in the other arts, was very far from finicky, and his pride in the fact that I could print at all sufficed to throttle such feeble qualms as he may have had. In February, 1888, he set off to one of the annual deliriums of the Knights Templar, and I applied for, and got, the contract for printing his fraternal *cartes de visite*. These cards were exchanged by brethren from North, East, South and West whenever two or more of them happened to be thrown together in the saloons of the convention town. They followed a rigid model. Each showed the name and home-town of the bearer, and a series of colored symbols representing his Masonic dignities.

The symbols were naturally lacking in my composing-room, and I had no idea where they were to be obtained. Moreover, my Baltimore No. 10 Self-Inker was hardly fitted for work in six or eight colors. But such impediments could not stump a really up-and-coming business man. I simply put in the symbols by hand, and colored them with the water-colors that had also been among my Christmas presents. My father professed to be delighted with the cards, and on his return from the convention told me that he had presented specimens of them to Freemasons from points as far distant as Key West, Fla., Duluth, Minn., and Ogden, Utah, and that among the recipients were some of the most puissant and austere dignitaries of the order, including two Governors and a dozen United States

Senators. This was my first attempt upon a national audience. My bill for the job survives. It shows that I charged my father 8½ cents a dozen for the cards, including the hand-painting. Of the cards themselves, two or three also survive. They will go to the Bodleian after they have made the round of the American galleries.

In a little while I was branching out. On the one hand I issued a circular offering to print advertising at what, even in the primitive West Baltimore of that remote era, must have seemed to my competitors to be cut rates. And on the other hand, I launched into the publication of a newspaper in rivalry to the celebrated Baltimore *Sunpaper*, the news Bible at 1524 Hollins street as it has always been in every other respectable Baltimore household, then, now and forever. My circular offered to produce advertisements 2 by 2 inches in area, in any quantity below the astronomical, at the uniform rate of 4 cents a hundred. For an additional 2 cents a hundred I offered to blow them up to the magnitude of 3 inches by 3¼. This was as far as I could go, for it was the full size of the chase of my press. For business cards on plain white stock, " any size," I asked 5 cents a dozen, or 2 cents a quarter of a dozen. Why I assumed that anyone would want as few as a quarter of a dozen, or even a dozen, I don't recall: there must have been some reason, but it has slipped me. The " any size," of course, was only a euphemism: as I have said, my maximum size was 3 inches by 3¼. I never got any orders for these goods. I solicited my mother's trade, but she replied coldly that she was not in any commercial business, and had no use for cards or circulars. I also solicited my brother Charlie, but he was poor in those days, and believed that it was a kind of lunacy to lay out money on printed matter. He much preferred the black licorice nigger-babies sold by Old Man Kunker in Baltimore street, and commonly went about with his face mired by their exudations.

The newspaper I set up against the *Sunpaper* also came to nothing. It was doomed from the start, for it was afflicted by every malady that a public journal can suffer from — insufficiency of capital, incomplete news service, an incompetent staff, no advertising, and a press that couldn't print it. No copy of it survives, but I remember that it consisted of four pages, and was printed on scraps of wrapping-paper filched from the hired girl's hoard in the kitchen. I had to print each page separately, and to distribute the type between pages, for I hadn't enough to set up all four at once. Having no news service whatever, and not knowing where any was to be had, I compromised by lifting all of my dispatches out of my rival. In those days the Associated Press foreign report consisted largely of a series of brief bulletins, and the *Sunpaper* printed them on its first page every morning under the standing head of "Latest Foreign News." I chose the shortest, and when there were none short enough, chopped down the longer. Thus the most important item I ever printed was this:

Berlin, March 9 — William I is dead aged 91.

This came out in my paper on March 15 or thereabout, a week after the *Sunpaper* had made it generally known in Baltimore, Washington, Virginia, West Virginia and the Carolinas. My domestic news came from the same source, and consisted wholly of telegraphed items, for they were usually short. I made no effort to cover local news, though there was then plenty of it in West Baltimore. Almost every day Murphy the cop made one of his hauls of ruffianly Aframericans in Vincent alley, and I could sit at my third-story office-and-bedroom window and see him drag them through Union Square to the watch-house at Calhoun and Pratt streets. It was common, also, for car-horses to fall dead in their tracks, for children to get lost, and for great gang-wars among the neighborhood dogs to tear up the Union Square lawns. But I never attempted to report any of these things. I remain a bad reporter, in fact, to this day. During my term of servitude as city editor of a Baltimore daily, long after my own paper blew up, I blushed inwardly every time I had to excoriate a member of the staff for failing to get the age, weight, color and address of a lady jugged for murdering her husband, or the names of the brave cops who had tracked her down.

Rather curiously, I can't recall the name of my paper, if, in fact, it had one. The chances are at least even that it didn't, for I was chronically short of what printers call sorts, and never wasted a single piece of type if I could help it. A little while later, probably during the ensuing Autumn, I discovered a perfect mine of supplies in the hell-box that stood outside the printing plant of Isaac Friedenwald & Son, in Paca street, across narrow Cider alley from my father's factory. It was Mr. Maass who directed me to this Golconda, and I began to work it diligently. From it I recovered all sorts of mangey woodcuts, many empty ink-cans with a little ink remaining in them, a great deal of scrap paper and cardboard, and an occasional piece of condemned type, always badly battered. Unfortunately, this type was of small use to my newspaper, for the Friedenwalds were printers to the Johns Hopkins University, and laid claim to having the largest stock of foreign type-faces in the Western World, so when my eye lighted upon what looked to be a likely *E* it sometimes turned out to be a Greek *sigma* or a Hebrew *lamedh*. I could make nothing of these strange characters; in fact, I didn't know that they were characters at all, but took them to be the devices of unfamiliar branches of the Freemasons.

The Friedenwalds did not stop with such rela-

tively intelligible alphabets, but boasted that they
could print any language ever heard of on earth,
and often surprised and enchanted the Johns Hopkins professors by making good. They had fonts
of Arabic, Sanskrit, Russian, Coptic, Armenian
and Chinese, not to mention Old Norse runes and
Egyptian hieroglyphs. The specimens of these
types that I recovered were always cruelly dam-
aged, but nevertheless some of them were still legi-
ble, and if I had given them due study I might
have become a linguist. But I usually traded them
for marbles, chewing-tobacco tags or cigarette pictures with a neighbor who made lead soldiers of
them in a mold he had somehow acquired, so I made
no appreciable progress in the tongues.

Despite all these griefs and burdens, I stuck to
my printing press through 1888, and it remained
my favorite possession for several years afterward.
Why my father, seeing my interest in it, did not
buy me a larger and better one I do not know; probably it was because I wasn't aware that a larger and
better one existed, and hence did not ask for it. I
have found out since that Dorman had them with
chases up to 6 by 8 inches, and that his catalogue
listed two or three dozen different fonts of type,
some of them with highly ornate faces in the rococo
taste of the time. But though my press was a poor
thing and my type gradually wore out to the point
where all the letters printed like squashed O's, my
enthusiasm for printing did not die, and even when

a rage for photography and then for chemistry began to challenge it, in my early teens, it managed
to continue a sturdy undercover existence. When,
on my father's death, as I was eighteen, I was free
at last to choose my trade in the world, I chose newspaper work without any hesitation whatever, and,
save when the scent of a passing garbage-cart has
revived my chemical libido, I have never regretted
my choice. More than once I have slipped out of
daily journalism to dally in its meretricious sub-
urbs, but I have always returned repentant and re-
lieved, like a blackamoor coming back in Autumn
to a warm and sociable jail.

Aside from the direct and all-powerful influence
of that Baltimore No. 10 Self-Inker and the Friedenwald hell-box, I was probably edged toward
newspapers and their glorious miseries by two circumstances, both of them trivial. The first was my
discovery of a real newspaper office in the little
town of Ellicott City, where we spent the Summers
of 1889 and 1890. Ellicott City was then a very
picturesque and charming place, and indeed still
is, despite the fact that the heavy hand of progress
is on it. It is built along the two steep banks of a
ravine that runs down to the Patapsco, and many
of the old stone houses, though four stories high in
front, scarcely clear their backyards in the rear.
It is the local legend that dogs, pigs, chickens and
even children have been known to fall out of these
backyards into and down the chimneys. The Bal-

timore & Ohio Railroad's old main line to the West runs beside the river on a viaduct spanning the main street, and from this viaduct, in 1889, a long balcony ran along the second story of a block of houses, with an entrance from the railway station's platform. I naturally explored it, and was presently rewarded by discovering the printing-office of the weekly Ellicott City *Times*.

The *Times*, even in those days, must have been an appreciably better paper than my own, but its superiority was certainly not excessive. The chief article of equipment in its gloomy second-story office was a Washington handpress that had probably been hauled in on mule-back in the twenties or thirties, when the town was still Ellicott's Mills, and a famous coaching-station on the road to the Ohio. I have seen many Washington handpresses since, but never a hoarier one. Its standards were oaken beams, and it looked to a marvelling boy to be as massive as a locomotive. It was operated by a young man and a boy, and I watched enchanted as the white paper was placed on the chase, the platen was brought down, and the printed sheets were lifted off. The circulation of the *Times* at that time was probably not more than 400, but it took the man and the boy all day to print an edition, for only one side could be printed at a time, and yanking the huge lever was a back-breaking job. I noted that the young man left most of the yanking to the boy, and encouraged him from time to time by loud incitements and expostulations. I found out that Thursday was press-day, and I managed to be on hand every time. If my mother had no commission for me in the village on a Thursday I always suggested one.

I was captivated not only by the miracle of printing, but also by the high might and consequence of the young man in charge of the press. He was genuinely Somebody in that remote and obscure village, and the fact radiated from him like heat from a stove. He never deigned to take any notice of me. He might give me a blank glance when he halted the press to take a chew of tobacco, but that was all. He became to me a living symbol of the power and dignity of the press — a walking proof of its romantic puissance. Years later I encountered him again, and got to know him very well, and to have a great affection for him. I was by then city editor of the Baltimore *Morning Herald*, now dead and forgotten, and he was the assistant foreman of its composing-room. No man in all my experience has ever met more perfectly the classical specifications for that office.

On a rush night he gave a performance that was magnificent. Arising in his pulpit, he would howl for missing takes in a voice of brass, always using the formula hallowed since Gutenberg's time: " What --- -- - ----- has got A 17? " His chief, Joe Bamberger, was also a foreman of notable talents, and knew how to holler in a way that made even

the oldest printer gasp and blanche, but Josh
Lynch — for such was his name — could outholler
Joe a hundred to one, on the flat or over the jumps.
He was a grand fellow, and he taught me a lot about
the newspaper business that was not on tap in the
Herald editorial-rooms. Above all, he taught me
that a newspaper man, in the hierarchy of earthly
fauna, ranked only below the assistant foreman of
a composing-room, and that neither had any reason or excuse in law or equity to take any lip from
any ———— in the whole ———— world. He is dead
now, but surely not forgotten. If I miss him in
Hell it will be a disappointment.

The second experience that served to cake the ink
upon me and doom me to journalism took the form
of an overheard conversation. My father's Washington agent, Mr. Cross, paid a visit to us at Ellicott City one Sunday, and he and my father and
my uncle Henry put in the afternoon drinking beer
on the veranda of our house. They fell to talking
of the illustrious personages they were constantly
meeting in Washington — Senators who had not
been sober for a generation, Congressmen who
fought bartenders and kicked the windows out of
night-hacks, Admirals in the Navy who were re-
puted to be four-, five- and even six-bottle men,
Justices of the Supreme and other high courts who
were said to live on whiskey and chewing tobacco
alone. They naturally admired these prodigious
men, and I crept up to hear them described and

praised. But in the end Mr. Cross, who knew Washington far better than my father or my uncle, permitted himself a caveat of doubt. All such eminentissimos, he allowed, were mere passing shapes, as evanescent as the morning dew, here today and gone tomorrow. They had their effulgence, but then they perished, leaving no trace save a faint aroma, usually bad. The real princes of Washington, he said, were the newspaper correspondents. They outlasted Senators, Congressmen, judges and Presidents. In so far as the United States had any rational and permanent government, they were its liver and its lights. To this day, though reason may protest bitterly, I still revere the gentlemen of the Washington corps.

Other Christmas presents came and went, but there was never another that fetched and floored me like Dorman's Baltimore No. 10 Self-Inker Printing Press. The box of water-colors that set me to painting I have mentioned, and I have also alluded to the camera that aroused in me a passion for photography, and then, by way of developers and toning solutions, for chemistry. But my career as a water-colorist was brief and not glorious, and the camera came after the period covered by this history. I recall a year when some one gave me a microscope, but it, too, held me only transiently, for one of the first things I inspected through it was a drop of vinegar, and the revolting mass of worms that I saw kept me off vinegar for a year after-

ward, and cured me of microscopy. Another year
I received an electric battery, and for a while I had
a swell time with it, but I began to neglect it when
I discovered that it could not work a small arc-
light that I had made of two charred matches.
Yet another year I was favored with a box of carpenter's tools, but they must have been poor ones,
for the saw would not saw, the plane would not
plane, the hammer mashed my thumb, and the
chisel cut my hand. Nor was I greatly interested
in the steam-engine that appeared at Christmas
1889, or the steam railroad that followed the year
after. The latter, indeed, was probably my brother
Charlie's present, not mine, for he spent much more
time playing with it than I did, and in later life he
took to engineering, and laid many a mile of railroad line, and worked on many a bridge and tunnel.

It was the printing-press that left its marks, not
only upon my hands, face and clothing, but also on
my psyche. They are still there, though more than
fifty years have come and gone.

XIV

FROM THE RECORDS OF

an Athlete

IT always astonishes people familiar with my present matronly figure to hear that I was a fast runner as a boy. It not only astonishes them; it also makes them laugh. Nevertheless, a fact remains a fact, no matter how much infidels may mock it, and I like to recall this one whenever a steep stairway blows me, or I begin to choke and gurgle in the act of lacing my shoes.

Toward the end of the year 1890, when I was ten years old, I made the 100 yards in $12\frac{2}{5}$ seconds, wearing heavy Winter underwear and timed by my father's Swiss repeater watch, then the great glory of his jewel casket — that is, next to the massive gold chain that anchored it to his person, the ruby-studded Shriner's button that he wore in his coat-lapel, and the diamond solitaire that screwed into the façade of his boiled shirt. To be sure, the distance for my dash was estimated by the eye, not laid off by geometers, but all the same it must have been accurate to within 15 or 20 yards. I made it in less than 13 seconds, not once but six or eight times in close succession, and would have gone on running all afternoon if my mother had not intervened on what I gathered to be hygienic grounds. I recall clearly only her suggestion that my father must be going crazy.

He himself was surely no athlete. Once, seeking to edify my brother Charlie and me, he essayed to jump over a bale of hay, but only succeeded in landing on top of it belly-down, kicking and hollering. When the mood to inspire us by boasting was on him he liked to tell us that he had been a powerful swimmer in his youth, but I never saw him in actual water save once, and he then came out very promptly, shivering and upset. When a natatorium was opened in Baltimore and I demanded to be taken to it and taught the art, he kept on postponing the visit until the place finally went bankrupt and closed. He also claimed to be gifted as an oarsman, but on the only occasion when I ever saw him enter a rowboat he upset it at the first stroke, and got a good dousing, and was upbraided by my mother for resorting to the cup on a fine Summer afternoon, better fitted for nature study and other such sensible recreation.

As I have noted in a previous chapter, he was completely devoid of all the usual small skills. Never once, to my knowledge, did he ever undertake any of the repairs that are needed so incessantly in a dwelling-house, with children running wild in it. If a plank got loose in the backyard fence he had to send for a neighborhood handy-man to nail it tight, and if a spigot needed a washer it was a job for the plumber. If my brother and I, playing in the yard, tossed a ball into a rain-gutter, he sent us to the alley to find a colored boy to recover it. If the family dog choked on a bone he hustled it to Reveille's livery-stable two blocks away, to be succored by the Aframerican barber-surgeons there in practise. The grape vines in the backyard needed tying up now and then, what with blowing winds and climbing cats, but my father never undertook the job. My mother told me years later that he had tried it once, standing on a chair, but that the chair legs had sunk into the soft ground, and tumbled him head over heels.

He and his brother often sat in the Summerhouse below the arbor on warm Sunday mornings, drinking beer and discussing the infamies of Terence V. Powderly, the Chicago anarchists, and other such scamps. The beer was usually Anheuser-Busch from St. Louis, and it came in flour-barrels holding 96 bottles, packed in straw. When a new barrel arrived my uncle would sometimes suggest waggishly that my father open it. Now and then he rose to the bait, but when he began work with a hatchet he made so much noise, broke so many bottles and so inevitably cut his hand that my uncle always had to finish the job. My uncle was more or less clumsy too, following the pattern of all the Menckenii since their escape from the Teutoburgerwald, but compared to my father he was almost a prestidigitator.

I have hitherto noted his prowess with firearms. All Winter long, throughout my nonage, the side-yard between our two houses was hung with the carcasses of wild ducks that had fallen to his aim. He would turn out before dawn, proceed to the Chesapeake marshes by train, and come rolling home in the late afternoon with dozens of them, mainly canvasbacks. They often hung in the yard for weeks, for his own family revolted against them by Christmas, and my mother had them on her blacklist, mainly because picking them was a painful chore and had the effect of filling hired girls with subversive ideas. Thus I grew up unaware that wild duck was a luxury open only to millionaires. Indeed, I was amazed years later to find it priced at $3 a portion on Delmonico's bill-of-fare. It was a quite common victual in the Baltimore of my youth — not so common, to be sure, as soft-crabs or shadfish, but still very far from something to get excited about.

My uncle's hunting trips extended much further than the shores of the Chesapeake. Whenever he made a business journey, which was pretty often, he always took his guns along, and usually he would come back with many souvenirs and tall tales of the chase. He went all the way to Florida, which was then only a wilderness, to shoot alligators, and returned with the story that he had lured them out of the bayous by tying Negro babies to stakes along the bank. Whether or not this story was true I do not know, but my brother Charlie and I believed it firmly at the time.

On one of these Florida trips my uncle took along one of the drummers of Aug. Mencken & Bro., by name Christian Abner, a magnificently handsome Rhinelander who some years later returned home, married a wife with a substantial *dot*, and set up a carpet-sweeper factory. Abner sent his relatives in Cologne a glowing account of alligator-hunting in Florida, and urged them not to be upset by the use of Negro babies· as bait. At first, he explained, he had shrunk from it himself as incompatible with Christian principles and German *Kultur*, but travel had a tendency to broaden the mind, and he had come to the view that it was bigotry to judge the *mores* of a new and progressive country by those of Europe, now so old and decadent. In later letters he confessed confidentially that he had proceeded experimentally to actual nigger-shooting in Georgia, but added in excuse and avoidance that he did not like it. To this day there is no taste for

American ways among the bourgeoisie of Cologne, and no belief in American idealism.

Despite his brother's enthusiasm for the chase my father disliked it, and never owned a gun. The only lethal weapon I could find in his effects after his death was his Knight Templar sword, a sleazy blade that would have curled up if jabbed into a tub of butter. It has now vanished, and I suspect that my mother either had it buried in the back-yard, or gave it to the Salvation Army. A pair of dumb-bells survived in the cellar for many years, but my father never touched them to my knowledge. They were of cast-iron, and weighed 15 or 18 pounds apiece. My brother Charlie and I began to feel almost grown-up when we could so much as lift them, but that is as far as we ever got.

Our chief sports in those early days were running, climbing backyard fences, and making long exploratory tramps to Steuart's Hill or the other open country west of Hollins street. With the boys of the neighborhood we played at least half a dozen different running games, and very often there were match races. It was in these races that I developed the speed aforesaid. The prime of my talent was reached before the age of twelve, but I remained pretty fast until I had passed twenty and began to put on blubber. Even to this day I could probably run down a horse-car if there were any left in the world, and I still had my old facility for sucking in air. All my muscles are in my legs. My biceps are puny, and my fingers are so weak that a couple of hours of playing the piano at high voltage makes them ache and itch.

This relative feebleness above-decks prevented me from shining as a boxer. Like every other boy in Hollins street I had ambitions in that direction, for Jake Kilrain opened a saloon in nearby Baltimore street after John L. Sullivan finished him in 1889, and his familiar proximity inspired us all. We were free to look at and venerate him as he stood in front of his place on balmy days, his coat off and his shirt sleeves rolled up. His forearms looked to us to be quite as massive as the hind legs of elephants. But he was a very reserved and solemn fellow, and never paid any attention to us. What little we learned of boxing we learned by pummelling one another. But this was poor sport, for there was one boy in the gang, Chauncey West by name (the Chauncey was always pronounced *Chance-y*, not *Chawnce-y*), who could lick any of the rest of us, or any two of us, or indeed all of us put together.

One Summer day, while we were in the country, my father came home with two pairs of boxing gloves, picked up at a bargain from an insolvent pugilist encountered in a saloon. They were much too big for my brother Charlie and me, but we finally managed to tie them on, and proceeded to bang each other all over the place. My mother was scandalized by these barbarities, and insisted on amending the house statutes by forbidding us (*a*) to clout each other above the neck, or (*b*) to fight at all unless my father or some other grown man was on hand to referee. Our first formal combat under these rules was our last. We staggered on for twenty rounds, with my father refereeing and keeping time, but I was in trouble after the tenth round, and in the twentieth Charlie floored me with a right hook to the neck, and I couldn't get up. After that I had no more stomach for boxing.

The one sport my father was really interested in was baseball, and for that he was a fanatic. This, of course, was before the days of the celebrated Baltimore Orioles, but nevertheless Baltimore had a very good team, and he attended its sessions at Oriole Park whenever he and it were in town together. When it was on the road, he would slip away from his office in the late afternoon to glim the score at Kelly's oyster house in Eutaw street. There were, in that era, no baseball extras of the newspapers, so the high-toned saloons of the town catered to the fans by putting in telegraph operators who wrote the scores on blackboards. Kelly's operator was supposed to be the fastest and most accurate in town. He sat in a little balcony half way up the wall of the barroom, and was so greatly respected that on a busy afternoon, with the Baltimores winning, he harvested treats running to twenty or thirty beers, and perhaps half as many cigars.

I often went with my father on his visits to Kelly's, for in those days I spent many of my free afternoons in his cigar factory in Paca street, watching and envying the stripper-boys, stealing cigar-bands, cigar-box nails and other such negotiable commodities, and excavating the wastebaskets in the office for postage stamps, worn-out pens and rubber bands. When he set out he would take me with him, and while he stood at the bar with one eye on the blackboard and a beer before him, I would be parked on the brass rail, with a glass of sarsaparilla in one hand and a pretzel in the other. I figure that before I was nine years old I had put down at least 5000 bottles of sarsaparilla and the same number of pretzels. In the end I got so used to sitting on brass bar rails that I could do so without holding on.

My father had a branch of his business in Washington, at the corner of Seventh and G streets, and connected with it there was a cigar-store. This cigar-store became the baseball headquarters of Washington, and he got to know all the principal ball-players and managers of the time. Eventually, he bought an interest in the Washington club, and became its vice-president. In his papers I find a letter from its secretary, dated July 27, 1891, and running as follows:

Last time we went West rate was $30 each for 13 men. The R. R. Agents here have since formed a combination to squeeze us and now make the rate at $40.50 for each man. We understand this applies only to Washington. Won't you kindly see Barnie and see what rate he pays and see if you can't get same rate for our men from Baltimore? Route will be Balto to Cincinnati, to Columbus, to Louisville, to St. Louis, and then home.

Barnie was the manager of the Baltimore club. He and my father had frequent palavers in those days, not only about the extortions of the railroads, but also about the outrageous demands of the players, some of whom, though they were getting $1500 and even $1800 a year, had the impudence to ask for more. These palavers were usually held in the Summer-house in Hollins street on Sunday mornings, and the Bolsheviks were summoned there, and put on the mat. Many a time I have seen six or eight head of stars assembled together, drinking beer and smoking ten-cent cigars in their uncomfortable Sunday clothes, and quailing under the moral indignation of Barnie and my father. The boys of the neighborhood flocked to the back-gate to get glimpses of them, and my brother Charlie and I would open it a few inches for particular friends, and so convert friends into slaves.

The most eminent of all the stars who suffered the correction of their false thinking in the Summer-house was Matt Kilroy, a pitcher now somehow forgotten, though he was as vastly admired in his day as Amos Rusie afterward. He was an Irishman with eight brothers who were also ball-players, and my father toyed with the idea of organizing them into a nine and sending them on a tour of the country. Unfortunately, Kilroy belonged to Barnie, and Barnie hung on to him. My father sought surcease from this bafflement by naming a five-cent cigar after the great man, and employed his catcher, Sam Trott, to sell it. Sam was a novice to *Geschäft*, but he developed a considerable gift for it, and the Kilroy was thus a big success. When Kilroy himself blew up the five-center went with him, and Sam became Baltimore agent for a cigar factory in Philadelphia. He continued in the trade to the end of his life, and I often encountered him on the streets in his later years.

He was a handsome, four-square fellow with enormous shoulders, and every finger of his two hands was as gnarled as a cypress-tree. This was a souvenir of the days when catchers caught with their bare paws. He adopted a glove toward the end of his career, but it was too late either to save his hands or to change his technic. When a ball came zooming in from the outfield and an enemy player tried to steal home Sam always threw aside his glove and planted himself at the plate *au naturel*. He was an amiable man, and when my brother and I began to major in baseball he gave us a lot of useful advice. But he never managed to make a good player of either of us.

We could do little playing in the Winter, for the cops of West Baltimore objected to anything more serious than one-two-three in the street, and the nearest grounds were disputed by other boys, including, now and then, brigandish fellows from the vicinity of the Baltimore & Ohio railroad shops. When these ruffians were in a relatively mild mood they were content to chase us off the diamond, but when their glands were flowing freely they also cabbaged our bats, balls and gloves. In the Summers beyond the period I here embalm we had a better chance, for just behind our newly-acquired house at Mt. Washington there was a large hay-field, and the farmer who owned it was glad to rent us room enough for a diamond, once he had got in his hay. Along with the neighbor boys we paid him $15 a year for it, and had the place all to ourselves, morning, afternoon and evening, on Sundays as well as on week-days. Years ago our baseball field became part of the first golf course ever seen in Baltimore. That course is still in operation, but it now seems so far downtown that most of the members of the Baltimore Country Club, which owns it, prefer the newer links ten miles out in the country.

The four Lürssen boys, who were our next-door neighbors, were baseball fans of the first chop, and there were plenty of other enthusiasts nearby, so we had games going on all the time. In the middle of Summer we often played until eight o'clock in the evening, and when formal play had to be stopped we put in another hour catching flies from the darkening sky. Two miles nearer the city there was a little mill-town, Woodberry by name, that turned out an amazing number of first-rate ball-players, for most of the jobs in the mills were for females, which left the bucks all day to practise. One of the prodigies thus given to humanity was Frank Foreman, a pitcher who developed the widest and wickedest curves I have ever seen. He got into the big leagues, and for all I know may be still living in Baltimore, though very few Baltimoreans now recall his once immortal name.

On Sundays he would sometimes bring his nine to our field, and play a couple of games with scrub nines from Baltimore. Inspired and inflamed by his incomparable virtuosity, I set up for a pitcher, but nothing ever came of it, for I had little speed and no control at all. When I ventured on an in-shoot it was apt to be recovered, not by the catcher, but by the third baseman. So the Lürssen boys, who were older than my brother and I, retired me to the outfield, or, as it was then called, the farm, and from there I slowly worked my way back as far as the position of short-stop. One day a sizzler gave my left little finger a terrific clout, and I was out of the game for weeks. The finger remains slightly cauliflowered to this day — another reason, perhaps, why I have never made much of a shine as a piano virtuoso.

My father seldom took any part in these games,

though some of the other men of the vicinity often did so. Once he bought us an outfit of uniforms, but they didn't last long, for we younger players quickly outgrew them, and the visitors who were invited in from time to time had a habit of making off with those issued to them. My own I'll never forget. It was made of a woolen material as thick as a Scotsman's Winter underwear, and as I gradually increased in stature and bulk the breeches pulled up until their bottoms were halfway between my knees and my hips, and the shirt began to bind my chest like a surgical bandage. My brother and I used to go to Mt. Washington on Sunday afternoons early in Spring, long before the family had moved out for the Summer, and there get in a lot of hard practice. I recall that we were always stiff in the legs and arms until the Wednesday following. But all this diligent work got me nowhere, and I began slowly to grasp the humiliating fact that I was not earmarked for a career of glory on the diamond. When the Baltimore Orioles started out to astound mankind with their new prodigies, in 1894, I withdrew in despair, though I remained a fan for a few years longer. Since 1900 I have seen but two professional baseball games.

XV

THE CAPITAL OF THE

Republic

My father, in the days when I first knew him, visited his Washington office every Friday; after I went into pants he occasionally took me along. I recall standing between his knees as the train conductor came round, and hearing him protest that I was too young to pay any fare, even half-fare. Whether these protests were serious or not I don't know, but in all probability they were not, for the conductor was always in a very affable mood, and sometimes he let me work his ticket-punch on one of my father's business cards. The candy-butcher also showed me some attention, but that had plain self-interest in it, for he carried a basket containing oval boxes of figs, little red railroad lanterns full of candy pills, gumdrops in red, white and green, and other such favorite refreshments and souvenirs of the era, and my father was always good for a sale.

At that early period Washington was hardly more than a blur to me, and I divided my four or five hours there between admiring the meerschaum pipes and cigar-holders in the cigar-store connected with the branch office of Aug. Mencken & Bro., and accompanying my father on his subsequent rounds of his customers, many of whom kept either restaurants or saloons. He disappeared into his office the moment we got to Seventh and G streets, N.W., and spent the next hour or so auditing its books, with his agent standing by to answer questions. By that time I was half starved, so a great wave of hosannahs rolled through me when we started off for lunch. We usually ate, of course, in the restaurant of some customer, and no doubt we visited, first and last, a great many, but the one I remember best was kept by Mr. Burkhardt, who had once been my father's agent himself, but had now, by dint of diligence and thrift, acquired a business of his own. He always instructed his carver, a coal-black man called Snowball, to give me extra-large portions, and I always got them down. Indeed, I commonly ate so heartily that during the subsequent tour of saloons I had relatively little stomach for the pretzels that were handed down to me at my perch on the brass rail, and even gagged at drinking more than two or three bottles of sarsaparilla.

As I emerged from the fog of infancy Washington began to take on shape and substance, and pretty soon I was wallowing delightedly in its marvels. The greatest of them, in that era, was not the Capitol at the end of Pennsylvania avenue, nor even the Washington Monument, but the asphalt streets. Asphalt was then a novelty in the United States, and Washington was the only city that could show any considerable spread of it: in Baltimore it was still thought to be dangerous to horses. What I remember of it chiefly is the dreadful heat it threw up in Summer. The cobblestones of Baltimore, with their lush interstitial crops of grass, oats and Jimson weed, were cool in the warmest weather, but in Washington the white asphalt bounced the sun back into people's faces, and every stranger was told that in July and August the inhabitants abandoned their kitchen stoves altogether and cooked their meals on the street. This tale still pops up whenever there is an extraordinarily severe spell of heat, and it has probably gone out over the wires at least forty times. It was untrue when I first heard it as a small boy, and it remains untrue to this day, but for some reason or other people like to believe it, and so it hangs on.

Of my first trip to the top of the Washington Monument, which must have been made soon after it was opened in 1888, I recall only the fact that we descended by walking down the long, dark steps, and it seemed a journey without end. There was in those days a bitter debate as to whether a base-ball thrown from the top of the monument could be caught by a catcher on the ground, and my father was much interested and full of mathematical proofs that it couldn't be done. Some time later it was tried, and turned out to be very easy. He also had a hand in a long and acrimonious discussion of curve pitching, one faction holding that the path of the ball was actually a curve and the other main-taining that the whole thing was only an optical il-lusion. Which side he took I don't recall, but I remember him coming home with the news that the reality of curves had been proved by setting up three stakes in a straight line at the Washington baseball grounds, and putting a pitcher to work on them. After knocking them down or missing them altogether for half an hour running he finally succeeded in pitching a ball clearly to leftward of the two end ones and as clearly to rightward of the middle one. This feat attracted a large crowd and was dealt with by the newspapers as if it had been some great public calamity or first-rate murder, but I was in school that day, and so had to miss seeing it. Later on my father undertook to show me how to curve a baseball, but inasmuch as he never could do it himself I made very little prog-ress.

Most of my visits to Washington, at least from 1886 onward, must have been made after school

let out in Spring, for I remember the town as always warm, and both my father and me as always
thirsty. As he proceeded from one restaurant or saloon to another, usually with his agent, Mr. Cross,
and palavered amiably with their proprietors, I
sat on a long succession of brass rails, munching
my pretzels and drinking my sarsaparilla. This
life had its moments of boredom, especially when
the visit to any given place was prolonged, but on
the whole I enjoyed it, and to this day I retain a
friendly feeling for saloons, though I seldom stand
up at their bars, for I long ago associated myself
with the Chinese doctrine that it is foolish to do
anything standing up that can be done sitting
down, or anything sitting down that can be done
lying down. In the days before Prohibition, which
were also the days before air-cooling, I doted on the
cool, refreshing scent of a good saloon on a hot
Summer day, with its delicate overtones of mint,
cloves, hops, Angostura bitters, horse-radish, *Blut-
wurst* and *Kartoffelsalat*. It was always somewhat
dark therein, and there was an icy and comforting
sweat upon the glasses. The huge, hand-painted
oil painting facing the bar, nearly always of Venus
stripped for her weekly tub, was covered with netting to keep off the flies, and the mirror that framed
the bartender was decorated with Winter land-
scapes drawn in soap. I have visited in my day the
barrooms of all civilized countries, but none that I
ever saw came within miles of a high-toned Ameri-

can saloon of the Golden Age. Today the influence
of the cocktail lounge has brought in blue glass,
chrome fixtures, and bars of pale and puny woods,
but in the time I speak of saloon architects stuck
to mirrors as God first made them, to honest brass,
and to noble and imperishable mahogany.

My father sometimes took an afternoon off from
his calls on restauranteurs (for that is what they
all liked to call themselves, including the unmistakable saloonkeepers) to show me the salient sights of
the capital, or, perhaps more often, sent his office-
boy with me while he struggled with accounts in his
office. The majestic spectacle of the United States
Senate was thus a commonplace to me before I was
eight years old, and by the time I was ten I was
a familiar of the Smithsonian and the National
Museum. Both of the latter were even more meagre
and measly then than they are now, but I was too
young to know it, and hence enjoyed them immensely. There were two exhibits in the Smithsonian that fascinated me especially. The first,
perhaps naturally, was the skeleton of a prehis-
toric monster, ten or twelve feet high at the shoulder. The second, rather curiously, was a primitive
ox-cart with wheels made of solid slices of tree
trunks. Why this last should have struck me so
powerfully I do not know, but there is the fact. I
wrote a description of it in my composition-book,
and gained thereby the praise of Mr. Willie, son
to the chancellor of F. Knapp's Institute. I also

got his favorable notice by exhibiting a small bust of Abraham Lincoln, made of condemned and macerated paper money from the Treasury. Such busts are still obtainable in Washington, and honeymooners from the remoter villages of Virginia and Maryland often take them home. Their price runs in proportion to the face value of the deceased greenbacks in them. One containing the remains of mere $1 bills goes cheaply, but one made of $1000 bills costs a pretty penny. In my day the little hill on which the Washington Monument stands was still bestrewn with large chips of marble left by the builders. I recovered, first and last, at least a hundred pounds of them, and my brother Charlie and I hoarded them for a long while, for it was believed in Hollins street that soda-water could be made of them, though we never found out how. They disappeared eventually into a rockery that my mother made in the backyard.

At the Capitol and in the other public buildings of the town its magnificoes could be viewed only at a distance, but in the saloons they came down to earth, and laid themselves open to intimate inspection. Their principal resort was Shoomaker's oldtime groggery in Pennsylvania avenue, but my father seldom visited it, so I had to get my eyeful of them at other places, notably Mr. Burkhardt's. Mr. Burkhardt, I conclude on reflection, must have specialized in the judiciary, for I recall a great many customers who were addressed as Judge, or even as Mr. Justice. These eminent men were quiet drinkers, but assiduous. They apparently had short working-hours, for they showed up at the bar early in the afternoon, and stuck around until it was time for us to return to Baltimore. There was a very old one, in a long-tailed black coat and white chin-whiskers, who one day lifted me to speechless veneration by slipping me a quarter. But the next time I encountered him he failed to give me another, so I transferred my devotion to other gods. There were also several Senators in the Burkhardt stock company, and a great many Congressmen. I noticed, boy as I was, that Mr. Burkhardt kept his deference and solicitude for the Senators and the judiciary, and had none left for Congressmen. He addressed them familiarly as George, Jack and Bill, and once I heard him invite one of them to get the hell out of the place, and stay out. My father explained that this was because Congressmen were too numerous in Washington to be of any note; moreover, not a few of them were given to caterwauling and wrestling in barrooms, a habit that he always deprecated. They yet linger, I believe, in their lowly station, and are regarded by most Washingtonians as hardly worthy of common politeness.

Of all the eminent men I had the honor of witnessing in those days, the only one who ever showed me much personal attention, and hence the only one I remember with any vividness, was Mr. Mc-

Carthy, a member of the higher joboisie of the State Department. Mr. McCarthy was a hunchback, but his infirmity did not damp his spirits, which were naturally very gay. I can see him yet as he stood at the stately bar of Mr. Burkhardt's restaurant, with his head scarcely reaching the mahogany rail but his good right arm plenty long enough to keep a firm hold on the glass of beer that the bartender had just drawn for him. He could get down five or six in a row, and yet retain both his courtly manners and his wide knowledge of international affairs. My father relied upon him for confidential information about the filthy schemes of the chancelleries of Europe, and I relied upon him for a steady supply of foreign postage stamps. He seemed to have something to do with handling departmental mail, for his pockets were always full of stamps from the farthest and most outlandish places, many of which have long since disappeared from the stamp catalogues, at least as current producers — for example, Korea, Montenegro, and Thurn und Taxis. He never failed to hand me a handful, and I never failed, on returning home, to paste them carefully in a blue-covered stamp-album that my mother had given me. When, in the course of human events, I tired of stamp-collecting, I turned over the album to my young sister, Gertrude, and when she, in her turn, took to other concerns, its contents passed to our niece Virginia, the daughter of my brother Charlie, and she then handed it on to one of her cousins, and so on and so on. I suppose that Mr. McCarthy's stamps are still cherished somewhere by some youngster or other. As for Mr. McCarthy himself, he appears to have been absorbed into the cosmos long years ago, but in my mind his memory is still green.

Mr. Cross, who had succeeded Mr. Burkhardt as my father's Washington nuncio, was another of my favorites, for he saved up rubber-bands for me, let me inspect and handle the florid meerschaum pipes in his showcase (one of them, I recall, was priced $300), and was always good for a piece of cash money. In those days the custom of tipping boys was as widespread in the United States as it still is in England, and my brother Charlie and I derived a considerable revenue from it, especially in Summer, when visitors often came to the country for all-day visits. These visits sometimes strained my mother's housekeeping dangerously, and once or twice broke it down altogether, but they were highly agreeable to Charlie and me, for that was a scurvy fellow who did not fork up at least a quarter. One Sunday when we were still at the Vineyard Mr. Cross staggered us by slipping us a dollar each — a large sum for any boy to have in his hands in the eighties, and perhaps roughly comparable to a couple of shares of Eastman Kodak or Am. Tel. & Tel. today. What is more, Mr. Cross kept to his mark thereafter, so we were always rich during the week following one of his visits, and regarded him at all times as a gentleman of surpassing elegance, which indeed he was. He was a handsome man with a brisk coal-black mustache and prematurely white hair, and he made a striking figure in the somewhat advanced tailoring that he affected. One day he surprised us by bringing along a beautiful lady in a small bonnet and large bustle: in the course of time, I believe, they were married. But that must have been after he retired from the service of Aug. Mencken & Bro., and we saw him no more.

The old office at Seventh and G streets still stands, and when I last saw it it had changed little since 1889. There was the same areaway beside it, with the same pipe railing, and across the street the old building of the Patent Office looked exactly as I remember it as a boy. In the eighties the building next door was occupied by Mr. Voigt, a jeweler and one of my father's friends. On September 26, 1890, as I find by my father's bill-file, he bought a Swiss repeater watch from Mr. Voigt, paying $200 for it in cash — a strange transaction for him, for he commonly preferred barter, and settled most of his major bills in either cigars or leaf tobacco, or both. Even his tailor's bills were commonly paid that way — not directly to the tailor, but to a curious *entrepreneur* named Mr. Butke, who seems to have carried on a complicated series of similar transactions with half the business men

of Baltimore. He would start out by finding someone who wanted the cigars or tobacco that he had
got from my father, and end by finding someone
who had something that the tailor wanted. The
number of his intermediate trades varied from time
to time, and often ran to many. He lived at Ellicott City, and was supposed to have mortgages on
half the farms in the circumambient county. My
father had some gifts as a trader himself, and so
did his brother, but they were always a bit wary of
Mr. Butke, for his talents began where theirs left
off. They considered him, in fact, a public menace,
but for many years they kept on dealing with him,
hoping against hope that some day he would slip
a cog and they would be able to throw him.

Mr. Voigt got cash for the Swiss repeater watch,
I suspect, simply because Mr. Butke's diocese did
not extend to Washington. The watch itself was
my father's proudest possession until his death.
It not only had a hand that made five jumps to the
second; it was also fitted with a device which could
be made to strike the hours, halves and quarters,
thus telling the time in the dark. But my father
never quite mastered the code of this device, so he
could never really find out, in the dark, just what
time it was. Moreover, it was always much easier to
strike a match. In the days after his death, when I
began to wear the watch myself, this apparatus
got out of order, and the best watchmakers in Baltimore failed to cure it, though they sent me very

large bills. In the end the rest of the works also went flooey, and I retired the piece to a safe-deposit box which houses a series of family watches running back to the year 1700. At my own exitus they will be thrown into the market. Meanwhile, I receive a bill from the bank every six months, and they thus waste my substance and help to hold me in the literary sweatshop.

I find by the bill-file that Mr. Voigt supplied many of the articles of *virtu* that engauded our house in Hollins street in my early days. There are bills for a cuckoo-clock, a music-box, and other such things, beside a gold watch for my mother, and a chain and locket for it. Mr. Eckhardt, who was our neighbor in Hollins street and operated an art works in downtown Baltimore street, was also active in this trade. His contributions included the pier-glass that still stands in the old house; a photograph album bound in plush, with a music-box inside; a pair of sombre steel engravings from paintings by Turner, showing the English seaports of Hastings and Dover, each with a heavy walnut frame; another steel engraving entitled " King Solomon and the Iron Worker," apparently of Masonic significance; and " 1 pce. statuary " billed on October 19, 1885 — unquestionably the Rogers group, " Fooling Grandpa," that stood on a rococo table in the parlor for many years, and is still cherished by my sister. The music-box that came from Mr. Voigt's emporium in 1887, at the price of $125 cash in hand, was as large as (and much resembled) a child's coffin,[1] and my father had to have a special hollow-topped table made to accommodate it. It not only played ten loud and swinging tunes — including Johann Strauss's "Rosen aus dem Süden," and selections from "Boccaccio," "The Mascot" and "The Tales of Hoffmann"; it was also outfitted with drums and bells, and when my brother Charlie and I set it going on a Sunday morning it shook the house. We employed it, boylike, to build up advantage in the neighborhood. Boys and girls who were polite to us were let in to listen to it perform, and a favored few of extraordinary amiability were permitted to wind it, and to turn the drums and bells off and on.

I always enjoyed the train ride to and from Washington, and in fact still prefer railroad travel to any other mode of conveyance by land. We used the B. & O. exclusively, not only because its ancient Baltimore station, Camden, was convenient to my father's office, but also as a matter of local pride and patriotism. The B. & O. made Baltimore, and Baltimoreans have never forgotten the fact. The company is tax exempt in Maryland to this day, and Baltimoreans going to New York would use its trains almost invariably if it had a tunnel through

---

1 It still exists, and after writing the above I measured it. It is two feet, seven and a half inches long, fourteen inches wide, and ten inches high. It seemed much larger as I recalled it from infancy. Indeed, I'd have guessed that it was nearer four feet long.

the North river. Its once famous flyer, the Royal
Blue, did not go into service until 1890, but it had
fast trains running between Baltimore and Washington so long ago as 1881, and by the middle
eighties they were making the forty miles in fifty
minutes, including the time wasted in getting in
and out of the two cities. My father began to sell
cigars to the B. & O. back in the seventies, when it
added the first dining-cars to its star trains, and
this business, along with the accompanying station-
restaurant business, helped to put his firm on its
feet. He died convinced that B. & O. trains were
somehow superior to all others. If it were argued
in his presence that they shipped a great deal of
ballast dust and locomotive ash, then he would
reply that those of both the Pennsylvania and the
New York Central shipped even more, and that in
any case no rational man could object to a nuisance
that had its origin in immutable natural laws, and
was thus in accord with the will of God. My father
placed, in general, very little reliance upon heavenly legislation, but in this and a few other difficult
situations he resorted to it to get rid of belly-achers
and casuists.

XVI

RECREATIONS OF A

𝔎eactionary

My father and his brother and partner, like most
reasonably successful American business men of
the eighties, always had plenty of time on their
hands. The business they were in had not yet been
demoralized and devoured by the large combinations of capital that were to come later on, and there
was room in their field, which was principally in
the Southeast, for all the firms in their line in Baltimore. They were thus on peaceful terms with their
competitors, and regarded at least some of them
with a kind of approval almost akin to respect.
They had a competent staff of drummers on the
road, their principal customers stuck to them
pretty faithfully, and, though they gave a great
deal of energy to excoriating labor agitators, they

had very little labor trouble in their own establishment.

My father's daily routine was no doubt quite typical of that of hundreds of other Baltimore employers of the period. He arose at what would be considered an early hour today, and immediately after breakfast proceeded to his office. If we were in the city he travelled by horse-car; if we were at Mt. Washington he drove his buggy, or, in impossible weather, went by train. In either case he tackled his mail the moment he reached his desk, which was a high one in the ancient mode, made for use standing up. If the mail contained enough checks and orders to content him he was in good humor all morning, and polite to the drummers who dropped in to sell him cigar-box labels, cigar bands, advertising novelties, wrapping paper, and other such minor supplies. But if the orders were light, or a letter turned up news that another dead-beat in Georgia or South Carolina had absconded, he would growl at these drummers in a most churlish way, and instruct the bookkeeper to write letters to all his own drummers, accusing them formally of wasting their time and his money on cards, dice, women and the bottle. This routine was broken only by his weekly trip to Washington.

On a normal morning all the cigars made in the factory the day before were waiting for his inspection in racks ranged in long rows. He would get to this job at about 10 a.m. and it took him probably half an hour. In theory, either he or his brother examined each and every cigar made in the place, but actually this was impossible; what they did was simply to draw out samples, feel of them critically, and set aside any plug or skipper that they discovered. A plug was a cigar so overstuffed with filler that sucking wind through it would probably be unfeasible, and a skipper was one so carelessly wrapped that the adjoining layers of wrapper did not overlap. There were plenty of days when my father found no case at all of either sort of pathology. When he encountered one he took the sick cigar upstairs, holding it at arm's length as if it had smallpox, and upbraided the offending cigar-maker. On his return he dropped it in a drawer which supplied complimentary smokes to truck-drivers, messenger boys who looked to be more than twenty-one years old, collectors for non-Masonic charities, bank runners, colored clergymen, and policemen below the rank of lieutenant.

The rest of the morning he devoted to a furious and largely useless figuring. He was immensely vain of his arithmetical capacities, and prepared elaborate cost-sheets long before they began to be whooped up at Harvard. They showed precisely what it stood the firm to produce 1000 of any one of the twenty or more brands of cigars on its list. Every time there was a ponderable change in the price of any kind of leaf tobacco, he recalculated those sheets. When the job was done he put them in one of the drawers of his desk, and that was the last anyone ever heard of them. His brother, who was not much interested in mathematics, gave them only a polite glance, and no one else in the place ever saw them at all, not even the bookkeeper.

A few minutes before one o'clock he suddenly clapped on his hat and dashed out for lunch. If the house in Hollins street was open he almost always lunched there; if not, he patronized one of the saloon-restaurants in the neighborhood, all of which advertised business men's lunches at the uniform price of twenty-five cents. When he went to Hollins street he made the round trip by horse-car and invariably took a nap after his meal. The scene or instrument of this nap was a frowsy old walnut and hair-cloth lounge in the dining-room, and the clearing off of dishes had to be deferred until a couple of Cheyne-Stokes snores notified the fact that he had passed out. After half an hour or so, he awoke with a start, looked about him wildly, reached for his hat, and started back to his office. To the casual eye he seemed to be in haste, but when he got to the office there was really next to nothing for him to do, and he usually spent the afternoon reading the *Tobacco Leaf* or the *Sporting Times* (this last for baseball news), searching out the ratings of prospective customers in the big Bradstreet book, or gossiping with his brother, the bookkeeper, or any caller who happened to drift in. At five-thirty he knocked off for the day.

I never knew him to visit his bank: all his routine business with it was transacted by the bookkeeper, and he never borrowed a nickel. Indeed, he regarded all borrowing as somehow shameful, and looked confidently for the bankruptcy and probable jailing of any business man who practised it regularly. His moral system, as I try to piece it together after so many years, seems to have been predominantly Chinese. All mankind, in his sight, was divided into two great races: those who paid their bills, and those who didn't. The former were virtuous, despite any evidence that could be adduced to the contrary; the latter were unanimously and incurably scoundrels.

He had a very tolerant view of all other torts and malfeasances. He believed that political corruption was inevitable under democracy, and even argued, out of his own experience, that it had its uses. One of his favorite anecdotes was about a huge swinging sign that used to hang outside his place of business in Paca street. When the building was built, in 1885, he simply hung out the sign, sent for the city councilman of the district, and gave him $20. This was in full settlement forevermore of all permit and privilege fees, easement taxes, and other such costs and imposts. The city councilman pocketed the money, and in return was supposed to stave off any cops, building inspectors or other functionaries who had any lawful interest in the matter, or tried to horn in for private profit.

Being an honorable man according to his lights, he kept his bargain, and the sign flapped and squeaked in the breeze for ten years. But then, in 1895, Baltimore had a reform wave, the councilman was voted out of office, and the idealists in the City Hall sent word that a license to maintain the sign would cost $62.75 *a year*. It came down the next day.

This was proof to my father that reform was mainly only a conspiracy of prehensile charlatans to mulct taxpayers. I picked up this idea from him, and entertain it to the present day. I also picked up his doctrine that private conduct had better not be inquired into too closely — with the exception, of course, of any kind involving beating a creditor. In the Breckinridge-Pollard breach of promise case, a nation-shaking scandal in 1892, rating columns of verbatim testimony in the newspapers, he sympathized openly with Breckinridge, whom he had met in the Washington saloons, and denounced La Pollard as a scheming minx. In the matter of polygamy among the Mormons, which kept all the moral theologians of the country in a dither down to 1890, he was a champion of the Saints, and argued that it was nobody's damned business how many wives they had, so long as they paid their bills, which seemed to be the case.

He had little truck with the Germans who swarmed into Baltimore during the seventies and early eighties, and regarded most of them as idiots, but, like his father, he admired the so-called Pennsylvania Dutch, with whom he had constant business, for many of them were tobacco growers. In various salient respects, he would say, they were so loutish as to be hardly human, but nevertheless they abhorred debt, and that was enough. Contrariwise, he had a low opinion of the Virginians who had flocked to Baltimore after the Civil War, for though many of them were elegant and charming fellows, and a few were even the aristocrats they all claimed to be, they were usually very hard up, and anyone who gave them credit had a hard time getting his money.

As I have said, my father's work-day was usually pretty well over by the time he got back to his office from lunch, and he had the rest of the afternoon for recreation. If the Baltimore baseball club was playing in town he would go to the game; if it were on tour he would go to Kelly's oyster-house to learn the score. In Winter he waited for a customer to drop in, or one of his own drummers, and if his hopes were realized he would propose a drink in the saloon next door. Getting it down, and the others that always chased it, would occupy the time until five-thirty, when the cigarmakers came downstairs with their day's produce, the bookkeeper locked the safe, and the day was over. In that era all American business was carried on to the accompaniment of such libations. To let a customer go without offering him a drink was an almost unheard of insult.

It was also considered unendurably boorish to refuse a drink when it was offered. There were bankers and brokers in South street, the Wall Street of Baltimore, who never got back from lunch at all. They ate in the luxurious bars of the neighborhood, and all their afternoon business, if they had any, was done in the same places.

My father preferred the saloon next to his office, not only because it was conveniently near, but also because it was kept by an old German named Ehoff, who pretended obligingly to be an extraordinarily innocent and credulous fellow. Many a time, as a small boy, I have sat on the brass rail, getting down my sarsaparilla and pretzel, and listened to my father complaining to Ehoff all over again, and. perhaps for the fiftieth time, that his ice was stale, or telling him that the Brooklyn Bridge had fallen down, or that the Dutch were being driven out of Holland, or that Cardinal Gibbons had joined the A.P.A., or that Bismarck was moving to Baltimore and proposed to open a brewery. Ehoff, I suspected even then, knew better, but he always professed to be astounded. Thus he was a favorite among the business men of the vicinity, who all tried their fancy upon him. They avoided very diligently a saloon a bit up the street, kept by one William Ruth, for over its door hung a sign reading *Union Bar*. No one knew then that this Ruth, by the exercise of his generative powers a few years later, was to become the father of the imperishable Babe.

On afternoons when nothing better offered, my father and his brother lolled in their office concocting hoaxes and canards. Their masterpiece was the creation of a mythical brother named Fred, who went on living in gaseous form for many years; to this day a rheumy old Baltimorean sometimes stops me on the street to ask what has become of him. Fred was supposed to be a clergyman. Everyone knew that my grandfather was an infidel, so my father and his brother represented that Fred was a cruel burden and disgrace to him, and warned all comers to avoid mentioning the clergy in his presence, lest his sorrow suddenly overwhelm and unman him. The Fred legend gradually took on elaborate embroideries. Fred had been invited to become chaplain of the United States Senate. He had converted 5,000 heathen in one week in Chicago. He had broken into the old man's house, and tried to pray him up to grace. He had bought Ehoff's saloon and Coblens's adjoining livery-stable and was planning to build a church or a Bible factory on the site. Finally, after my grandfather's death, they announced that Fred had been made a bishop, and there they let him rest.

My father's solo flights, I must say as a more or less honest historian, sometimes got perilously close to the line limiting the best of taste. When he

bought the Summer home at Mt. Washington, one
of the new neighbors asked him casually if he had
any plans for developing the place, which was somewhat dilapidated. He replied solemnly that he proposed to give over the long slope of lawn in front of
the house to the breeding of blooded hogs, a race of
cattle too much neglected in Maryland. This news
naturally staggered the neighbor, and he ran about
the vicinity spreading it. By the time the first dele-
gation of protest arrived my father was ready with
large blue-prints of the proposed piggery, prepared by a builder friend and showing the name
" Pig Hill " on a banner hung between two immense flagpoles at the main entrance. The excitement began to die down after we moved in and the
long ranks of pens continued *non est*, but there was
a revival of it every time workmen appeared to
gravel a walk or repair a porch. Worse, the name
of " Pig Hill " stuck to the place, and was gradually extended to the whole settlement. It survived,
in fact, until the city of Baltimore, proliferating
northward, finally obliterated both the settlement
and the name.

There was something of the same barbarity,
though it did much less damage, in an operation
against a German friend, a gentleman who owned
a wood-working factory. He was the most inoffen-
sive man imaginable, and his only known vice was
playing *Schafskopf* of an afternoon with a few
friends. One day he got into a row with a Maine

lumber company about a schooner load of lumber, and the company finally threatened him with a lawsuit. This alarmed him greatly, so he dropped in to consult my father. He was particularly concerned lest the noise and fumes of the dispute induce Bradstreet's, the commercial credit agency, to reduce his credit rating. My father offered at once to get a Bradstreet report on him to find out if anything of the sort had been done — and then spent the next two afternoons concocting a report that left nothing of him save a ruined name and his immortal soul.

This bogus report was typewritten on flimsy in exact imitation of a real one. It started off by saying that the old man was a once prosperous and respected *entrepreneur*, but that his gross neglect of his business had brought it down to the edge of bankruptcy. He left his office every day, it said, at 2 p.m., drove out to a notorious resort in the country (described so as to identify his own home), and there wasted what remained of his substance gambling with a gang of police characters. It added that he drank vast amounts of beer during this play, and was already showing signs of *mania à potu*. It ended by hinting that his family was considering having him put under restraint as *non compos mentis*, and that his creditors were forming a committee to join in the action.

The old man's response to all this nonsense was almost terrifying. He leaped in the air, began Goddamning horribly in English and German, and talked wildly of shaking the dust of the United States from his feet and going back to his native Bremen. He laid the whole blame upon the lumber company, which was operated, so he said, by Yankee swindlers of a kind that, in any civilized country, would be looked to by the *Polizei*. He became so excited that my father grew alarmed, and began to confess in haste that the report was spurious. But by this time the victim was so wrought up that he wouldn't listen, and it was not until the bookkeeper was dispatched to Bradstreet's Baltimore office for a real one, and it turned out on inspection to be highly complimentary, that he recovered any calm. Even so, he kept on denouncing the lumber company, and it retained first place in his menagerie of monsters so long as he lived.

About this time the half-grown son of a neighbor at Mt. Washington became stage struck and began to prepare himself diligently for his chosen art. His preparations took the form of dreadful howls and shrieks in the woods behind his home, designed to improve his breathing. This noise set all the dogs for half a mile round to barking, and scared the horses, cats, nurse-maids and small children of the settlement out of their wits. My father's characteristic device for getting rid of the nuisance was to complain to the police at the county seat that a wild man was loose in the woods, devouring rabbits raw and alive, and threatening cannibalism. The rural cops arrived on horseback and at a gallop, surrounded the woods, discharged their side-arms menacingly, and then rushed in and confronted the astonished actor. It took my father a couple of days and several boxes of Grade D cigars to convince them that some miscreant had played a joke on them.

But such designs and inventions were, after all, only small game. In his later years, reviewing his career as Münchhausen and Joe Cook from the serene pinnacle of the forties, my father dismissed them lightly as no more than inconsiderable impromptus. The true peak of his talent, he allowed, was reached in his successful scheme to wreck the cigarmakers' union of Baltimore, which called a strike along about 1889. In his own shop the strike lasted only a few days, but the men stayed out in some of the other shops of the town for weeks and months, and as a result large numbers of them began to fall behind in their rent and grocery-bills, and to hear unpleasantly from their wives. The union had a war fund, but it wasn't large enough to pay the strikers full benefits; the best it could offer, at least toward the end, was free tickets to Philadelphia, which then had so many shops that it was known as the Cigarmakers' Heaven. The union sent hundreds of the strikers there, and most of them got jobs, but other hundreds remained in Baltimore, and the war fund began to play out.

It was at this stage that my father formulated his

scheme to put the wounded enemy out of its misery. There were in the cellar of every cigar-shop in town a great many supernumerary cigarmakers' box-wood boards and cutting tools, left behind by tramp workmen who had come in from nowhere, worked a few weeks, got drunk and fired, and then vanished. The possession of such a board and set of tools was sufficient proof that the bearer was a ci-garmaker. The union was eager to clear out all such casuals of the trade, for they were always half starved when they arrived, and it was thus easy for the bosses to induce them to work as strikebreakers.

When my father's spies reported that a dozen or more of them were being shipped to Philadelphia every day the inspiration for his museum piece seized him. If a board and a set of cutting tools made a cigarmaker, why not fashion a whole regi-ment of them out of the abandoned boards and tools in the cellar? To get the men was easy: there were hundreds and thousands of them in the flop-houses of Baltimore — sailors who had gone on drunks and missed their ships, farm-boys come to town to make their fortunes, old soaks not yet quite ready for the morgue, and a dozen other kinds of miserable and hopeless men. So an agent was sent down to the region of Pratt street wharf to round up a squad, and in a little while he returned with twenty-five. Each was given a cigarmaker's board, a set of cutting tools, a drink of horse-liniment, and fifty cents in cash, and instructed how to find the headquarters of the union, and what to say on reaching it. The agent then started them off, and in an hour they were all aboard a train for Philadelphia, each with a ticket in his hand that had cost the union $1.85, and a quarter for refreshments *en route*.

When the boards in the cellar of the Metropolitan Cigar Factory of Aug. Mencken & Bro. gave out those in the cellars of other factories were levied upon, and in the course of the next few weeks at least a thousand poor bums were run through the mill. They cost the union $2.10 apiece, and its remaining funds swiftly melted away. Finally, the spies brought news that it could go on for but one day more. My father always lingered over this part of the story. The union was now wrecked, but how could the fiends in human form in charge of it be made to understand clearly *how* it had been wrecked, and by whom? How could its defeat be converted into shame and vain repining? His solution, though it strained his powers to the utmost, was really very simple. He sent his agents down to Pratt street wharf to round up a dozen *one-armed* men, outfitted them with the usual boards and tools, and had them marched to union headquarters. The instant they got there the fiends tumbled to the trick that had been played on them. With low cries of dismay, they gathered up the few dollars remaining, rushed to the Baltimore & Ohio dépôt, and fled to Philadelphia themselves.

The union sneaked back into Baltimore afterward, but it was a long time afterward. While my father lived it troubled him no more. He died full of a pious faith that he had finished it.

XVII

Brief Gust of Glory

In my boyhood in the Aurignacian Epoch of Baltimore the favorite bivouac and chapel-of-ease of all healthy males of tender years was the neighborhood livery-stable. I have since learned, by a reading in the social sciences, that the American livery-stables of that era were seminaries of iniquity, with a curriculum embracing cursing and swearing, gambling, cigarette-smoking, tobacco-chewing, the classical or Abraham Lincoln répertoire of lewd anecdotes, the design and execution of dirty pictures, and even the elements of seduction, burglary and delirium tremens. It may have been true, for all I know, in the pathological small towns that all social scientists appear to hail from, but certainly it was not true in West Baltimore. I was a regular student at Reveille's stable in Stricker street from the beginning of my seventh year to the end of my nonage, and as special student at Coblens's stable in Paca street, off and on, for most of the same period, but so far as I can recall I never heard a word uttered in either of them, or beheld any human act, transaction or phenomenon, that might not have been repeated before a bench of bishops.

On the contrary, they were both schools of decorum, operated by proud and even haughty men, and staffed by blackamoors of a generally high tone. No palpably dipsomaniacal or larcenous coon could survive more than a few days in any such establishment : there were too many valuable horses and rigs in hand to be trusted to the former, and too many valuable carriage-robes, buggy-whips, hassocks, etc., to be exposed to the latter. My father's No. 1 whip, hung up by the snapper in Mr. Reveille's office, had a gold band around the handle engraved with the insigne of the Ancient Arabic Order of Nobles of the Mystic Shrine, and in Mr. Coblens's office, where he commonly kept his No. 2 whip and his dayton-wagon, there was also a buffalo robe that he set great store by, although I should add that its hair had pretty well played out, and that after his death I gave it freely to the poor.

Mr. Coblens was a man of erect bearing, reserved manner, and great dignity. He wore none of the loud checks associated with his vocation, but was always clad in plain colors, and not infrequently appeared in a black cutaway. His only concession to the public expectation was a gray derby hat, very high in the crown. If you can imagine a Jewish colonel of a swagger cavalry regiment, then you have got him to the life. My father had a high regard for him, and often paused to discuss horses with him — a subject about which he knew everything and my father next to nothing. He seldom descended from his heights to speak to my brother or me. He knew us very well, and would indicate by a vague flicker of his eyes that he was aware of our presence, but it was not often that he said anything.

His cousin Felix was a far more cordial fellow. Felix was a bachelor in those days, and apparently a somewhat gay one, for more than once I saw him set out of an afternoon in a buggy shining like a $100 coffin, with sometimes a blonde lady beside him and sometimes a brunette. My brother and I, boylike, regarded his ease and success at gallantry with great respect. He was, indeed, one of our heroes, and also one of our friends. He was never too busy to explain to us, with the use of living models paraded by his blackamoors, the points of a harness horse, and he also had illuminating ideas about buggy architecture. When my father gave my brother Charlie and me the pony Frank, it was Mr. Felix who taught us how to handle him — no mean art, I assure you, for Shetland ponies not only kick like mules, but also bite like dogs, and no doubt would scratch like cats if they had claws. To this day I have a scar on my bosom, often passing for a war wound, that proves how effectively Frank could use his teeth.

In 1890 or thereabout my father traded two cases of Zimmer Spanish leaf tobacco for a gelding bearing the strange name (for a horse) of John. John was a trotter, and supposedly of some speed in harness, but my father could never get it out of him. The two did so badly together, indeed, that my father concluded that John must have rheumatism, and thereafter, for two or three months, the poor beast was the patient of a veterinarian who sent in large bottles of a fiery, suffocating liniment and even larger bills, but never did John any good. Mr. Felix, it appeared, had suspected all the while that the trouble was predominantly in the driver rather than in the horse, and eventually he volunteered to go out with my father some afternoon, and make a scientific review of his driving. He returned downcast. " Your pa," he said to me the next time I dropped in, " is hopeless. It would take him two or three hundred years to learn to drive a cart-horse, let alone a trotter. He holds the lines like a man dealing cards. If he ever got John to really stepping he would fall out of the buggy and break his neck."

A few days later, as if reminded by conscience that he may have been hasty in dismissing his duty to the family, he amazed and delighted me by offering to give *me* a few lessons. It was a colossal opportunity to a boy of eleven, for Mr. Felix was an eminent figure in the trotting world of Baltimore, and seldom condescended to pedagogy. I had, as I recall it, only four or five lessons, but when they were over Mr. Felix was so complimentary that I developed on the spot a complacency which still survives after nearly fifty years, protecting me like an undershirt of concrete from the contumely of mankind. Indeed, he said flatly, and I believe he meant it, that I had in me the makings of a really smart harness driver. " By the time you begin to shave," he concluded, " you'll be showing 'em."

By that time, alas, I had turned from equestrology to chemistry, and a little while later I abandoned chemistry for the kind of beautiful letters on tap in newspaper offices. But for a couple of years I drove John every day, and so gradually improved and mellowed my technic. On Summer afternoons, when my father and I were driving home to Mt. Washington, and the clomp-clomp of a trotter's scissoring hooves began to sound behind us on the Pimlico road speedway, he would silently hand me the reins, and settle back to be torn between parental pride and personal repining. I seemed to hear him groan now and then, but he never said anything. When John, who was really very fast, had left the other nag behind, and the brush was over, he would quietly relight his cigar and resume the reins. He never complimented me: it was too painful. Despite the unction to my vanity that flowed out of these episodes, there was also

melancholy in them, and they implanted in me a
lifelong conviction that children, taking one day
with another, must be damned pests.

But it was not the Coblens stable but the Reveille
stable that was my chief haunt in boyhood. The
Coblens stable was downtown in Paca street, a few
yards from my father's place of business, but the
Reveille stable was only two blocks from our home
in Hollins street. My brother and I spent many
happy hours there, watching the blackamoors cur-
rying, feeding and watering the horses, plaiting
their tails, excavating and blacking their hooves,
dosing them with Glauber's salts and condition
powders, and treating their lampas (pronounced
lampers) with red-hot pokers. This last was a horrifying spectacle, for lampas is an overgrowth of
tissue behind the upper incisor teeth, and burning
it out involved thrusting the poker into the poor
horse's gaping mouth. But I learned before long
that horses have very little sense of pain, if indeed
any at all; and years afterward I saw one with a
leg cut off in an accident munching the grass between the cobblestones as it lay on a Baltimore
street, waiting for a cop to come out of a saloon to
shoot it.

Mr. Reveille was a Frenchman who seemed ven-
erable and even ancient to my brother and me, for
he wore a long beard and always had on a black
coat. He had two grown sons, both stout and
hearty fellows, but, like their father, very digni-

fied. There was a period when both the trotter
John and the pony Frank (whose stable at the bottom of our backyard was transiently shut down)
were quartered in the Reveille establishment, along
with two buggies, a pony cart and several other
rigs, so my brother and I had plenty of excuse for
hanging about. The Reveilles always welcomed us
gravely, and let us warm up, in Winter, in their
tiny office, which was so filled with robes that there
was scarcely room for the stove, always verging
on white-hot. We admired especially the rack of
whips, which included some virtuoso pieces by the
Baltimore master-craftsmen of the time. A good
whip might cost as much as $25, and we figured that
the whole lot must be worth at least $1000.

The colored brethren who pontificated at Reveille's have all faded, with the flight of the years, into
a brown smudge — all, that is, save Old Jim. Jim
was the carriage-washer, and a fellow of vast size
and unparalleled amiability. He was coal-black
and built like a battleship, and when he got into his
hip-high rubber boots and put on his long rubber
apron he looked like an emperor in Hell. Jim's
atelier was a skylighted space at the rear of the
carriage-house, paved with cobblestones and always flowing with water. He got to work at six in
the morning, and was sometimes still going hard at
nine at night. He had the care of fifty or more
buggies, and of perhaps as many other vehicles,
and he kept them clean and shining. His hardest

time came on Sunday morning, when he had to wash and polish all the buggies in preparation for the pleasure jaunts of the afternoon. For this business he brought out his newest sponges and cleanest chamois-skins. Also, he put on a black derby hat, never worn on week-days.

In the intervals of his washing and polishing Jim took out rigs to the homes of clients of the stable, and thereby sometimes acquired quiet brannigans, for it was the custom to reward him, not with money, but with drinks. My father kept a special jug for the purpose. It was shared by the ice-man, but Jim got most of it, for in view of his great bulk he was given a much larger drink than the ice-man. He always downed it at a gulp, and after it was down he would blink his eyes, rub his belly, and say " Ah-h-h-h-h-! " This was a Baltimore custom of the time, practised by most of the nobility and gentry and imitated by serving folk. Sometimes Jim also got a cigar. He would light it at once, and stalk back to Reveille's smoking it at an angle of forty-five degrees. When he reached the stable he would choke it carefully and deposit it on a high ledge in the brick wall, out of reach of his less Himalayan and reliable colleagues.

My brother and I greatly admired Jim, and delighted in watching him at work. He had a way of spinning buggy-wheels that was really magnificent, and he worked with larger sponges and broader chamois-skins than any other carriage-washer in West Baltimore. The buggies of those days all had carpets, and when there was nothing else to do he would get out a dozen or so of them, and beat them. Sometimes he would find a nickel or a dime under one of them. It always went into his pocket, for it was the theory among the colored proletarians of Baltimore in those days that whatever a white person lost or mislaid he really didn't want. If he wanted it, he would ask for it, and probably raise hell about it. Jim's income from this source was not large, for he found a great many more pins than nickels. He always laid them aside carefully and then threw them into the manure-pit, for a pin in the frog of a horse's hoof might bring on calamity.

One day my brother and I were astonished to find Jim missing; it seemed almost as strange as finding Mr. Reveille missing, or the stable itself. His *locum tenens*, a short, spotty colored man named Browny, ordinarily a hostler, told us the sad news. Jim's youngest son, a youth of sixteen, had been blown up by an explosion in a one-horse soda-pop factory up a nearby alley, and Jim was off for the day, arranging for the interment of the few fragments that had been recovered. We had never heard of this son, but we were full of sympathy, and when Jim returned we tried to tell him so in the shy manner of boys. He replied that it was God's deliberate act and will, and that he did not mourn beyond reason. The son, he went on judicially, was not really bad, at least as sons went in an age of moral chaos, but nevertheless there was some worry in him, for now and then, like any other high-spirited colored boy, he got into trouble with the cops, and when that wasn't going on he wasted his substance on trashy yallah gals. Now he was far, far away, riding some cloud or rainbow, and hence safe from the hangman forever. He had even escaped, by the unusual manner of his death, the body-snatchers.

Two or three days later we saw a brisk-looking white man in a short yellow overcoat talking to Jim, and the day following Jim again disappeared. We heard from Browny that the brisk-looking man had been a lawyer, and that the talk had been of damages. Another talk, he said, was now proceeding downtown. Jim was gone a week, and then suddenly reappeared, but not to resume work. He showed up one morning in a stove-pipe hat and a long-tailed black coat, carrying an ebony cane with a bone head in the shape of a horse with widely distended nostrils tinted red, and green gems for eyes. His right-hand coat pocket was bulging with at least a quarter's worth of peanuts, and he invited all his old colleagues to thrust in their paws and help themselves. In his other coat pocket he had half a dozen apples for horses he especially liked, including the pony Frank but not the trotter John, and in the hand unburdened by the cane he carried a two-pound bag of lump-sugar. In all four pockets of his white waistcoat were five-cent cigars, standing in rows like cartridges in a belt. He offered the cigars freely, and recommended them as the best in West Baltimore. He even offered one to Mr. Peter Reveille. His hip pockets were stuffed with chewing-tobacco.

Such was Jim in the full tide of his bereavement. Mr. Peter Reveille told us that the lawyer had offered him $250, but that Jim had stuck out for $300, and got it. He let it be known that he had demanded the money in $1 bills, but where he kept them we didn't know until later. Some of the hostlers were of the opinion that he had sneaked into the stable-loft by night and hidden them in the hay, and for a week or so a vain search for them went on. Browny insisted that they were in Jim's stove-pipe hat. He knew, as all of us knew, that policemen always kept their valuables in their helmets; *ergo*, why not Jim? But this theory blew up when Jim dropped in, a week or so later, without his hat, and complaining that two bad niggers from Vincent alley had knocked it off with clubs, and run away with it. The hat was gone, but Jim continued in funds for a long while afterward — indeed, for fully a month. He dropped into the stable almost daily, and never failed to distribute cigars, peanuts, and chewing tobacco, with sugar and apples for the horses. He appeared, at different times, in no less than five hats, and was often mildly in liquor. But he never brought any liquor on the

premises, so the Reveilles, who had a large experience with the darker races, tolerated him patiently.

They knew that he would be back in his long
boots and rubber apron soon or late, and he was.
One morning early they found him at work, somewhat trembly and with a cut over his left eye, but
otherwise as he had been in the days before wealth
corrupted him. He had not been seen during the
preceding week, and for a while his final adventures
were unknown, for neither then nor thereafter did
he ever mention them. But the other colored men
gradually assembled and disgorged the story, and
the cop on the beat helped out with a fact or two. It
was really very simple. Jim, a decent widower, had
been ganged and undone by the massed yallah gals
of three alleys. They had all tackled him singly
and failed, but when they tackled him in a body he
succumbed.

The ensuing party raged for four days and four
nights, with continuous music by banjos, accordi-
ons, and bones. It began in a little saloon that was
the G.H.Q. of one of the alleys, but gradually
spread over the whole block, and ended at last in
a loft over an empty stable. There was no hint
whatever of carnality; the thing was purely alco-
holic. After the first few hours each of the yallah
gals sent for her regular fellow, and beginning
with the second day all sorts of gate-crashers
barged in. Thereafter there was a flow in and a
flow out. Every hour or two some guest would col-

lapse and roll home, and another would make the gate. Only Jim himself and a yallah gal named Mildred survived from beginning to end. Mildred, by that time, was in the first stages of *mania à potu*, and the cop on the beat, looking in, ordered her off the job, but Jim was still going strong.

Alas, he didn't go long, for a little while later the saloonkeeper's son Otto came in to say that time was called on the party. Otto and his brother Hermann had been hauling booze for it for four days and four nights, and both were badly used up. Hermann, in fact, had had to be put to bed. But it wasn't fatigue that made Otto call time; it was the fact that Jim's last dollar bill had been devoured. The father of Otto and Hermann was known to be a determined man, with the cops always on his side, so no one questioned the fiat. One by one, they simply faded away, leaving only Jim. He rolled himself in his long-tailed coat and lay down to a prodigal's dreams. He slept all the rest of that day, and all of the ensuing night to 5 a.m. Then he shuffled off to Reveille's stable, chased Browny away from his job, and resumed his station in life.

It was not until long afterward that my brother and I learned where Jim had kept his fortune while it oozed away. Mr. Reveille, worming the story out of the blackamoors, told my father, who told it to a neighbor, Mr. Scherer, whose boy Theodore, lurking about, overheard the telling, and brought it to us. The money had been in the care and cus-

tody of the saloonkeeper all the while. He doled it
out to Jim dollar by dollar, marking the score on
a blackboard behind his bar. He charged Jim a
dollar a day " interest " for keeping it. When the
final orgies began he charged a dollar for every
day and a dollar for every night.

The Scherer boy reported that, in telling about
this " interest," my father swore in a hair-raising
manner. He had, in fact, a generally suspicious
view of saloonkeepers. He would often say that
while he knew and respected some upright men
among them, only too many were disgraces to a
humane and even noble profession.

XVIII

THE CAREER OF A

𝕻𝖍𝖎𝖑𝖔𝖘𝖔𝖕𝖍𝖊𝖗

THAT learning and virtue do not always run together I learned early in life from the example of Old Wesley, a man of color living in the alley behind our house in Hollins street. Wesley dwelt in illicit symbiosis with Lily, the stately *madura* cook of our next-door neighbors, and once a year his younger brother, who pastored an A.M.E. church down in Calvert county, dropped in on him to remonstrate against his evil ways. But Wesley always won the ensuing bout in moral theology, for he had packed away in his head a complete roster of all the eminent Biblical characters who had taken headers through No. 7, beginning with King David and running down to prophets of such outlandish names that, as I now suspect, many of

them were probably invented on the spot. Moreover, Wesley could always floor his rev. brother
with a final poser: How could he marry Lily so long
as she had two other husbands, both of them united
to her by impeccable Christian rites? Did the pastor propose the commission of trigamy? If so, then
let him go down to the watchhouse in Calhoun street
and ask the cops to show him chapter nine, verse
twenty, in the big black lawbook behind the desk,
a foot or two east of the water-cooler.

The pastor, I believe, never went. He had too
healthy a respect for Wesley's scholarship in legal
science, and indeed in all the other sciences, including especially those of an ethical or sacred nature. Thus the debate always petered out into futile logic-chopping, and the other residents of the
alley, having crowded up to Wesley's open door for
the show, got only headaches for their pains. Wesley would thereupon suggest that the pastor preach
to them as a sort of solatium. Along with the other
white boys of Hollins street, I heard more than
one of those sermons, and I can testify that they
were very powerful. Each had not only a subject,
invariably the post-mortem dangers of sin, but
also an object — one of the congregation assembled.

I remember well the day when it was Old Aunt
Sophie's turn. She was the widow of a black barber from Fauquier county, Virginia, who had spent
the years 1863 and 1864 caring for the whiskers of

General George H. Thomas, and since her husband's death she had lived chastely on her pension,
attending (on the sidewalk) all the funerals, white
or black, in West Baltimore, and lending a hand
whenever special orgies were staged in the colored
churches. No more innocent person lived on this
earth. She had worn the same black veil for thirty
years, and it well indicated the sombre rectitude of
her soul. But the pastor lit into her as if she were
a child-stealer or a pirate on the high seas, and
after ten minutes of his discourse she was flat on
the cobblestones, suffocated by the fumes of brimstone and howling for deliverance.

Old Wesley himself listened to all these sermons
politely, though he was known to be an infidel, and
had a long argument to prove that there was not
enough coal and wood in creation to stoke the fires
of the Methodist Hell. He was, in fact, very proud
of his brother's homiletic talents, and when the
smaller colored boys on the edge of the crowd made
whoopee he would go among them with a lath and
paddle them far from gently. We white boys,
knowing that the prevailing *mores* forbade him to
paddle *us*, were bound in honor to keep quiet, and
this we always did. At the end of the sermon we
joined in the closing hymn — usually " Whiter
Than Snow " or " Are You Ready for the Judgment Day? " Then the pastor would suggest an
offering for his tarpaper tabernacle down in Calvert county, and the assemblage would disperse in

swift silence. But Wesley always put in a nickel, and sometimes a dime, and I recall one day when his sinister eye halted so many fugitives that the total plate was nearly thirty-five cents. This would be enough, said the grateful pastor, to replace a window-pane in the tabernacle, broken by agents of Satan. For three and a half years it had been sorely missed, for the butcher paper pasted over the opening shut out the light.

The pastor's visitations always came in the Summer, and usually in the afternoon. They quite upset Wesley's routine for hot days. His Lily had to clear out at seven o'clock to get breakfast for her white folks, but Wesley himself never arose before eight. The first sign that he was astir would be the appearance of their feather bed through the second-story front window of their four-room house. They apparently slept on it all the year round. On every fair morning, Wesley would shove it out of the window to air, and there it would remain until noon, unless storms came up in the meantime. He made his own breakfast, and then busied himself with undisclosed household tasks until eleven o'clock, when he took a walk around the block.

On his return, he had an armful of newspapers and other printed matter, dredged out of trash boxes on the way, and most of the afternoon he devoted to reading them. It was said that he could read any word, however hard. Colored schoolboys sometimes tackled him with appalling specimens, got from their teachers, but he was always ready to give them names, and to explain their significances. I myself, in the year 1889, sought to floor him with *phthisic*, then all the rage at my school. He called it off without a second's hesitation, and even offered to pronounce it backward. Its meaning? " It's one of them diseases," he said, " that you catch in the Fall of the year. It's something like what you call the heaves in a horse, and then again it ain't. There was a man up in Vincent alley died of it about the time the stockyards burned down. All the pallbearers took it, but none of them had it what you would call bad. Sometimes it don't amount to much."

In Summer, Wesley always did his reading across the alley from his house, in the shade of a white neighbor's backyard fence. He would bring out a kitchen chair shortly after noon, plant it carefully on the narrow and squidgy sidewalk, with its treacherous " she " bricks, and proceed solemnly to business. Years before, he had bought a pair of spectacles from a pack peddler, but he didn't need them, and seldom used them. He would read until three or four o'clock, and then he would be ready for easy and informative conversation until eight in the evening, when Lily returned from her place with a vast pan of victuals for their evening meal. Wesley, so far as I know, never ate lunch. Like most colored folk of the old school, he preferred to gorge at night, and to proceed direct from the table to bed. He was said once to have eaten a whole ham and a whole cabbage at a sitting, but I got that at third hand, and do not take responsibility for it.

I knew him best not as a gourmet but as a metaphysician. He had ready and overwhelming answers to all the questions that have baffled such professionals as Thomas Aquinas and Immanuel Kant, F. W. Nietzsche and William James. For example, What is truth? His answer, reduced to brevity, was as follows: "Truth is something that only damned fools deny." But how are you going to detect the damned fools? By the fact that they deny it. Is there a hole in this reasoning? Perhaps. But there are also holes, according to Kant, in the reasoning of Aquinas, and, according to Nietzsche and William James, in the reasoning of Kant, and so on to the end of the murky chapter.

Wesley had answers to all the other great riddles of the universe, and most of them were equally confident. He knew, for example, the causes of each and every one of the pestilences commonly afflicting Aframericans. Rheumatism, he explained, was due to bending over and lifting weights. The backbone, it appeared, crackled like a bent cornstalk. It could be restored to its natural shape and resilience only by adopting some sedentary avocation: this, in fact, was the reason Wesley himself lived at the cost and expense of Lily. His rheumatism, acquired during his former practice as a hod-carrier, still troubled him a bit, but sixteen years of ease had certainly improved it. He had got rid of the ague by carrying a horse chestnut in his pocket. Here the rationale was absurdly transparent. Horses and mules were notoriously immune to the ague; hence horse chestnuts would cure it. If there had been cow chestnuts or dog chestnuts, they would have cured it, too.

Wesley's pockets were full of many other such specifics. He carried a quince seed to hold in check the quinsy that beset him every Winter, some BB shot to prevent hiccoughs (the reasoning here I don't recall, or maybe never heard), and a small spring, apparently from a deceased firearm, to keep his wool in kink. This was before Aframerica began to patronize hair-straighteners. To Wesley, straight hair on a colored man was unearthly, and even alarming. The kinks, he taught, held the skull tight, and so kept the air out, and warded off headaches, blind staggers, and insanity. There had been a yellow fellow in Vincent alley with hair that was not only straight but also somewhat sandy. His fate was known to all. One windy night he went loony and cut his wife's throat, and a few months later, on a Friday that was the thirteenth of the month, he was hanged at the city jail.

Wesley seldom got farther than a block from his house in the alley behind Hollins street, but twice a year he went down into South Eutaw street near the railroad tracks to attend the meetings of a lodge that he belonged to. Its name I never discovered, or the character of its mysteries. Wesley always left home smoking a cigar, and, according to Lily, came back smelling of gin. The nearest route would have taken him past the University of Maryland Medical School at Lombard and Greene streets, but it was no secret that he always avoided the place by making a detour of six or eight blocks. This was not because he had any fear of the thousands of cadavers reported to be piled up like stovewood in the university deadhouse. As I shall show, he regarded the departed as beneficent presences, or, at all events, as harmless. But he held it to be manifest that medical students were indistinguishable from demons. They lay in wait in dark Greene street with their dreadful hooks, saws, lassos, and knives, and when they had roped a poor colored man they dragged him into their den with hellish shrieks, sawed off his legs and arms, scalped him, and boiled down what remained of him to make medicine. There were, of course, no witnesses to prove these obscene rites, for there were no survivors, but the facts needed no testimony, for they were admitted *quod ab omnibus, quod ubique, quod semper.*

Wesley's attitude toward the dead was one of easy confidence. He believed that the overwhelming majority of them turned into angels, and that these angels were invariably white. " Who would be black if he could he'p it? " he would ask solemnly, not without a touch of pathos. And then, as usual, he would answer himself, " Angels *can* he'p it." The non-angelic dead were simply probationers, roving the vicinity of their coffins (and hence extremely numerous in graveyards) until their cases could be adjudicated. Wesley rejected the idea of Hell, not only for the reason I have stated a while back, but also on legalistic grounds. There would be a profound irrationality, he argued, in punishing evildoers in one world for what they had done in another. Was a chicken thief in Calvert county jailed in Baltimore? Obviously not. The very cops would laugh at the idea. He had other reasons, too, but what they were I forget.

It was in the year 1891 that Wesley had a chance to test his faith in the beneficence of the departed. One day Lily came home from her place complaining of a terrible misery in the head. Wesley put her to bed at once, and sat up all night tearing towels and sheets into strips, soaking them in Dr. Jackson's Reliable Vinegar Liniment for Man and Beast, and binding them tightly to her head. But the air must have got in nevertheless, for by dawn Lily was out of her wits, and carrying on so loudly that the neighbors were all aroused, and came flocking in to assist at the bedside, and to tell one another when they had seen Lily last, and what she had said to them. Presently someone got word to Dr. Benson, the young white medico who had just

opened an office in Hollins street, and he came rush-
ing out of his back gate with his nightshirt stuffed
into his trousers, and his shiny new black bag bulging reassuringly. But the science of young Dr.
Benson, though it was extraordinarily fresh, and
indeed came down almost to that precise moment,
was insufficient to save poor Lily, and as the whistle
down at the Mount Clare carshops blew for seven
o'clock she gave up the ghost.

Wesley took his calamity like the philosopher
that he was. Nor did he blanch when word came
that the burial society to which Lily had belonged
for eighteen years, dutifully paying in fifteen cents
every week, was insolvent, and could not meet its li-
ability of forty dollars. He borrowed two dollars
from young Dr. Benson, produced eleven dollars
and some odd cents from a mysterious cigar box,
and talked the undertaker, Brother James Gadsden, into giving him credit for what was needed to
make up twenty-five. Thus Lily, though she missed
the gaudy Class A Nazarene funeral that she had
looked forward to for so many years, was at least
assured of dignified interment, and in an hour or
two Brother Gadsden and his son Joe arrived with a
neat black box, and she was duly laid out in the little parlor. A plate rested on her chest, and as the
neighbors and the public generally filed past there
was an occasional tinkle. Wesley raked in the
money from time to time, not wanting to expose
kindly friends to temptations beyond human en-

durance. By evening he had nearly a dollar and a half, and this he gave to Brother Gadsden to affix a copious but somewhat rusty crêpe to the spot on the front-door frame where a bell would have been if there had been one. A postal card was sent to the clerical brother down in Calvert county, inviting him to conduct the obsequies if his ecclesiastical and private engagements permitted. Wesley didn't expect him to show up, and he didn't. His professional view of Lily's morals was very low.

No less than two brave spirits, one of them the alley half-wit and the other a dubious-looking mulatto from the region behind Hollins Market, offered to sit up with Lily, but Wesley waved them away. There would be no death watch, he announced, and no wake. Along about nine o'clock in the evening he adjourned proceedings for the day, jammed a chair against the front door to keep it shut, made a solitary supper of cold meats, and went to bed in the little room above the chamber of death. The neighbors marveled at this fortitude. What if Lily should take to walking? What if her ghost began to moan? What if the Devil dropped in to look her over?

They listened cautiously for a while, but if they heard anything it was only Wesley's snores. His nursing duties the night before and all the excitement of the day had worn him out, and he was quickly asleep. There was no room in his philosophy for fear of the dead. If they became angels, they were, of course, harmless, and if they were put on probation, they naturally carried themselves very discreetly, in the hope of early release. It was only when those fiends, the medical students, disturbed them in their graves, dragging them out of the earth to rend and cook them, and leaving screwdrivers, broken knives, cigarette butts, and whiskey bottles in their empty coffins — it was only then that they went on in a riotous and alarming manner, and even so their worst screams were simply calls for help. Treat them with reasonable politeness, and they were no more evil than policemen, who responded in the same way to the same dose. Wesley had confidence in Lily. Living, she had paid his rent for many years, and provided him with nourishing board. Dead, she would certainly not afflict him.

But that, alas, is precisely what she did. The details are not all clear, but Wesley seems to have shown a brave and tolerant spirit. It was not until the grisly hour before dawn that he appeared at the door of his neighbors, the Perkinses, and rapped softly. Three of the seven Perkins children slept on pallets in the front room, and they let him in and called their father. Wesley was almost apologetic — not for himself but for Lily. " She don't seem to be restin'," he explained, " as well as she ought. Otherwise, I don't know *what* to call it. No sooner was I asleep than she pulled off my covers. Then I went to sleep again, and she pulled 'em off again. That went on six or seven times. Then she commenced to blow in my face. And then she buzzed like a mosquito. And then she meeowed like a cat. And then — well, I thought I'd better clear out, and maybe she could get some rest. I don't know *what's* troublin' her."

The Perkins children were scared half to death. It had been bad enough to sleep with only a thin wall between them and Lily; now that she was aprowl, the thing became appalling. But their parents, who told the whole neighborhood about it later, were not alarmed, or even surprised. They suggested that Lily, on her deathbed, had probably forgotten to tell Wesley something, and that it was still lying on her mind and driving her thoughts from celestial matters. Wesley himself had to admit the plausibility of the hypothesis. The next day he told Brother Gadsden, the undertaker, that she was most likely trying to tell him where he would find the cigar box and its hoard of nickels and pennies. In life, it appeared, she had never suspected that he knew about it all the while and had even burgled it modestly once or twice. But Brother Gadsden, though naturally a stupid fellow, came back with a series of disconcerting questions. " If she didn't know it when she was alive," he demanded, " is that any sign she didn't know it soon as she was dead? Can't a ghost *see*? And wasn't the box standing right there on the mantelpiece, plumb empty? "

So far as I know, Wesley never resolved the riddle. It seemed to bother him a great deal during the weeks following, and may have had something to do with his early demise. He was always bringing it up, and laboring it futilely. He even talked to himself about it. When the neighbors ceased to think of him as a lone and lorn widower, and so ceased to feed him, he turned anti-social, and was presently in the hands of the cops. Jailed for stealing two hams and a sack of flour from a grocer's delivery wagon, he came down with pneumonia in his damp dungeon. With the unhappy alacrity of his race, he was dead in five days, and a week later the medical students had him. I have never known a more gifted metaphysician, or one who came to a sadder end.

XIX

𝕵𝖓𝖓𝖔𝖈𝖊𝖓𝖈𝖊

IN A WICKED WORLD

BOMBAZINE is often spoken of by authors, usually in a sneering way, but the only person I ever knew to wear it was Aunt Sophie, the ancient colored woman mentioned in the last chapter. As I recall it, it was a somewhat stiff and shiny fabric, apparently black at the start, but converted by the oxygen of the air into a sinister, malarious polychrome like that of the waters of a stagnant frog pond. Aunt Sophie wore it on all public occasions, along with a long crêpe veil of the same unappetizing color. As the widow of a military barber, she was in receipt of a modest pension from the United States Treasury, and on it she lived at ease in her little four-room house, and even in a kind of opulence.

Her days were very busy. Whenever there was a funeral in West Baltimore, whether in a white street or a colored, she arrived in good time and planted herself on the sidewalk. She carried a white cambric handkerchief that, under the ravages of time, had taken on the texture of a lace curtain, and as the pallbearers emerged with the departed she always applied it politely to her eyes. If the cortege went to any church within walking distance, she hustled along beside it, and since the hack horses of those days were encouraged to move slowly, she usually beat them to the sacred edifice by at least a length, and grabbed a decorous seat near the door. There she mourned quietly in the character of an old friend, or even of a relative, if the departed happened to be colored, and in that of a family retainer if he or she were white. She was, in fact, more or less related to fully half the black folk in our neighborhood, for most of them had come from either Fauquier county, Virginia, where her husband was born, or Calvert county, Maryland, where she was born herself. And all the white folks knew and esteemed her.

This funeral-going occupied a large part of her time, and it was seldom that she got through two days running without putting on her uniform of woe. Among her own people her absence from the forefront of mortuary orgies was always remarked, and often it had a moral significance. For she was a woman of strict Christian principles, and per-

mitted herself no compromise with sin. Thus she
took her station at least five or six doors away from
the house of sorrow when Lily, the consort of Wesley the metaphysician, was laid to rest, for their
long association had been unblessed by any sacra-
ment. And when the yellow fellow in Vincent alley
ran amuck one night and slit his wife's weasand,
and was duly hanged for it at the city jail, she refused primly to patronize the ensuing ceremonials
in any way, shape or form, though they attracted
all the other colored people for a mile around, and
also all the white boys who could escape their mothers' vigilance. My brother and I both sneaked into
the tiny parlor to see the corpse, and were haunted
for many nights afterward by the marks of the rope
on its gaunt, felonious neck.

Old Sophie was made welcome at funerals, for
she was very well regarded throughout West Baltimore. The only time she was ever turned away, to
my knowledge, was when Joe Gans, the colored
pugilist, was buried. Joe was so eminent a character among his own people that his funeral had to
be divided into three cantos and held successively
in three different churches to accommodate the
immense concourse. Even so, many more appeared
than could get in to hear and see, and his heirs and
assigns, at the last moment, made a rule that only
those who arrived in carriages should be admitted.
This barred out Aunt Sophie, for she had no carriage and was too thrifty a woman to blow in four

dollars — the extortionate price for the day — on
a public hack. Worse, the baffled crowds outside
the three churches were so large and turbulent, despite the bellowing and scuffling of the police, that
she never got within half a block of poor Joe's
bones. Thus she appeared, unwittingly, to be operating her familiar moral boycott on him, but as a
matter of fact she admired him vastly, and had
proofs, as she said, that he had died in the bosom of
the A.M.E. Church and confident of a glorious res-
urrection.

The one curse of Aunt Sophie's otherwise peaceful and happy life was her fear of the murderous
villains she called body-snatchers. These body-
snatchers were not grave-robbers, but criminals
who engaged in the far worse business of manufac-
turing cadavers for the trade. Sophie's fear of
them actually had some ground in logic, for in the
early eighties one Emily Brown, another respectable old Baltimore colored woman, had been mur-
dered by two thugs, and her remains sold to the
janitor of the University of Maryland Medical
School for fifteen dollars. The pursuit and trial
of the assassins gave Baltimore, white and black,
a show that was remembered for years afterward.
They had represented to the janitor that they were
undertakers trying to get rid of an insolvent client,
so he was cleared of all guilt, but they themselves
were hanged. The janitor was very careful after
that, but most colored people believed that he still

had murderers in his employ, and only the bravest or craziest ever ventured to pass the Medical School after dark.

Aunt Sophie held the view that his agents were on the prowl, not only in the immediate vicinity of his grisly den but also all over West Baltimore. Thus, when she had to be abroad by night she kept to well-lighted streets, and whenever it was possible induced someone else to go along. When she was alone her eye was alert for policemen, and after she had passed one she always looked back over her shoulder two or three times, to make sure that he was still there, and ready to protect her if necessary. Most of the cops knew her, and now and then one of them would have some fun by letting off a fearful whoop after she had gone by. In such cases it was hard for her to make up her mind whether she should rush back to him or gallop on.

One dismal Autumn night, on her way down Hollins street to her A.M.E. tabernacle in Stockton street, she was suddenly alarmed by the sound of stealthy footsteps behind her. She quickened her pace, but the steps continued close; in fact, they gradually came closer. Finally she broke into what, in spite of her rheumatism, must be described as a kind of run, but there was no speed in it, and the sinister steps still followed her. She was convinced that her last hour had come, and was preparing to die howling and scratching when suddenly she saw a policeman on the other side of the dark street.

At once she swung round, and confronted her pursuer, who turned out to be a young white man.

" I know what you is! " she screamed. " You's a body-snatcher! Begone, you wicked rapscallion! Don't you lay none o' your dirty hands on *me!* "

But the young white man only laughed, and when the cop ambled across the street to see what the uproar was about, he laughed too. It was a disconcerting dénouement, certainly, and as Aunt Sophie thought it over during the days following, she began to read very unpleasant significances into it. In the end she went about the neighborhood warning all persons of color that the police had entered into a corrupt compact with the body-snatchers, and that the streets were more unsafe by night than ever before. She became, like all other persons with grievances against the government, somewhat extravagant in her denunciations, and playful cops liked to set her off when a crowd of loafers was at hand. Before her scare wore off, she went to the length of threatening to arm herself with her late husband's sword, and to run it through anyone who approached her after nightfall, whether cop or layman. It was news to most people that colored barbers in the Union Army had been armed with swords, but so far as I can recall, no one ever raised the point. Nor did anyone ever see the sword.

The little parlor in Aunt Sophie's house remained substantially as her husband Jeems had left it. He had practised his profession intermittently, charging five cents flat for shaving either a face or a scalp, but his pension put him above worldly cares, and most of his time had been given to the art of painting in oils. There were several examples of his genius on the walls of the room — one a picture of a full-rigged ship laboring in a pea-green ocean. Jeems had to pick up his paints and brushes where he could find them, usually in trash cans, so his color schemes were sometimes very unusual. He once did a portrait of Old Wesley, using coal-black paint for the face. This greatly offended Wesley, who was of a rich chestnut color and liked to believe that he had Indian blood.

Sophie left Jeems's mirror on the wall after his death, along with the wooden shelf beneath it bearing his razor, comb, and brush. His operating chair presented no problem, for it was an ordinary cane-seat chair of the period, with the lost canes replaced by strips of wood from a soapbox. A large wooden spittoon filled with sawdust still stood under the mirror; for Jeems had chewed tobacco in the Army to relieve his frequent toothaches, and never gave up the practice afterward. Against the farther wall stood a scuffed Victorian side table with a cracked marble top, and on it were the *objets d'art* that Sophie had collected in her tours of the kitchens and backyards of the adjacent white folks.

The most striking of these ornaments was a large Dresden cupid with both wings missing and a crack across the face which gave it the appearance of a prizefighter staggering up for the twentieth round. There was also a glass bell covering a stuffed canary that had lost its tail and one of its eyes. Propped against the bell were several pieces of curved colored glass, all relics of deceased goblets or bottles. Some souvenirs of the Philadelphia Centennial of 1876 were also in the collection — one of them an oyster shell embellished with a sketch of Independence Hall in full color. Sophie had not visited the exposition herself; in fact, she had never been farther north in this world than Harlem Square in Baltimore. But as its white frequenters gradually discarded their souvenirs of it, she acquired them and, having acquired them, cherished them.

She used to make regular rounds of all the white folks' kitchens in the neighborhood — that is, of all wherein she was reasonably sure of a welcome. The cooks of her own race were glad to see her, for she knew all the gossip, both white and colored, and was full of wise advice to those having trouble with their husbands, their children, their madames, or the police. She usually appeared at mealtimes and always refused the first ten or twenty invitations to have a bite. But in the end she would sit down, and if she happened to be in good form she devoured enough to feed a longshoreman, though she couldn't have weighed much more than a hundred pounds. If anything was left over, she wrapped it in a newspaper and took it home. No one ever saw her buy anything, whether food or clothing. She ate, so to speak, on the country, and her wardrobe had been fixed and complete for years. Her pension went (*a*) for her rent, which was $1.25 a week, (*b*) to the funds of the A.M.E. Church in Stockton street, (*c*) to funeral collections, and (*d*) into a dime savings bank down in Baltimore street. When she died at last, and a young white lawyer in the neighborhood volunteered, as *amicus curiae*, to investigate her affairs, he found that she had amassed the substantial sum of $67.10.

Her visits to our kitchen were always made at about four o'clock in the afternoon, for she knew that my mother had tea at that time, and that she was sure of four or five cups of it, and a slab of whatever cake happened to be current. Her favorite was raisin bread, which she liked with plenty of powdered sugar. A whole dynasty of our hired girls, white and black, thus fed her. Sometimes, in the course of her formal refusals to have any refreshment, she would rush out of the kitchen door, but she always returned before the teapot was cold. In Summer, however, her refusal of iced tea was real, for she regarded ice as a poison almost as deadly as cucumbers. She liked her drinks very hot, and one of our hired girls once told me that she could eat a red pepper straight out of the tarragon-vinegar cruet without batting an eye.

Aunt Sophie lived to a great age, and in her last

years was somewhat shaky. One day, in my hearing, my mother asked her how old she was, precisely. She thought sombrely for a minute or two, and then answered that she must be well along toward thirty. This was in 1897 or thereabout, and she had been married to her Jeems some time before the Civil War. Another day my mother asked her why she didn't move back to Calvert county, where she had nephews to look after her, including two preachers, and her pension would make her a grand lady. Again she gave herself to meditation, and then answered simply, " They ain't never no parades in the country."

XX

STRANGE SCENES AND

𝔉𝔞𝔯 𝔓𝔩𝔞𝔠𝔢𝔰

To my brother Charlie and me our father seemed
to be a tremendous traveler — indeed, almost a
Marco Polo. His trips to buy tobacco ranged from
New York State and Connecticut in the North to
Cuba in the South, and from the wilds of the Pennsylvania Dutch in the East to Wisconsin in the
West, and he also made at least one journey a year
to some national potlatch of the Freemasons. In
this last mysterious order he never attained to any
eminent degree or held any office, but he was en-
rolled in both of its more sportive and expensive
sub-divisions, the Knights Templar and the Shriners. At the orgies of the Knights Templar he appears to have arrayed himself in a uniform resembling that of a rear-admiral, for in the wardrobe

that he took with him there were a long-tailed blue
coat with brass buttons, a velvet chapeau with a
black feather, a silk baldric, and a sword. With
them he carried the red fez that marked him a member of the Ancient Arabic Order of the Nobles of
the Mystic Shrine. Whether or not the Shriners
and the Knights met jointly I don't know, but every time he returned from a muster of either the one
or the other or both he brought back souvenirs of
the convention and the convention town, and these
entertained Charlie and me in a very agreeable way,
and gave us considerable credit, when they were
exhibited, among the boys of the neighborhood.
Other such objects of art and instruction flowed in
from his tobacco-buying trips, so that the house
was always well supplied. I recall especially some
ornate fans from Havana, some jars of guava jelly
from the same place, a large book illustrating the
objects of interest in St. Louis, a photograph of
the bar of the Palmer House in Chicago, showing
(not very clearly) its floor of silver dollars, and a
book of views along the French Broad river in
North Carolina, apparently a souvenir of a visit
to Asheville. My father's traveler's tales were full
of thrills to Charlie and me, especially those that
had to do with bullfighting in Cuba. My mother always protested against them as horrifying and
brutalizing, but we never got enough of them. Or
of his accounts of strange victuals devoured and
enjoyed in far places. I well remember his return

from Kansas City, probably in 1889 or thereabout, with the first news that had ever reached Hollins street of a dessert called floating-island, then apparently a novelty in the world. We made him describe it over and over again, and in the end some effort was made to concoct it in the family kitchen, but that effort came to naught.

Our own travels, down to the end of the eighties, had been very meagre. I had been to Washington often, and Charlie rather less often, but neither of us had ever been far enough from home to have to stay overnight, and neither of us had ever eaten in a dining-car or slept in a sleeper. It was thus a gaudy piece of news when, in the first days of 1891, my grandfather Abhau let it be known that he had some long-neglected relatives in faraway Ohio, and was of a mind to pay them a visit, and take me along. These relatives were new to me, and even my mother had only the vaguest idea of them. They were the descendants, it appeared, of my grandfather's elder sister, who had been so much his senior that she might have been his aunt. On arriving in the United States at some undetermined time in the past, they had bought a lottery ticket on the dock, won a substantial prize (my grandfather's estimate of it ranged up to $20,000), and used the money to buy a couple of fine farms on the borders of the Western Reserve in Ohio, not far from Toledo. My grandfather now proposed to wait upon them, and to stop on the way to see some

303

friends in Cleveland. Himself of no experience as
a land traveler (though he had made some sea voy-
ages as a youth), he wanted companionship for the
journey, and as his oldest grandchild I got the
nomination. It was to me as exciting a surprise as
being appointed hostler to Maud S. or president
of the Foos candy factory down the alley behind
Hollins street.

The preparations for the journey took a couple
of weeks, at least. There was, first of all, the matter of my trousseau. What was the climate of
Northern Ohio in Winter? No one seemed to know,
so my mother proceeded on the assumption that it
must be pretty terrible. I thus drew a new and
well-padded overcoat from Oehm's Acme Hall, and
a new Winter cap with ear-flaps from Mr. Garrigues, the Bible-searching hatter in Baltimore
street. Simultaneously, my mother began assem-
bling a large stock of extra-heavy stockings and
underclothes, and a great battery of mufflers, mittens and pulse-warmers, and to it was added a pair
of massive goloshes. All these things had to be tried
on, and some of them were broken in by being worn
on my daily journeys to F. Knapp's Institute, for
the weather in Baltimore had conveniently turned
very cold. But I had no appetite in days so electric
for the proceedings at F. Knapp's Institute, and
for the first and last time in my school life I came
home at the end of January with bad marks. Of
the many sciences taught there that month, the

only one that I really paid any attention to was geography, and in geography my studies were confined to the State of Ohio. I learned to my satisfaction that Toledo was very near its western
frontier, and hence within handy reach of the spot
where Sitting Bull had just been killed; that the
village we were bound for was only a few miles from
Lake Erie, which was twice as large as Chesapeake
Bay and probably jammed to the brim with oysters, crabs and shad-fish; and that Cleveland was
celebrated all over the world for the magnificence
of its Euclid avenue, lined with the *palazzi* of
Christian millionaires.

My father entered the picture in the closing days
of our preparations. He came home one day with
the tickets, including the Pullman tickets, and proceeded to instruct me in the technic of getting to
bed at night and up again the next morning on a
sleeper. He said that he would see us off at Camden
Station, Baltimore, and, if there was time enough,
make sure that we were properly stowed, but on
the chance that the train would not halt more than
a few minutes, he would also request his Washington agent, Mr. Cross, to take a look at us when we
reached Washington. We were to travel, of course,
by Baltimore & Ohio, and the route ran through
Washington and Pittsburgh. I recall nothing of
our actual departure, nor of Mr. Cross's inspection in Washington, but I remember very well my
father's last-minute fears that I might not have

enough money for possible expenses. My grandfather was the treasurer of the expedition, but inasmuch as he was an ancient of sixty-four there was always the chance that he might stray off and get lost, or fall into the hands of bunco-steerers, or succumb to amnesia, or lose his faculties otherwise, so it was necessary for me to be financed on my own. Every time my father thought of another of these contingencies he gave me another dollar bill, and urged me to store it safely. By the time we finally shoved off I had them secreted all over my person, and on our return two weeks later I managed to omit a couple from my settlement of accounts. With these, after a discreet interval, my brother Charlie and I bought a new air-rifle. The marks of its darts are still in the door of a cupboard on the third floor of Hollins street.

My grandfather and I changed trains at Pittsburgh in the morning, and I had my first glimpse of a quick-lunch counter. The appearance of a white waiter behind it was a piquant novelty to me, for all the restaurants I knew in Baltimore and Washington were served by blackamoors. I remember that the white coat of this Caucasian appeared to show a certain lack of freshness, but I forgot the fact when he shoved a huge stack of wheat cakes before me, with a large pitcher of syrup beside it, and then politely turned his back. At home the syrup pitcher was rigorously policed, and emptying it over a pancake brought a reprimand, if not a box of the ears, but in Pittsburgh there seemed to be no rules, so I fell to in a large and freehand way. Once or twice I noticed my grandfather looking at me uneasily, and making as if to speak, but he actually said nothing, and by the time we had to rush for our train the wheat cakes were all gone, and so was most of the syrup. There was also a plate of bread on the table, but I never touched it. As we left I saw the waiter return the slices to a pile on a shelf behind the counter. This gave me a considerable shock, and set me to wondering if the wheat cakes had also passed over some other plate before they reached mine. But I was too full of them to worry much, and after what seemed a very brief ride through country covered with snow, we reached Cleveland and were met by my grandfather's friend, Mr. Landgrebe.

Mr. Landgrebe turned out to be a very pleasant man, and when we got to his house he produced a young son, Karl, slightly older than I, who was agreeable too. How long we stayed in Cleveland I don't know, but it must have been no more than two days. But though the time was short, Mr. Landgrebe showed us all the marvels of the town, including not only the millionaires' elegantly hand-tooled castles along Euclid avenue, with every lawn peopled by a whole herd of cast-iron deers, dogs, cupids and Civil War soldiers, but also the infernal valley wherein the oil of these millionaires was processed and barreled, and a lunatic asylum in which, presumably, the victims of their free competition were confined. My grandfather, a man of tender heart, was much upset by the carryings-on of the Napoleons, George Washingtons and Pontius Pilates in the wards, and shushed me with some asperity whenever I ventured to giggle. It was my first visit to a lunatic asylum, and I enjoyed it in the innocent and thankful manner of any normal boy of ten. There was one poor maniac who entertained me particularly, for his aberration took the form of rolling up thin cylinders of paper and sticking them in his nose and ears. When I got home and told my brother Charlie about the wonderful things I had seen on my travels, he pronounced this lunatic the most wonderful of all. My own first choice, after mature reflection, was the trolley-car that ran past the Landgrebe house in Cleveland. There had been one in Baltimore for six months, but its route lay far from Hollins street, so I knew nothing about it. What struck me especially about the Cleveland car was the loud, whistling buzz that its trolley made as it came down the street. This buzz could be heard *before* the noise of the car itself was detectable — a marvelous indicator, to me, of the unearthly powers of electricity. But Charlie, who was less than nine years old, stuck to the lunatic.

When we finally got to the farms of my grandfather's kinfolk the snow had melted and the whole countryside was an ocean of mud, but by the next morning I had forgotten it, for by that time I was on easy terms with the boys and girls of the two houses, and thereafter they showed me what, in those days, was called an elegant time. I had already spent two Summers at the Vineyard, and was thus more or less familiar with rural scenes, but the Vineyard, after all, was only ten miles as the bird flies from Baltimore, and we were only Summer sojourners. Here were real farms inhabited by real farming people, and in their daily life there was something every minute that was new to me, and full of fascination. I got to know cows and hogs familiarly, and learned to esteem them. I helped the younger Almroths (it was at their house that we stayed) to crack walnuts in the barn, to fetch up apples from the cellar, and to haul wood for the great egg-stoves that kept us warm. The enormous country dinners and suppers, with their pyramids of fried chicken and their huge platters of white home-cured hog-meat, swimming in grease, stoked and enchanted my vast appetite, and I rolled and wallowed at night in the huge feather-beds. It was pleasant to go out of a morning with Mr. Almroth, and watch him (from a safe distance) blow out stumps with sticks of dynamite. It was even more pleasant to go into the woods with his two older sons, and help stack the firewood that they cut. One day I labored so diligently at this task that I got into a lather and picked up a sore throat, and the next day Mrs. Almroth cured it with a mixture of honey and horse-radish — a prescription that went far beyond anything Dr. Wiley ever ordered. The days ran by as fast as the Cleveland trolley-car, and the evenings around the egg-stove in the parlor were trips to a new and romantic world. The youngsters and I stuffed doughnuts, tortured the house dogs and swapped riddles out of Dr. Ayers' Almanac while my grandfather and the elders searched the remotest reaches of their genealogy, and the village schoolma'm (who boarded out during the term, and was the Almroths' guest that Winter) sat by the lamp on the table reading a book that seemed to me to be the thickest on earth. Before we left I sneaked a look at its title, and when we got back to Baltimore I borrowed it from the branch of the Pratt Library in Hollins street, but I never managed to get beyond its first chapter. It was " St. Elmo," by Mrs. Augusta Jane Evans Wilson.

The Almroths, it appeared, were professing Christians, and on the Sunday following our arrival they took my grandfather and me to their church, which stood in the midst of a slough in the village, and was, as I recall, of some branch or other of the Lutheran communion. We got in late and my grandfather diffidently declined to go forward to the Almroth pew, but slipped into a seat near the door and dragged me with him. But if he thought to escape the glare of notoriety by that device he was badly fooled, for at the close of the proceedings an officer arose near the pulpit and read a report on the attendance for the day. When he came to " Number of visitors present : two " the whole congregation arose as one Christian and rubber-necked East, West, North and South until we had been located. There was indeed such a hubbub that my grandfather was induced to arise and make a bow. As we were passing out afterward he was introduced to the pastor and all the notables of the congregation, including many who welcomed him in German, for the whole Lake Erie littoral was full of Germans. The pastor eyed me speculatively and seemed about to try me out on the Catechism, but just then a female customer began to whoop up his sermon in high, astounding terms, and I escaped under cover of his grateful thanks.

But of all the incidents of that memorable journey to the Wild West the one that sticks in my recollection most firmly was the last, for it was aided in gaining lodgment by an uneasy conscience. My grandfather and I, on our return, were hardened travelers, and dealt with train conductors, Pullman porters and such-like functionaries in a casual and confident manner. We arrived at Washington very early in the morning, and my father's plenipotentiary, Mr. Cross, was there to meet us. His face, when we sighted him on the platform, was very grave, and he approached us in the manner of a man charged with an unhappy duty. It took the form of handing us a telegram. My grandfather blanched when he saw it, and passed it to me without reading it, for telegrams always alarmed him. I opened it at his nod, and then proceeded to read it to him in a chastened whisper, as follows:

Frank Cross,   Baltimore, February 26, 1891
   Aug. Mencken & Bro.,
     Seventh and G streets, N.W.,
      Washington, D.C.

        Mr. B. L. Mencken is dead.
                      Habighurst.

Mr. Habighurst was my father's bookkeeper, and Mr. B. L. Mencken was my other grandfather, the progenitor, chief justice and captain general of all the American Menckenii. My grandfather Abhau was silent on the short trip back to Baltimore, and remained silent as we boarded a horse-car at Camden Station and rode out to Hollins street, our bags piled beside the driver. We got off at Stricker and Lombard streets, and made for the house across Union Square. As we came to the fishpond in the center of the square I saw that there was a black crêpe on the handle of the doorbell, in token of filial respect to the dead patriarch. The sight made me feel creepy, for that was the first crêpe I had ever seen on a Mencken doorbell. But I was only ten years old, and the emotions of boys of that age are not those of philosophers. For a brief instant, I suppose, I mourned my grandfather, but before we had crossed the cobblestones

312

of Hollins street a vagrom and wicked thought ran through my head. I recognized its enormity instantly, but simply could not throttle it. The day was a Thursday — and they'd certainly not bury the old man until Sunday. No school tomorrow!

A NOTE ABOUT THE AUTHOR

H. L. Mencken was born in Baltimore in 1880 and died there in 1956. Educated privately and at Baltimore Polytechnic, he began his long career as journalist, critic and philologist on the Baltimore *Morning Herald* in 1899. In 1906 he joined the staff of the Baltimore *Sun*, thus beginning an association with the *Sun* papers which lasted until a few years before his death. He was co-editor of the *Smart Set* with George Jean Nathan from 1908 to 1923, and with Nathan he founded in 1924 the *American Mercury*, of which he was editor until 1933. His numerous books include *A Book of Burlesques* (1916); *A Book of Prefaces* (1917); *In Defense of Women* (1917); *The American Language* (1918; 4th edition, 1936); *Supplement One* (1945); *Supplement Two* (1948); six volumes of *Prejudices* (1919, 1920, 1922, 1924, 1926, 1927); *Notes on Democracy* (1926); *Treatise on Right and Wrong* (1934); *Happy Days* (1940); *Newspaper Days* (1941); *Heathen Days* (1934); *A Mencken Chrestomathy* (1949); and *Minority Report* (1956). Mencken also edited several books; he selected and edited *A New Dictionary of Quotations* (1942). He was co-author of a number of books, including *Europe after 8:15* (1914); *The American Credo* (1920); *Heliogabalus* (a play, 1920); and *The Sunpapers of Baltimore* (1937).

Library of Congress Cataloging-in-Publication Data

Mencken, H. L. (Henry Louis), 1880–1956.
  Happy days, 1880–1892 / H. L. Mencken.
    p.   cm. — (Maryland paperback bookshelf)
  Originally published : New York : Knopf, 1936.
  ISBN 0-8018-5338-9 (pbk. : alk. paper)
  1. Mencken, H. L. (Henry Louis), 1880–1956—Childhood and youth.
2. Authors, American—20th century—Biography. 3. Baltimore (Md.)—
Social life and customs. I. Title. II. Series.
PS3525.E43Z464   1996
818'.5209—dc20
[B]   95-45208